D1106429

SOCIAL ETHICS

# SOCIAL ETHICS

ROBERT T. HARRIS

MIAMI UNIVERSITY, OXFORD, OHIO

PHILADELPHIA AND NEW YORK

J. B. LIPPINCOTT COMPANY

*Library of Congress Catalog Card Number: 63–7027*
*Printed in the United States of America*

To my Father and Mother
and to my Wife

# Preface

The unexamined life is not worth living, Socrates said. The unexamined society is hardly worth living in, he might have added. The members of a good society are aware of their values and their habitual ways of deciding and acting. In this time of rapidly changing social relations, it is hoped that this book will supply the present need for a guide to study which will stimulate the reader's interest in social ethics and the philosophy of action.

Give us principles, and give us facts. A social philosophy that is not *au courant* has doubtful utility. The facts about social groups and processes, however, are gathered by social scientists.

To some persons, facts alone seem enough, and anything more seems more than enough. But then why are so many leading social scientists "optimistic" or "pessimistic," "conservative" or "progressive," concerned about our "emotional health" and "social sanity"? We need their experience, interpretations, and perspectives, along with the facts, but not in place of our own self-analyzed intentions and standards. Scientists cannot, in their professional capacity, tell us what is virtuous and what vicious, what right and wrong mean, or sound and unsound.

Policy should result frankly from wise and knowledgeable choice among all the alternatives. Let us learn again openly (and not under the *cloak* of science) to value and disvalue, judge, and decide.

I wish to thank Wayne A. R. Leys for advice. I also thank Raymond E. Olson and my other colleagues; the administration of

Miami University; F. P. Locke and Jerome Ellison; Jack Taylor, Peter Kratt, and other helpful students; and I happily acknowledge fine preparation of the manuscript by Mrs. Jill Nethercot Mulliken. All failings are my own.

OXFORD, OHIO
FEBRUARY 22, 1962

ROBERT T. HARRIS

# Contents

PART IV

EQUALITY: SOCIAL ORDERS AND MEANINGS OF "EQUALITY"



PART V

THE INDIVIDUAL IN LIBERAL DEMOCRATIC SOCIETY

# PART I

# Introductory

# 1

# VALUES

## THE IMPORTANCE OF VALUES

The person who knows his own values gets the most out of life. He also gives the most to it. A person is worth more both to himself and to others if he has observed and weighed his values and considered their contribution to his whole life. Our world needs people who know what they want and what they stand for.

### DO YOU KNOW WHAT YOU WANT?

Many people today have memorized what certain psychologists and sociologists say about values. They can tell you about the values of suburbia and of underdeveloped countries, about the values of introverts, of anxious siblings and of "organization men." But often these same well-informed people cannot tell you what they themselves value.

If someone tries to tell you about his (or her) values, he may present you with the picture of a bohemian, of someone who is "old family," or of someone who is "socially mobile upward." But are his verbal responses in themselves reliable evidence? The "progressive" or "conservative" image that he has of himself may be inaccurate. He may feel that he is "concerned" or "indifferent" about community affairs. He may think of himself as "competitive," or "sociable," as "interested in the finer things of life." But how dependable are such judgments? Do they tell us what we most need to know about values?

The libertarian point of view, from which this book is written, affirms the universal desirability of freedom for individuals to discover their own values. The *libertarian thesis* here means an insistence on the desire, need, and right to grow according to one's own pattern, individual or institutional. It means stress on the opportunity to hear all sides, to get acquainted sympathetically with all perspectives, to get at the full facts and to get at all facets of the meaning of issues that are in conflict. The word *libertarian* has been selected, in preference to *liberal,* just because it is so ugly: The thesis of this book is libertarian, and *libertarian* means what the author means by it, as stated above.

However powerful cultural or other influences may be, the libertarian believes that the intelligence of human beings keeps them from being doomed to value stereotypes and gives them the possibility of learning and deciding in the first person what is valuable for themselves and for their communities. That individuals frequently do not value the things they *say* they value is a conviction of the libertarian, based on centuries of experience. Furthermore, human beings are in many instances capable of valuing activities, experiences, and objects which it has never occurred to them that they might value. There's the man who habitually plays gin rummy and wouldn't think of cracking a book, the girl who "loves" operettas and wouldn't think of listening to jazz, or to classical or contemporary music.

If we seriously aim to understand ourselves, the first thing we shall want to know is *what pleases us.* What kinds of experience, what purchases in the market, what investments of our time can be counted on to gratify us? When Socrates made "Know thyself!" his motto,[1] this precept already meant to him, "Know what you really value, Know what your values are and know them in their order of importance." The self reveals itself primarily in the interests it takes, the appraisals it makes: It is a valuer.

A valuer values something, and he is known for what he values,

[1] Socrates, an Athenian philosopher and the founder of ethics, lived from 469 to 399 B.C. The precept antedates him, having been stated by the Delphic Oracle; it was already used by Chilon of Sparta about 600 B.C.—(Sir Ernest Jones said that Sigmund Freud was the first man ever to achieve this self-knowledge, and that he did so through the famous self-psychoanalysis which began in his early forties.)

how he values it and how much. A wrestling fan is one who values wrestling, an arsonist is one who likes fires and likes them too much and too indiscriminately, and a philosopher (in one view) is a man who loves wisdom. In what equally important sense can we understand ourselves? *Webster's Unabridged Dictionary* gives the following technical meaning to *self-conscious:* "3. Psychol. Aware of oneself as an individual that experiences, desires, and acts." In this definition the important word for us as valuers is "desires."

If a student thinks he wants a college education, but really doesn't, the learning and doing assignments are hard, and the everyday work is frustrating rather than pleasing and successful. If he thinks he wants to study mathematics, but really doesn't, he will find it "abstract," useless, and boring—none of which reveals as much about mathematics as about the student. We can also easily understand that parents who love their children will find it easier to put up with their foibles and that professors will work harder if they really like their subjects and tolerate students. Men who look back on a long career of money-making but who really wanted to be professional people, we shall expect to find frustrated and cheerless in their old age; and the same for scientists who really wanted to be artists, and *vice versa*. Nothing seems more important to living well than knowing what one wants.

Such self-knowledge implies reflection. We can find out what pleases us only if we observe, notice, and analyze the enjoyment that we take in various things, activities, and persons. Do we like gay and noisy friends more than the quiet kind? Sympathetic companions less than stimulating ones? If we know ourselves, we can make fairly reliable predictions about what things will give us the relatively larger gratification. If we just move with the wind and with the gang and don't observe, reflect, and make comparisons of one day's events with those of another, then our experiences will fail to provide orientation. "First among the signs of intellectual maturity we would wish for an ideal person is the achievement of an insight into his own make-up, a realistic understanding of his own assets and liabilities, an understanding of his own dominant trends and motivations . . ."[2]

Self-knowledge comes only with experience. In order to understand ourselves, we must *have* experience and trends and motivations. Self-knowledge implies experiences *had,* experiences felt to be better or worse than others. It implies interests and aversions

[2] Lawrence E. Cole. Quoted by Roger H. Garrison in *The Adventure of Learning in College*. New York: Harper & Brothers, 1959, p. 11. Reprinted by permission.

that have grown out of experiences that were satisfying and other experiences that were not. Who can sympathize with the person who makes no demands on life, who has no interests to protect and foster? Who can respect the person who mimics his brothers, plodding along behind them in a stupor. Esthesia, or sensibility, frightens some people. They put off having any experience for fear that they might enjoy it, might want to repeat it, might be induced to work to achieve it again. It is true that nothing begets human energy like sensibility and desire. "Strong impulses are but another name for energy. Energy may be turned to bad uses; but more good may always be made of an energetic nature, than of an indolent and impassive one." [3]

The Puritans of a former time were greatly energetic and made singular contributions to the history of Britain and the United States. But it ought not to be forgotten that they expected—and with abundance of fertile imagination—to be rewarded. The great characteristics of Puritanism today are its emptiness and wintry negativity. It will prohibit, inhibit, slap the lover, soak the rich, scorn and abuse every innovation and enjoyment. Today's Puritan is the man or woman who shuns experience, knowledge, and pleasure and who fears life, energy, and work. We do need a purer, more rigorous moral code, but one inspired by positive energy and desire, not by negative repressiveness.

The man who wants nothing, or whose wants are obscure and unclear, is not dependable. He is truly the lost soul. We can't characterize him and, hence, can't count on him. To him, changing values and contemporary reappraisals mean nothing; but then again neither do accepted and traditional ones. Adventure is not his game, but no more so is an active and vigilant defense of past and present.

If we must brush one pole or the other, complete insensitiveness is worse than hypersensitiveness. Epidermis and the smallness of our sense organs protect us against too great sensitiveness. We can say with Henry James: "Be one of those on whom nothing is lost." The pay-off is always and exclusively in consciousness; we ought neither to fear experience nor to be insensitive to the least germ of life or value.

Nor ought we to miss our time: "Better late than never," yes, but "Still better punctual than late!" James has his great fictional hero Strether think and say:

[3] John Stuart Mill, *On Liberty*. New York: E. P. Dutton & Co., Inc., Everyman Edition, p. 118.

> There were some things that had to come in time if they were to come at all. If they didn't come in time they were lost forever. . . . 'It's not too late for *you,* on any side, and you don't strike me as in danger of missing the train: . . . All the same, don't forget that you're young—blessedly young; be glad of it, on the contrary, and live up to it. Live all you can; it's a mistake not to. It doesn't so much matter what you do in particular, so long as you have your life. If you haven't had that, what *have* you had? . . . The right time is *any* time that one is still so lucky as to have. You've plenty; that's the great thing; you're, as I say, damn you, so happily and hatefully young. Don't, at any rate, miss things out of stupidity. Of course, I don't take you for a fool, or I shouldn't be addressing you thus awfully!' [4]

The very expression, "having experience," brings John Dewey to mind. "There is no immaculate conception of meanings or purposes," he wrote.[5] They arise out of impulses, habits, sensations, and thoughts. Without experience a man can have neither important ends nor means. Looking for philosophical support for Strether's advice, we find that it exists in plenty. All men should go to the theater, Spinoza said, in order to learn about life and to extend their imagination and experience. "Innocence is indeed a splendid thing; only it is very much to be deplored that it is hard to maintain it and it is easily led astray," in the opinion of Immanuel Kant.[6] The same point was recently made—but much more bluntly —by Sir Charles Snow: ". . . the worst crime is innocence." [7] Plato and Hegel despised innocence and its correlative, a habit of laziness and incompleteness. May we illustrate in terms of college life?

> In China I once saw a man cut in half by a machine gun. At the time I thought it the most melancholy sight I would ever see. But as a professor I have seen a sight even more melancholy: the spectacle of Christian students, including pre-ministerial students, coming to class day after day and performing indifferent, nonchalant work.[8]

[4] Strether to little Bilham in *The Ambassadors.* New York: Harper & Brothers, 1902, pp. 149–150.

[5] John Dewey, *Human Nature and Conduct.* New York: Henry Holt and Company (Modern Library edition published by Random House, 1930), pp. 30–31. Reprinted by permission.

[6] Immanuel Kant, *The Fundamental Principles of the Metaphysic of Ethics.* New York: D. Appleton-Century Company (Manthey-Zorn, translator), 1938, pp. 20–21.

[7] C. P. Snow, *The Two Cultures and the Scientific Revolution.* New York: Cambridge University Press, 1959, p. 49.

[8] Leland Miles (Hanover College), "What Do You Mean, 'Religious Emphasis Week'?" *Bulletin* of the American Association of University Professors, Vol. 42, No. 4 (Winter 1956), p. 681. Reprinted by permission.

In any case, the reluctance of students to aim at scope and excellence in their work and experience is appalling. A senior who is president of his Omicron Delta Kappa (national honorary) chapter was recently relating that, in his freshman and sophomore years, he could not and would not bring himself to attend a symphony concert. It was too high-brow, perhaps also vaguely effeminate. After finally being persuaded to go, he quickly learned to enjoy not only symphonic but even chamber music. This senior will spend next year in India on a fellowship, broadening and deepening his experience, before entering law school.

Do students think it effeminate to enjoy the hardest won achievements and values of our civilization? Don't they know that Bach, Haydn, Mozart, and Beethoven, and Rembrandt and Rubens, too, were *more* masculine and virile than the long-forgotten commercial men, powerful blacksmiths, and so on, who were their contemporaries? Or do our more vigorous young people wish, perhaps, to turn over the highest values in our civilization to those who *are* effete and effeminate? We cannot afford such a collegiate tradition of ignorance, mediocrity, and slothfulness.

This apathy and lack of nerve even affect students' choices of courses and majors, sometimes prejudicing them against the more far-ranging subjects, for instance against philosophical and classical fields. Our society needs young people who have the foresight and courage to envision themselves twenty, thirty, and forty years ahead in major leadership roles. Because of our materialistic, and hence somewhat unimaginative, ideology, the problem of the full maturation of our college population is especially pressing. College undergraduates may properly be expected to learn things and to acquire habits useful to society and valuable to themselves as persons *in the long run*. How much value will there be in my whole life, in my life taken as a whole?

If students just learn how to get the first job, how to enjoy the faddish music and dance of the moment, how to escape into the fantasy world of adolescent movies, the likelihood of their having a full life and adding up to much is surely small. If they do have skills and advance materially, if the bitch-goddess, Success, does smile on them, they will be only the more frustrated. (The most successful alumni of engineering schools are the strongest advocates of the humanities. Witness the revised programs at Massachusetts Institute of Technology and California Technical Institute.)

> You want to spend your life for something important, but you are not sure what is important and what is not. (This is why 'core studies' programs include philosophy and the history of ideas.)
>
> . . . I think of the earnest and hard-working student who has learned only mechanical skills and material information, and who has not been asked to consider the moral or cultural value of these skills. Such a person is a cheated student, potentially unhappy and possibly even a future danger to the society in which he will work . . .[9]

### DO YOU MAKE IMPORTANT VALUE JUDGMENTS?

We have said that self-understanding implies reflection on our experience, and that if this reflection is not to be sterile, we must *have* experience, and we must be sensitive to its qualities. This kind of recognition and emphasis characterize *libertarian* ethics. The individual cannot, in the end, depend on anyone but his own growing self. Value judgments, if they are to have any living significance, must be those of the individual; here the student cannot even depend on his professor. This strongly *individualistic* bias is also characteristic of libertarian ethics. As Alburey Castell has put it, "Every man his own moralist." [10]

In the nature of things, everyone *is* his own moralist; everyone values that which he values and approves that which he approves. Of course, not everyone faces up to the responsibility that accompanies being one's own moralist. The alternative of "trusting authority" and depending on someone else is a pseudo-alternative, because in fact the man who depends on an external authority is making a decision (at least, a tacit one) of his own in favor of the authority. Those who follow an authority have in effect decided for an authoritarian type ethical theory, as well as for some concrete person or institution that they accept as authority. Admittedly, the man whose ethics are authoritarian may be in the position of the gentle bourgeois who spoke prose all his life without knowing it. A good reason for studying ethics and value theory is precisely in order to become aware what kind of values and ethics one is committed to, what one's principles and presuppositions are, and what the alternatives are, too.

Nor is there any question that the judgments of authority are themselves sometimes of value as a part of our experience. Re-

[9] Roger H. Garrison, *op. cit.*, pp. 54, 57. Reprinted by permission.

[10] Alburey Castell, *An Elementary Ethics*. New York: Prentice-Hall, Inc., 1954, pp. 11–18. (The quoted phrase is a section heading.)

cently we hear much of the father image, often with the impression that it's a sign of weakness or of lack of orientation. But a boy needs his father for a guiding star. Freud himself said that the worst day in any man's life is the day he loses his father.

Although students commonly think of themselves as strikingly modest in refraining from making value judgments and as even more hesitant to pass moral judgments, they in fact not only make such judgments just as frequently as do other classes of people, but also they tend to make them more severely. Often the Dean of Men, or some such official, has to appear before the Student Discipline Board and plead mercy for the poor student defendant. The severity of student boards may well remind one of the French tribunals of 1793.

On the other hand, students exhibit a degree of judgment in their appraisal of the conduct of non-students, and they are almost kindly, sometimes, in their attitude towards faculty and officialdom.

During the final examination period, seven girls in Hogg Dormitory were still studying at 2:00 A.M., and they had become very hungry. They were not allowed to leave the dormitory. One of them, who waited table in the dining room at the time, knew where there was ice cream in the kitchen. After a little discussion pro and con, they reached a unanimous decision to steal down to the kitchen and each have a dish. They in fact succeeded in eating almost two gallons from a five-gallon container.

When the expected inquisition began the next day, the girls confessed their guilt. Now, the house mother took it in stride and was satisfied with the promise that it would not happen again. She accepted the suggestion of one of the girls that they all seven skip desserts, or at least ice cream, during the next month. But the dormitory director, whose rank was the same as that of the house mother, was enraged that the girls had been "sneaky" and had "stolen," and she knew of no way in which they could pay for the ice cream or otherwise make up to the University (and its founders!) for their inexcusable theft. She "realized" that if this kind of action were allowed to go unpunished, it could end by bankrupting the institution.

Then the girls in turn became annoyed, and two of them opined to higher authorities that the dormitory director was immature. On request, they did not publicly repeat this opinion. Fortunately, after a few days, little more was heard of the incident. Within two weeks, the girls were being served dessert again, and no one mentioned it.

All the girls in Hogg Dormitory were at that time busily making value judgments and moral judgments. Some of their judgments, it is true, were hasty and not well authenticated; but others were sound and carefully supported. Is it not true that students are forever making such judgments about values and morals? The faculty gets judged one by one. Many of the higher administrative personnel are subject to clear-cut student ratings, however based. Student leaders are rated, also often by obscure means. And courses get rated, too. In our system of higher education, students choose many of their own courses and professors and thus have more power than they usually are aware of. But are students not also concerned with what they are going to do after college, after graduation, and about the use of it all? With economic and political traditions, and perhaps above all, with personalities and classes of personalities? Students may well be the chief remaining cracker-barrel philosophers in our whole moral economy.

So the question is not whether or not value judgments and moral judgments get made. They do. The question concerns how well they get made. A reason for commencing this book with a preliminary discussion of values and value judgments is that if one is not aware of his own values and of the principles that actually operate in his choices, his moral habits and ethical decisions cannot have personal meaning, cannot relate directly and vigorously to his own wish and will. Of course, not everyone is an expert in self-knowledge, but everyone ought to strive to be. No one else can have as good an opportunity to understand me as I do myself, to take my own internal perspective, to become directly aware of my own needs. (There is a major difference between an expert and an authority, namely that an authority is one whose decisions get followed, while an expert is one who knows what problems are worth examining and how to attempt solutions.)

Libertarian ethics affirm that we must know what we want and, as far as possible, what is good and what desirable before we can take up a moral position. And it affirms that the individual should determine for himself what he wants and what he finds good. Can we apply this doctrine without exception? Perhaps no doctrine is unexceptionable. The libertarian doctrine supposes development, education, a certain subtlety in decision and in application to individual instances; in a word, it supposes maturity. It functions well for mature people who will strive to be consistent in their actions and who will consistently aim to understand themselves and the world and to make the most of it. As a political principle, it also supposes enough practical wisdom so that citizens of their own volition will compromise with necessity—compromise interest, that is, not compromise principle. The expectation is that free people will realize more value in their lives than people can, in the long run, under any arrangement in which authority is arbitrary or merely traditional. The doctrine and the expectation apply to us all, to the extent that we are mature. On those who are immature, a pressure is exerted toward maturity.

Incidentally, application of this view to college students is difficult, because college students are not quite sure whether or not they are mature. Proverbs 22:15 states, "Folly is bound up in the heart of a child, but the rod of discipline drives it far from him." Shall we say, then, that the doctrine is not meant to apply to foolish children, that it won't work in reform school? Certainly we won't advocate the foolish use of the rod; the rod is not the only instrument for driving out folly. At the college level, the difficulty is all the greater, because we ought to want our students to be energetic, and "energy" is but another name for strong impulses. John Stuart Mill, quoted above, continues:

> Those who have most natural feeling are always those whose cultivated feelings may be made the strongest. The same strong susceptibilities which make the personal impulses vivid and powerful, are also the source from whence are generated the most passionate love of virtue, and the sternest self-control. . . . Whoever thinks that individuality of desires and impulses should not be encouraged to unfold itself, must maintain that society has no need of strong natures—is not the better for containing many persons who have much character—and that a high general average of energy is not desirable. . . .
>
> Human nature is not a machine to be built after a model, and set to do exactly the work prescribed for it, but a tree, which requires to grow and develop itself on all sides, according to the tendency of the inward forces which make it a living thing. . . .
>
> It is not because men's desires are strong that they act ill; it is because their consciences are weak.[11]

Energetic individuality is a most important social value. Not only the higher pleasures, to which we made a low bow above, but also the lower pleasures warrant a measure of social defense. If society needs energetic characters, it needs men and women of strong impulses. Society needs strong characters with their own strong consciences. We should not have to draw our future leader-

[11] *On Liberty,* Everyman Edition, pp. 117–118. John Stuart Mill (1806–1873) was a leading British philosopher and Utilitarian and a major executive of the East India Company.

ship classes from among the spineless. If we bow the lower pleasures off the stage with faint praise, the raw material of human nature is betrayed. The amount of drive that an individual is going to have depends at certain stages of life on not suffering too much curbing, pruning and frustrating, just as at other stages it depends on undergoing enough curbing and controlling. Of course, the energy released in rebelliousness was generated under repression.

Moreover, we ought to have a degree of respect for both tradition and criticism, and even for foolish or misguided criticism, since one must *learn* to be critical, *become* a competent critic. Progress depends on a critical understanding of tradition. As V. Gordon Childe wrote of cultural progress:

> The human child is taught rules and precepts for action that members of his group and their ancestors have found beneficial. . . . the body of traditional rules is *not* fixed and immutable. Fresh experiences may suggest to individuals additions and modifications. These, if found useful, will be communicated to, discussed, and tested by, the community as a whole, and eventually incorporated in the collective tradition. In reality, of course, the process is not nearly so simple as it sounds. Men cling passionately to old traditions and display intense reluctance to modify customary modes of behavior, as innovators at all times have found to their cost. The dead-weight of conservatism, largely a lazy and cowardly distaste for the strenuous and painful activity of real thinking, has undoubtedly retarded human progress even more in the past than today. Nevertheless, for the human species progress has consisted essentially in the improvement of the social tradition, transmitted by precept and example.[12]

Perhaps the greatest value of the exercise of criticism lies in the application of it to ourselves. Bernard Baruch spoke of "the age-old conflict that every ambitious youth experiences between the reckless impulse to shoot the works and the cautious desire to mass one's resources for the morrow." How hard it is to know and control one's self! "I have known men who could see through the motivations of others with the skill of a clairvoyant, only to prove blind to their own mistakes. In fact I have been one of those men." After telling how, after a major undertaking, he would leave Wall Street and go to some quiet place where he could review what he had done and where he had gone wrong, Baruch adds:

> Periodic self-examination of this sort is something all of us need, in both private and governmental affairs. It is always wise for in-

[12] *Man Makes Himself,* New York: The New American Library of World Literature, Inc., 1951, p. 31. My italics. Reprinted by permission of English publisher, C. A. Watts & Co., Ltd., London.

dividuals and governments to stop and ask whether we should rush on blindly as in the past. Have new conditions arisen which require a change of direction or pace? Have we lost sight of the essential problem and are we simply wasting our energies on distractions? What have we learned that may help us avoid repeating the same old errors? Also, the more we know of our own failings, the easier it becomes to understand other people and why they act as they do.[13]

The effort at understanding ourselves is rewarding, among other reasons, because it helps us to understand others. Serious effort spent on understanding others may also prove rewarding, by giving us insight into ourselves. Fortunately, we don't by any means have to have every experience in the first person singular. Not only can we learn from the experiences of others, but we can extrapolate beyond the experiences that we do have personally. There are also such instruments available as biographies and autobiographies and works of fiction. To achieve an understanding of theory of value or of social ethics will of itself constitute a certain extension of our experience.

In a book devoted primarily to social ethics, to describe all the kinds of approaches to the understanding of value that are current today is not possible. Instead, having now emphasized valuing—desire and aversion—as the clue to personality and self-understanding, let us briefly analyze the value situation itself.

### WHAT MAKES UP A VALUE SITUATION?

The two major poles of every value situation are obvious: (1) There will be some object, generally an external thing or event, that pleases or displeases us, attracts or repels us. (2) There will be our liking or disliking itself: the second pole is our inner and personal, felt response *to* the object. It may be a feeling of repulsion or attraction. The goodness or badness of the *experience* as such and as a whole—its beauty or ugliness, glamour or drabness, its moral character—is a product of the object intersecting with our sensibility. Of course, value situations are often highly complex.

Value in objects, in things, is potential only.[14] We impute value and disvalue to external things and events because we recall experience of them as pleasant or unpleasant, or because we reckon on the basis of some other experience and evidence that the things *would* give us pleasure, under certain circumstances. The main

[13] Bernard Baruch, *My Own Story*. New York: Holt, Rinehart, & Winston, 1957, p. 91. Reprinted by permission.

[14] My debt to Professor C. I. Lewis in this section is acknowledged.

point is that all *actualized* value is value brought home to individuals, is value in the experience of somebody. Undiscovered gold makes no one rich. Schoenberg's later compositions give pleasure only to those who who have somehow learned to hear musical values in works constructed on the twelve-tone scale by his peculiar genius.

From the point of view of actual value, all objects, states, properties, and even ideals, are instruments, occasions, and causes, but never final nor consummatory.

Moreover, value can be realized only in the here and now, though this will not exclude, of course, values in present anticipation and recollection.

Final verification of value in objects, also, must wait upon its being incorporated in some actual, present, and immediately felt satisfaction or dissatisfaction. The value that we impute to objects is imputed as a result of our imagining and estimating what the experience of those objects would be like. The same holds in respect to imputation, verification and realization of value in the services of other persons. I judge the barber hopefully, but see the haircut!

This view, no matter how "subjective," is the tough-minded view of value realization: For object and sensibility are not values in themselves, but come into relation to one another and become realized as values only in personal experience.

### (*1*) *The Object*

The object that causes the experience may be something which happens to appeal to our capacities for lower pleasure: bread and butter, herring in cream; roller-skating, skip-rope, or jacks; driving with the top down, dancing, or holding hands. (Are the pleasures of driving or sailing or walking into a fresh breeze lower or higher pleasures? Do some things and actions interest us at certain ages only, or at only certain stages of development? [Yes, but why?] Are there some things that we could not possibly enjoy, not under any circumstances? To what extent is enjoyment of various things a matter of conditioning? Of reflection? Do all enjoyments ultimately, albeit indirectly, rest on bodily needs?)

The object that we aim at, and in which we seek our gratification, may be some ideal that appeals to our highest feelings: liberty and fraternity, justice, the strength and nobility of our country. Such larger ideals are naturally of interest to us in social ethics.

Sometimes the object will lie nearer the middle of the scale, between higher and lower: in the quality of our studies, the immediate welfare of our family, the salaries paid to our employees. (Can we successfully rank our interests and gratifications in this way, one above the other? Are some objectives "higher" than others? What does "higher" mean? Or do we perhaps need some other kind of model for our thinking about values, since we seem to need for the good life *both* everyday physical pleasures, the ordinary necessities and luxuries, *and* over-arching ideals and aims that give longer-range orientation to our existence?)

### (2) *Our Sensibility*

The other element in value situations is the sensibility of the person or other creature. It is precisely our capacity for higher or lower pleasure, and for higher or lower pain. So here we have experiencers with their widely varying sensibilities, individuals of all ages, at various stages of intellectual and emotional maturity, persons of all kinds and degrees with their loves, hates, commitments, entrapments, and foibles. Now, unless the object can affect the sensibility of some experiencer or experiencers, unless it can be appreciated, there will be no value experience of it.

Passing nameless and unnoticed faces on the street is not having a meeting, and contact or encounter with an object or an ideal that means nothing to us does not constitute an actualization of value. There is value experience and at least a degree of realization when the person's sensibility is such that he can and does count the value, react to it, make it his own. For value experience, consequently, the cultivation of sensibility is of crucial importance. (Just having the developed capacity for enjoyment does not give the experience either. There are required both the sensibility and the occasion and means, the object. The capacity to read French novels with enjoyment may lead only to frustration if you cannot get hold of any French novels.)

## CAN YOU IMPROVE YOUR VALUING?

Can sensibility be cultivated? And if so, how then? The answer is affirmative; but just as wisdom does not come cheaply, nor in merely routine ways, and is not in practice entirely teachable, so also is sensibility difficult to acquire and not easily taught.

> In *Crime and Punishment,* the murderer Raskolnikov is finally brought to the very brink of confession through the offices of a gentle, pious, and uncondemning girl, Sonia. And just before he opens his

> lips to tell his awful story, Raskolnikov feels a violent hatred for his confessor. And then the author [Dostoevski] says, "It was not hatred at all; he had mistaken one feeling for another. It merely meant that *the* moment had come." Here is a comment that might bring us up short with questions; for instance: Could he, can anyone, be *mistaken* about his own feeling? Can one have a feeling that seems like hatred but is not hatred? The notion that one can may be rather startling. But now what is one to do with such a question? The author says no more at least directly. He is not writing a systematic psychology. It is at precisely such a point as this that one may, even quite deliberately, *think,* think about one's own feelings and the interpretations of those feelings. And thinking, one may decide that it does sometimes happen: a feeling is not really what it first seems to be.[15]

We can by careful reflection on our own feelings, by armchair study, learn a great deal about feelings and about our own feelings. We can sometimes correct our understanding of them.

This power of correction has a bearing on ethics. Our "purely" subjective feelings and attitudes are subject to correction and improvement; they can be made more or less healthy.[16] The fact that a given feeling has moral tone, a moral aura, is not sufficient to establish it as correct, as really moral. Feelings are subject to validation procedures.[17]

However, we should not wish to give the impression that armchair strategies are the only, or even the primary, means of affecting our feeling capacities. The usual and more obvious way of cultivating our sensibilities is by increasing our experience: by stopping to look at the sunset, by going into the theater, by standing before good paintings, including modern ones, and contemplating them; by trying our hand at writing, sculpturing, fiddling;[18] by judging, but especially by being involved in, moral situations and moral decisions, and by hearing how other people say they react to moral problems.

Experience, of course, is ongoing; and it is not all passive. We have feelings which are typically associated with doing things. The satisfactions available to us do not all attach to mere bits and pieces of experience; more important gratifications attach

[15] James L. Jarrett, *The Quest for Beauty.* Englewood Cliffs, N.J.: Prentice-Hall, Inc., 1957, p. 169. Copyright 1957. Reprinted by permission.

[16] Cf. R. Collingwood on Spinoza in *The Principles of Art.*

[17] We can decide that our feeling is right or shameful or appropriate or shallow. (There may be a sense in which the decision itself rests on feeling, too.)

[18] There are lively and elementary enough discussions of means of cultivating our feelings in Curt Ducasse, *Art, The Critics and You,* and Stephen C. Pepper, *The Principles of Art.* Both emphasize the importance of *having* experience and of moving gradually from "simpler" to more difficult feeling responses.

to the larger flow of events, to our efforts to face up to the greater challenges, to "statements about life so all-embracing that they can't be split up into separate words." We would not want to over-discount the gratification that comes with success in major undertakings: Success may be a bitch-goddess, but that isn't the whole story. *Failure* is the Witch of the West! We can suffer terrible frustration in the failure to achieve final accomplishment, not to mention the lesser and perhaps anticipated frustrations en route. Success is better than failure! [19]

There may indeed be no quite uncolored success. Major successes grow on great mounds of failures and frustrated efforts. Success and victory, if real, are then all the more exciting and gratifying. Shocking failure sometimes pays off, and handsomely. Courage and strength grow out of transcending difficulties from which our first impulse is to run and keep running.[20]

To say that experience is ongoing may also suggest that many of our needs are recurrent and call for satisfaction and re-satisfaction. The author wants to write not just one book, but another and yet another. "Three meals a day" is banal, but that is not the whole story. We are prodded by need into being active, and much of our pleasure and displeasure is connected with necessary activities. Aesthetic education is as important a kind of education as there is, but it should be conceived broadly so as to apply not just to contemplation, but also to intellectual and active pursuits. Aesthetic education should relate naturally to our whole lives, contemplative, theoretical, and practical and both individual and social.

We may now roughly summarize our position respecting the two poles of value experience in a brief quotation that also succinctly presents the essential merit of much recent discussion among Objectivists and Subjectivists—and Cultural Relativists.

> (1) The fact underlying Subjectivism is that without a gratified, "good-feeling" person present, no event can properly be said to contain actual beauty [or value of any kind].
>
> (2) The fact underlying Cultural Relativism is that feeling responses of individuals become conditioned toward uniformity within a given culture.
>
> (3) The fact underlying Objectivism is that beauty [or other value] is a quality of the things we call "beautiful" and not of the experience that prompts the judgment.[21]

[19] Can any generation of men need to be reminded of that?

[20] Recall Stephen Crane, *The Red Badge of Courage.*

[21] Jarrett, *op. cit.*, p. 31. Copyright 1957. Reprinted by permission.

Let the reference to Cultural Relativism remind us that many, many things may affect our sensibility: personal make-up, personal history, the quality of our judgment and the amount of our reflection, the number and kinds of experience available to us. But surely above all other influences are the overwhelming effects of other persons. When we value things and when we make judgments of value, we are forever looking over our shoulder to see what other people think, especially to see what they think of *us*. There is considerable personal advantage in substituting "*We* like Schoenberg's quartets" for "*I* like Schoenberg's quartets." Willis Moore suggests that it may be just this kind of reinforcement by others that leads us eventually to say—objectively!—"Schoenberg's quartets are good." [22]

We may also see that, as Hegel sometime remarked, every beginning is relative. For, although you and I begin with valuing, and also begin this book discussing values, still the relation of value and value theory to social ethics is not a one-way street. Our social ethics and social policy act reciprocally on our valuings and valuations. What is or is not allowed and what is encouraged or discouraged by society, especially by our own sub-group, make a great difference, and make a difference that affects our innermost subjectivity. That is one reason why social ethics is so important to every one of us. It is also a reason why the libertarian will vigorously insist on his kind of broad-gauged ethical principles as against every sort of totalitarianism, puritanism, and asceticism. He will strive consistently, persistently, to achieve a world in which the real values can be actualized and in which values can be rated and scaled according to their true order of merit. He wills maximum elbowroom for the fullest, deepest, and highest enjoyments, for himself and for all men, so far as possible. He knows that others are looking over his shoulder, but he doesn't let it embarrass him; and he doesn't approve of too much looking over shoulders. If some of it is legitimate and necessary, yet the rest is misguided. His attitude is reinforced by the thought that all actualized value is

[22] "The social factor, in the form of opinion of others, may so operate as to affect the intensity or even to change the direction of the value component of the individual's experience. In effect, society is looking over our shoulders down that same continuum, its value reactions so merging with ours as to alter appreciably the character of our individual reactions. Usually, and within limits, the consciousness that others feel about *x* as we do serves to *heighten,* and an awareness that they disagree with us to *depress,* our feelings about that same object." Willis Moore, "The Language of Values." In *The Language of Values,* ed. Ray Lepley. New York: Columbia University Press, 1957, p. 15.

value realized and felt in individual, personal experience, and that persons, fortunately, differ one from another.

The most significant question a young person can ask himself is, "What do *I* want, and what do I want more than anything else?" When he can answer it, he is, at least for the time being, oriented in life and to life; he is on his way to some energetic accomplishment in the world and to a wise consistency in his own personality. But it is a hard question to ask one's self.

* * *

A few words about social values.

In most popular discussion, social values are discussed non-analytically. There is much heat and fury, but sometimes not much light. A revival of interest in problems attaching to social values on the part of analytical philosophers is very much in order. Who is to command the performance? [23] Very few good books and articles in social ethics have been published in recent times. The confusion of our aims grows apace. Henry Wriston has said that "Scientific advance has always been hampered by popular scepticism." [24] Philosophic and academic scepticism is a major cause of the lack of analysis of questions and problems in social ethics. There is so much business with preliminary questions, so much analysis of usage, that one hardly gets around to the analysis of serious issues in social philosophy. Bertrand Russell has pontificated, to be sure:

> I have two messages [for the future generations]—one on the intellectual level and the other on the moral level. On the intellectual level: when you study any matter ask yourself, 'what are the facts?'
> On the moral side—love is wise and hatred is foolish.[25]

And so we can only speak about social values with the utmost modesty.

Let us anyway take a preliminary glance at ultimate social values. We have already said that we hold the ultimate end of society to be the actualization of maximum value in the lives of individ-

[23] Professor Morton White has tried in *Religion, Politics, and the Higher Learning.* Cambridge, Massachusetts: Harvard University Press, 1959, p. ix. Sometimes a word to the wise does not suffice.

[24] *Bulletin* of the American Association of University Professors for June 1939, p. 337.

[25] Associated Press Dispatch, London, January 30, 1960. Of course, it's good advice. In fairness to Lord Russell, one should add that he not only authored *Proposed Roads to Freedom,* with its brilliant introductory chapter that is consistent with his later views, but he has published several insightful little books in the last decade that touch on social values. It is a minor part of his work.

uals.[26] This ideal implies extensive individual liberty, and that means the establishment of social freedom and its enforcement by society. But this ideal also implies the support of circumstances under which individuals can cultivate their sensibilities and implies the creation and social production of objects worthy of developed susceptibilities and sufficient in quality and quantity to gratify them. There's the rub: Our ideal implies liberty, but it also implies organization, educational and other institutions—even prisons—and social production.

Our thesis will be that liberty is the basic value, and that other considerations, no matter how weighty and essential, should not be given precedence. Liberty and correlative human dignity are not to be violated: Institutions and social actions must be so aligned that their ends are achieved without diminishing liberty or lessening human dignity.

None of us knows what is best for future society.[27] For the most part, we don't know what is best for other persons. We cannot accurately predict future circumstances and what opportunities and perils will present themselves. (Who could predict in 1910 what was going to happen in the next five decades? Who can now predict a generation ahead?) The very *least* that we can do, then, is not to constitute ourselves "the dead hand of the past."

"The beauty of the American republic is that the past provided for the future by permitting the present to take care of itself."[28] America has grown up now, has won a position of power and responsibility. And Russia is rapidly doing the same. In America, we will have to exert our power and fulfill our responsibility by healthily and critically being ourselves, by staying, in the dangerous state of full bloom, true to ourselves and to our deepest traditions.

Our ideal certainly does not force us to stand idly by, while events take care of themselves. We can affirm enough about the future to stand as a basis of action. (1) If the men of the future are strong and wise, they will want to act as to them seems fit. (2) Their basic bodily and psychological needs will be like our own, even if their ways of filling these needs are different. (3) Their knowledge and power ought to be much greater than ours. (4) And we may be permitted a degree of confidence, a tentative and

[26] In principle, this ideal is applicable to heaven and earth. Economists study this subject of optimization in a secular and proficient but perhaps restricted way in the division of Economics that they call "Welfare Economics."

[27] Hitler thought he did.

[28] James A. Farley, "What I Believe." *The Atlantic Monthly,* June 1959, p. 37.

undogmatic anticipation, that the more carefully wrought cultural values of today will not entirely go by the board. In brief, if we grant a decent respect for future mankind and for *its* present, then our own problem, for the rest, is the problem of *our* present. For good and real reasons, our intermediate social ideals should be oriented toward the solution of the problems of the immediate future.

In order to draft a fundamentally sound Constitution for the United States, its authors did not have to predict the invention of the railroad, use of electric power, development of the hydrogen bomb, and admission of Alaska and Hawaii. But they did have to provide for modification (amendment) and judicial interpretation. They did have to provide a method of making decisions that assured flexibility. What they had to solve, for the most part, were the pressing problems of the states *at that time*. Fortunately, we do not have to face the problem of initial federation of the states. We have enough to do. Let our social ideals find their relevance in the needs of the present, in securing world peace, in maintaining, under new circumstances, both cultural progress and individual liberty.

# 2

# CONTROL

Our century has been fascinated by questions about how to get people to do things. We have learned much, no doubt, in recent times about how to persuade, direct, manage, "reorient," and "psychologically compel" by use of techniques based on impressive new knowledge of man and especially of his irrational behavior. Our questions have chiefly concerned the control of man as an irrational animal, and we seem to be convinced that man *is* essentially irrational. The nineteenth century was already beginning to suspect as much, but it did not yet know how to convert suspicion into science. Nor was it yet able to construct a systematic technology for the control and utilization of human beings.

## IS REASON DEAD?

We have learned to find our enjoyment in snake dances, the Twist, and the Hully Gully, and to look on intelligent debate and rational inquiry as Victorian or worse. We understand mass meetings and the television audience of a hundred million; we are not shocked to see political conventions opened with ukuleles, silly songs, and Hollywood celebrities. We tolerate or even enjoy manipulation just as if we were ourselves the new supermen and not the minions of fate and public relations.

Perhaps we don't so well understand and appreciate the independent thinker and agent, "the man who owns himself," the student closeted and alone. Were it not that we know that "today everybody has to get a degree," we should look on the serious college student as someone who has "indeed renounced the world." (To some extent we make an exception of students of natural science and engineering.) We too easily accept that all should act alike, and we are at least a little amazed ever to find anyone—ourselves included—acting from conviction. Voluntary and rational deportment is, in many contexts, looked on as something eccentric. Or in today's bold language, something "queer." The concept of "the man who thinks for himself" is just one more advertising gimmick.

We seem too little, and there appear to be too many of us, to be anything but mass-handled, pushed around psychologically, and taken hold of by that natural handle, our unconscious mind. We are so persuaded to suasion that only a great war could convince us that Hitler and Dr. Josef Goebbels' propaganda were plain old-fashioned evil.

Such an attitude, the passive acceptance of amoral, or even immoral, persuasion and propaganda techniques is cynical. It is indicative of a vulgar materialism: People don't mind having their wants titillated, so long as they get satisfied. People are coasting too far with the Madison Avenue huckster, the subliminal hidden persuader, and even the manipulative TV politician.

### IS THERE AN IMPELLING NEW NEED FOR ORGANIZATION?

From a quite different perspective on the same tendencies, however, some people are aware of a vast need for organization and social control in our society and throughout the world. Because of great physical and social forces recently released—hydrogen bombs, the newer nationalism, racism, and antiracism—the desire for social control has become intense. Some in their fear and provincialism want unrestricted regional or national controls, and their fears are channeled into such directions as sectionalism and chauvinism. Others press for international or even global control "mechanisms." Still others really do despair and sometimes cynically favor measures of desperation.

Certainly the world no longer has the same degree of confidence in reason that it had in the eighteenth century, or for that matter, in the early twentieth. Our confidence in the reasoning power of individuals has weakened, but especially our confidence in reason as a force affecting social conduct. We no longer trust its power to bring numbers of people together and hold them together. We now suppose that agreement must be achieved by other means, or that at least the force of reason must be substantially supplemented.

We are aware of the imperative necessity of lining people up in order to achieve local, national, and international purposes. We are aware of the stakes, of the price of major failure. We also realize that some of the brilliant devices for lining people up are morally devious and that but few of them convince us by appeal to our best judgment.

Oftentimes these devices are in the hands of institutions and their officers. They are in the hands of corporations wanting to sell, to employ, to issue stock; of bureaucracies both civilian and military; of political parties; labor unions; churches. Anyone can pass judgment on the devices of persuasion and control, but, for the most part, only organizations of numerous forceful people can control the controls or can even hope significantly to affect them.

Obviously, many of these devices get abused. In a free society, in which individuals and institutions are counted on to look after their own interests, abuse is not invited, but it is perhaps to be expected. As a matter of social policy, the admission of a little incidental abuse may be better than extreme regimentation and control. If there is absolutely no possibility of abuse, there will also be minimal occasion for invention and progress. Progress entails change, and for change to take place in society, there must be individuals courageous and energetic enough to induce the change, operating under free conditions—under conditions not wholly unfavorable. Consequently, one of the facts of life is that where there is no "abuse," there is no progress either. China under the Mandarin system exemplified a social order almost without flaw and static; much as we may admire the Mandarin system, it does not in the end appeal to us. In the present world, progress is essential to survival.

To try to explain the presence of abuse is not to support any concrete abuse. For instance, advertising is easy to justify in principle, as it is prerequisite to the building of large markets and the economies of intensive division of labor, the assembly line, and automation. But it does not follow that all the advertising for competing brands is justifiable and that it produces economic benefits. No doubt much of it represents only economic waste. No doubt much of the political hullabaloo is also false and misleading, and we have to hope that the public is able to see through it.

In spite of all the abuses, and in spite of all the false claims made for "togetherness," we do need organization; we need it more than ever, both within the nation and throughout the world. There must, in many areas, exist the kind of practical and working unanimity that allows of major social processes and changes. Our big institutions must be allowed to breathe and live, so that we may count on their vigorous performance and proliferation. We desperately need better order and arrangement on the global scale, *e.g.*, effective agreement that there shall not be unlimited global war and procedure for avoiding it. The public instinct that we must stick together is eminently sound; the live issue concerns rather what shall be our orientation, our joint program.

## INSTITUTIONS AND INSTITUTIONAL CHANGE

Aristotle once said that political science should not be taught to young men, for they are inexperienced in the actions that occur in life. While we do not accept Aristotle's maxim, certainly there are difficulties in teaching young persons about political institutions—or about any kind of institutions. The difficulties are today greater than ever; but so is the need. The traditional difficulties lie in youths' lack of awareness of the extent to which human life—including their own lives—is structured by institutions, the extent to which our attitudes are products of the family, community, school, and state. Our existence is shaped and played out in institutions: Our personality is largely determined by the social environment, whether we live in St. Louis or in central Africa. One needs time, moreover, to learn the shifting and sometimes devious turns and twists of adult maneuvering. Any social science or social ethics appropriate to the present day stands in close affinity to the liberal arts, for it rests on (*at least* intuitive) understanding of the conscious and unconscious ways of men.

The newer difficulties lie in youth not having a developed sense of the radical speed with which institutions change. In the beginning, youth does not have much historical sense. Institutions are dynamic and always changing in response to their members and to internal and external circumstance. Age and experience sensitize one to change; one may gradually become aware even of basic transformation in his culture. It's a truism that institutions have never changed faster than they do today.

Especially in America, young people tend to take what comes as their one eternal right and to look to the future as the serious time of life; they are joyous and conservative, and merrily turn over all institutional responsibility to their elders—we have plenty of campus politics; but we don't have many young people in real political life. With false modesty, they confess to knowing too little to fight for progress and justice, with the result that their interest, the interest of the new generation, has usually been underrepresented.

How can inexperience in the actions that occur in life be transcended? How can historical sense be quickly acquired? How can young persons bring home to themselves their peculiar responsibilities precisely *as* young persons? How, indeed, in a nation where most young people themselves think that they are not wise enough to vote until twenty-one? Where they take more interest in movie stars than presidents? Where the social sciences may be found intriguing for their exposés of social fact, but where every serious social action is avoided on the ground of immaturity—an immaturity self-proclaimed and doggedly prolonged?

Extensive and intensive transformations are taking place in the world today. May we speak briefly—perhaps for some readers vacuously—of a few historical facts?

(1) Except for the United States, Switzerland, and, if you please, Britain, no country in the world has been without at least one radical change of political form since 1790. Until 1860, Italy was a number of little states; Germany was unified in 1870, but it consisted beforehand of three hundred principalities (kingdoms, duchies, independent municipalities, *etc.*). Since 1790, France has been twice an empire, twice a monarchy, and several times a republic. Russia was slower to change, but then by revolution became the first great Communist state. Two times since 1918, the political map of the world has undergone vast revision. Now all our political atlases have built-in obsolescence. Even so the outer shell revealed by political maps does not so much reveal as conceal the actual wrenching of institutions. This violent wrenching is (unfortunately) veiled from us in the United States, where (fortunately) we have a stable form of government. What task of ours could be more urgent than to learn these metamorphoses and their causes?

(2) There has been change inside the United States. In 1790, one white male in ten voted. In Jackson's era the suffrage was extended to all white males. Now it reaches to all adults—except where it "just doesn't stretch." [Negroes, youths, urban populations, migrants, and visiting professors are inadequately represented in our

elections.] Other great changes are the addition of states and the growth of political parties: Arizona became a state in 1912, and the Republican Party was first organized 1854–1856.

(3) Economic, industrial, and financial changes have been even more rapid and far-reaching. The United States Steel Corporation was established by merger in 1900. The vast vertical unions rose to power in the thirties. The great building and loan associations have grown big in the forties and fifties.

(a) There is the revolution in agriculture: A century ago the economist, John Stuart Mill, thought that at least 90 per cent of the working population would always be found in agriculture; today in America less than 10 per cent is in agriculture.

(b) A fascinating new movement is the emigration of American industry.

(c) Change in marketing is just as radical.—All these industrial changes imply other kinds of change: in work habits, buying habits, and attire; in living quarters and style of living; in political behavior, taste, religion, and ideology. New kinds of personality prove advantageous and come to succeed better than old ones in the struggle for advancement. Occasionally, it is true, change is reactionary.

(5) International frictions exist on a vast new scale, and further frictions can be "safely" predicted. The consequences of these events will affect us greatly. They eventually reach into every nook and cranny. Not only our careers and prospects but even our personalities proper are affected. Every detailed prediction finds its reliability reduced by the larger event that may upset it. For instance, population trends are carefully calculated; but the trends are modified by war, depression, and change of habit. In the Great Depression, the birth rate of the United States shrank. Since the Second World War, it has increased explosively. *How many children there will be in your family may depend less on your individual or family decision than on the state of our larger institutions.*

## "SOCIAL STUDIES?"

A principal thesis of this book is that we ought to know our own values. If we would know ourselves and our values, then we must also understand the institutional environment. The social sciences can teach us a great deal about institutions, but to date, they have proved somewhat limited [not impotent!] as guides to judicious personal and social decision, and to role-finding and involvement.

Knowledge increases fast, but wisdom increases slowly. Of course, *wisdom ought* to permeate all our thinking, deciding, and acting. An ideal education would affect our efferent impulses as much as our afferent ones.

Sophistication concerning institutions, but above all sophistication concerning participation in them, is important. The social sciences and psychology are properly felt to be of vital significance on the contemporary scene. Whether they are doing their work adequately is an open question. Some observers keep suggesting that the social sciences may sometimes have provided powerful instruments to the wrong people,[1] and instruments beyond necessity to the right people.[2]

If people think of higher learning as nothing more than accumulating more and more knowledge and sensory experience, but never as something that bears on choice, decision, and action, how can they learn to act wisely and responsibly? Is there no higher learning that concerns performance and participation? "We think of an imperative only when there is either an actual or a possible discrepancy between what we are doing and what we should do." [3] There is a discrepancy in the social sciences—and elsewhere—that suggests the imperatives, "Learn to use your knowledge, learn to use all your instruments, practice choice, practice wisdom!"

### WHO TAKES CARE OF THE CARETAKER'S DAUGHTER? [4]

As our institutions become larger and larger, the control of them may seem to concentrate in fewer and fewer hands. In a way this is the case. Of necessity, technical decision and military decision must be made by competent personnel. However, there is no need to exaggerate the point until it encourages deviation from our fundamental democratic convictions and proved principles and pro-

[1] One frequent charge against the social sciences is that, in their deliberate evasion of moral orientation and even of action orientation, they have failed to give us the most important knowledge of which they are capable: How to improve the human lot. Dr. Goebbels used *his* knowledge to *worsen* the human lot.

[2] A second charge is that social scientists are unimaginative. The election of 1960, in which (then) Senator Kennedy and Vice-President Nixon drafted their speeches in the light of acceptance or rejection of propositions by the American people, as reported by opinion pollsters, was doubtfully as informative and decisive as it might otherwise have been.

[3] George A. Schrader, "Responsibility and Existence." *Responsibility,* Ed., Carl J. Friedrich. New York: The Liberal Arts Press, 1960, p. 51.

[4] "Who takes care of the caretaker's daughter, when the caretaker is busy taking care?"

cedures. Some of the demands made for supercontrol and secrecy have been overstrenuous, and a few of them may have been attempts to avoid public scrutiny. Those who press the public in the direction of social hysteria or liberticide can sometimes be shown to have either a personal or an institutional axe to grind.

We need an orientation that is less strenuous and more consistent with our underlying attitude of good will toward all men.

The public, in a democracy, is the watchman over the watchmen, the control on the controllers. The reaction that is called for is a reaction in the direction of stronger individualities and firmer *self*-control with consequent elimination of hysteria. Trends toward subjugation and the meek acceptance of authority, undue security measures, and weakening of civil and social liberty have been fed by external pressures. Our longer and deeper tradition has taught us, however, better ways of reacting to strain and pressure than subjection.

There exists, moreover, a major theory about the origin of control and authority and about the ultimate causation of historical events that today merits our special attention. This more democratic theory says that it is the common people anyway who make the effective decisions. People at the top give the commands, buy and produce the televison shows, determine what car models shall be manufactured, select candidates in smoke-filled rooms, and the like. But you and I interpret and obey the commands according to our own lights, watch or turn off the programs, buy or don't buy the automobiles, and vote or do not vote for the presented candidates. Our country's tradition is free contract, free election, free men.

The theory is in large degree applicable, however, even to totalitarian states and autocracies. One of Tolstoy's celebrated paradoxes, enunciated in *War and Peace,* specifically referring to the generalship of the Russian and Napoleonic armies, was that

> the higher soldiers or statesmen are in the pyramid of authority, the farther they must be from its base which consists of those ordinary men and women whose lives are the actual stuff of history; and, consequently, the smaller the effect of the words and acts of such remote personages, despite all their theoretical authority, upon that history.[5]

A related idea, an interpretation of what has happened in our own mass age is this: "So great is the power that society can exert against

[5] As stated by Sir Isaiah Berlin in *The Hedgehog and The Fox.* (New York: A Mentor Book, 1957), p. 30. (Originally published in England in 1953.) Copyright 1953. Reprinted by permission.

the individual that it even subjects to dominance those very élites who seem to rule." [6]

The fact very probably is that both the higher affect the lower, and the lower the higher, so far as any chain of authority is concerned. The relation is one of reciprocity. As Hegel long ago pointed out, where there is master psychology, there also is slave psychology: If there are masters, there must be slaves. The same holds today, and if master persuaders "get away with murder" in the areas of commerce and politics, it is because the persuaded put up with them and their devices. A kind of intellectual inertia must have set in, in the public mind.

How different is our tradition from this lethargy. How opposed is the American political and moral heritage to this being swayed by any strong wind that blows. Our normal ethic implies the individualization and the internalization of decision. It supposes the free and full acceptance of personal responsibility and liability for action. It intends that action shall arise out of studied and persistent individual motives and interest. And this applies not only to individual conduct and decision, but also to social decision and action, which are expected to represent a consensus and summation of individual interests and perspectives.

This tradition has always recognized that men must act together: "We must all hang together or hang separately." But it conceives that men can find in rationality a basis for agreement. It conceives that individual men can form a sound opinion on the practical necessities of the time and spontaneously reach agreement on what course to pursue jointly. It supposes that they can then locate and loyally fill their various roles and find them both individually rewarding and socially useful.

Control and effective social decision and action do not entail regimentation. From this perspective, our first fear today should be lest we lose confidence that free citizens can succeed in working together and fighting together on a basis of individual initiative and thought. Is the sane and reflective individual, as citizen, voter, consumer, producer, powerless to affect society? Is the intelligent member of an institution just the tool of that institution?

No one who will become a member of the leadership group will answer these questions in the affirmative. No man is a leader until he has strong interests and convictions and the energy to promote them. [The thesis of Chapter 1.]

[6] George P. Grant, *Philosophy in the Mass Age* (New York: Hill and Wang, 1960), p. 16. "The proposition that the individual makes society is as much a half-truth as its converse," pp. 26–27.

Neither is a man a leader unless he has cultivated his judgment, his practical intellect, the capacity to determine rationally his own actions, and of course the self-discipline to hold to his policy. Unless our energetic man has a strong conscience, he may not be socially desirable.

### SUMMARY ON CONTROL

Our age has been fascinated by books like *The Hidden Persuaders,* obsessed with fact and fiction about Madison Avenue, propaganda, "public relations," and generally with the control of people by *sub rosa* techniques that appeal to the subliminal, the subconscious, the irrational mind. Our age has also been fascinated by the notion of historical inevitability, the unconscious influence of culture and political forms over individual mentality, the role of social and economic status, and such psychological influences as mother-and-father-orientation. Many have believed fanatically in destiny, the "inevitable" class-struggle, inescapable progress, (or, more recently, inescapable decline), the unavoidability of totalitarianism, and so on.

Yet our basic institutions are rationalistic and individualistic. Our official and traditional ideology supposes that man is a rational animal, proclaims the freedom of man, and assumes individual responsibility and the capacity to recognize and defend one's own interests. In principle we accept the Greek and Judeo-Christian conception of the individual man as having immense worth. We put confidence in individual deliberation and choice and foster free education and development. We have aimed to minimize state intervention and control, aimed to maximize self-control; and we have placed our trust in individuals and voluntary organizations. We have counted on an internalized morality.

The libertarian view is able to accept and absorb all the findings that point to irrational society and irrational man. Enlightened self-control in our day means self-control in the knowledge of available facts about our real nature as man and folk. Our recognition that we must work together in great masses and our interest in the science of human relations are wholesome, but they do not entail the impossibility of intelligent individual and social decision.[7] The great challenge of today is the mastery of social stress. We are not absolutely doomed to subjection, defeat, and ruin.

[7] That men can sometimes be controlled by strings does not prove that our social and political institutions are asinine. A hundred years ago, Abraham Lincoln strongly implied that most men can be fooled most of the time, but he retained his faith in liberal democracy.

# 3

# IMPERATIVES

That is imperative which is expressive of command. An imperative is an order, or any kind of demand or requirement, to do something or not to do something. Imperatives may be conceived broadly to include not only commands by other people and pressures generated by natural and historical situations, but also demands of conscience and sensitivities to obligation. We do not ordinarily speak of imperatives as true or false; but we do think of them as well- or ill-founded, justifiable or not justifiable, and sometimes as adequate or inadequate.

## WHAT ARE RATIONAL IMPERATIVES?

We are all quite clear about simple imperatives that have the form of direct orders, and we are all well acquainted with the kinds of question common sense raises about them. The sergeant shouts at us, "Pick up your feet!" It's a clear and meaningful order, and we know what we have to do, and why we have to do it. We recognize a difference between such shouted phrases and the quiet indicative sentences of science. Meaningful indicatives are true or false, and truth is something to which scientists may be more sensitive than sergeants. Sometimes, however, imperatives imply an indicative meaning. For instance, we might think to ourselves when ordered to pick up our feet, "But we weren't dragging them." And if we weren't, we might complain (under our breath, of course) that the sergeant's command did not rest on fact. So we can raise questions of fact and of truth about imperatives, and this difference between imperatives and indicative statements is not absolute.

Another kind of question that we often raise about orders relates to their authoritativeness. Is the sergeant from *my* company? Does he have jurisdiction, and the right to tell me what to do? "Who said so?" we bluntly ask. Under certain circumstances we may well insist on seeing the papers that ascribe authority, before we are prepared to respond. Questions about jurisdiction and spheres of authority become highly intricate and complicated in organized societies, so that lawyers must sometimes ponder to what court to appeal, and administrators feel called upon to issue orders about how to issue orders and spell out just what kinds and amounts of authority are vested in various positions. Management firms offer expert services in the reorganization of corporate structure and the reassignment of authority. Special "earthmoving" commissions dredge new channels of command through federal bureaus and agencies.

Imperatives interest ethicists for several reasons: (1) Because every custom, every rule or maxim that is invested with moral significance is an imperative commanding all those who are subject to it to do something or to refrain from doing something. (2) Because various ethical systems feature various *kinds* of imperatives: Authoritarian ethics will support and give emphasis to the commands of some accepted authority like God and his priests or the monarch; rationalist ethics will stress rational imperatives. (3) Because moral imperatives often conflict with other kinds of imperatives; thus, if I aim to get rich, I may sometime be tempted to follow prudential and moral imperatives that do not jibe. Moral imperatives, moreover, may conflict with one another: A man's duty to his father may come into conflict with duty to his church.[1] Ethicists take interest both in imperatives-in-general and in moral imperatives in particular: In questions about their meaningfulness, in questions about their validity, and in their relations one to another and to fact.

We are all of us ethicists. Expanding intelligence asks broader and broader questions about the value and reasonableness of acts and about their merit and likelihood of success in view of real situations.

Whence the imperativeness of imperatives? It does not lie in the

[1] An instance of such a conflict is narrated in Plato's *Euthyphro*.

value sought, the act commanded, or the state of affairs. It seems to lie rather in a *relation* between value and act, or authority and act, in some given context. Constraint, imperativeness, and obligation are *relational.*

*Rational* imperatives are imperatives that have been through the crucible of intelligence and judgment; they are to be distinguished from mere impulses, whims, customs, and the foolish orders of foolish sovereigns. Rational imperatives make their appeal directly to our free judgment—both in distinction from our impulses and selfishness and in distinction from rules supported by old tradition, external authority, or physical force. The imperativeness of a rational imperative as such lies in its presenting a sensible answer to some discrepancy between need and fulfillment. It may, of course, be supported by custom or law.

## TECHNICAL IMPERATIVES

Kant held that, to whatever extent we are rational in practical life, we are following imperatives that are generalizable. A practical rule is an instruction that can in principle be followed more than one time and by more than one individual.

Technical imperatives are rules of procedure that tell us how to go about satisfying various kinds of purpose that we might, from considerations of value, be inclined to adopt as our own. Technical imperatives have to do with the practical arts of life and industry, but also with the social arts and the organization of human activities aiming at social accomplishment. Kant called all these "imperatives of skill." He said that their *universal form* is: "Whoever wills the end, also (insofar as reason has a decisive influence upon his actions) wills the indispensable means at his disposal." [2]

[2] Immanuel Kant, *The Fundamental Principles of the Metaphysic of Ethics.* Translated with an Introduction by Otto Manthey-Zorn. New York: D. Appleton-Century Company, Inc., 1938, p. 34. Immanuel Kant is one of the greatest philosophers. He was born and died in Koenigsberg, East Prussia, 1724–1804. His teaching career at the University of Koenigsberg encompassed not only philosophy, but also anthropology, of which he was the first teacher; his first publication was an important work in astronomy. His primary fame rests on his origination and development of the critical philosophy—a philosophy that aims to discover the limits of human knowledge, especially of metaphysical and ethical knowledge. His best-known work is *The Critique of Pure Reason,* 1781. His principal ethical treatises are the *Fundamental Principles* and the *Critique of Practical Reason.* Kant is perhaps less a product of Prussian Junkerdom than of the merchant class and the Hansa city of Koenigsberg, of the Enlightenment, and of the religious movement known as "Pietism." (The culture of the Junkers was, however, much deeper and broader than we Americans are inclined to admit; and some of the higher Prussian officials gave notable support to Kant in his need for freedom of teaching and publication.)

Typical technical imperatives, in full dress, are: "If you wish to stop the draft, then shut the window," "If it looks like rain, then carry an umbrella," and "If you are looking for sodium or chlorine, then break down molecules of table salt." As may be noted, the *object* of the possible action, the end, what we want accomplished, is stated in the antecedent clause; this is related in the consequent to some method or other of attainment. The technical imperative connects a possible objective, or value, with a possible mode of realization.

In practice we often do not bother to state the end, either because it is taken for granted or because any one of a number of ends will satisfy. In the case of an imperative like "Pick up your feet!" we might say that the objective was correct marching; but it would be equally cogent to say that the private's objective in obeying was to keep the sergeant off his back. In other words, from the action itself, we cannot always tell what the objective, what the "antecedent clause," is. If a man carefully drives on the right side of the road, it may be because of the imperative, "If you want to be safe, keep to the right," or it may be because, "If you don't want to be arrested, keep to the right." We don't care what technical imperative the man is following, so long as he keeps his car on the right side of the road.

The law, and custom and manners, often can and do abbreviate. They prescribe the action without stating the objective. The normal but often unstated antecedent of legal prescriptions is a threat of punishment. The law does not ordinarily physically restrain men from committing murder or burglary, but it warns them, "If you don't want to be executed or incarcerated, don't commit murder and don't commit burglary." So also in nonlegal cases: "Use the key attached to the bottom of the tin," "Wear white tie and tails," "R.S.V.P." The legal case and "R.S.V.P." are similar in that we are expected to obey without going into the motives of the prescriber. Whether the hostess wishes to invite someone else, if we aren't coming, or just wants to plan her place settings or her food and wine order is none of our business. And if the law has been laid down by legally constituted authority in accordance with legal procedure, *prima facie,* it is none of our business why we should obey. We ought to obey in any case, so long as it's the law.

Sometimes also we don't explicitly state the end, but suggest some fact that relates to a likely end. Thus, instead of saying, in proper form, "If you don't want your hand burned, don't put it there," we might instead say, "Don't touch that, it's hot." Or we may just hint at imperatives, as is commonly done in advertising, "The *best* goldfish food is Glover's Meal," "The *quickest* way to Chicago is by air," "The neat place to fulfill your military duty is the Coast Guard." In appropriate context, all these sentences imply imperatives.

### (*1*) *Imperatives and Child Learning*

Infants manage to grasp the meaning of orders even before they can talk. Mother says, "Hot, hot, hot!" and points at the top of the stove, all the time shaking her head negatively. "Hot" is sometimes the first word uttered by children, and it then carries a decided imperative flavor. An interesting early introduction to imperatives may be found in toilet training, perhaps the earliest major set of imperatives that require substantial *self-command,* in this case, control through the efferent nervous system over one's own body.[3]

Most child learning is learning technical imperatives (rather than simple sensing). A factor in much of it is *self-imitation.* The child reaches the point at which he is anatomically and physiologically ready to learn to walk; at the same time he develops an immense urge to try walking. He repeats his successes more and more, until at last he can walk about. The primary principles in the whole development probably are trial-and-error and self-imitation (of successes). The urge to walk and the urge to talk are, in human nature, very powerful; attainment of the very highest artistic success in speech and graceful locomotion are, incidentally, among the most difficult human achievements. We tend, most of us, to settle for too little excellence in movement and communication. Ordinary powers of locomotion and speech typically reside in mere *habit* and demand but minimal attention (except under extraordinary circumstances, as in mountain climbing and after illness or in preparing an address).

A vast number of maxims is painstakingly acquired and verified in use; then the whole set is retained in the unconscious. The same procedure and eventuation are exemplified in learning to read and write, to drive an automobile, to eat with knife, fork, and spoon—or with chopsticks—to dress, to sweep, and to scrub. Vital imperatives are thus imprinted deeply in our minds and bodies where they function well enough, generally speaking, and do not cause us much bother. If, when we think of technical imperatives, we tend to think

[3] It has a special meaning in the psychology of the individual and may affect his lifetime emotional attitude toward authority. Educated parents are circumspect in the issuance of orders to their children, never asking the impossible but insisting on obedience.

of more sophisticated, more technological ones, it is only because the more elementary maxims demand so little attention.

### (2) *How We Learn Complex Technical Imperatives*

How and where do we learn the more advanced technical imperatives? We learn counting and penmanship in school, piano-playing from a private teacher, laboratory technique from manuals and in the laboratory under instruction. We learn technological imperatives most frequently on the job, over long periods of time, and through necessity, experience, and apprenticeship. We learn them in the most intimate relationship with work and science. At the very highest level, there is usually considerable trial-and-error mixed with skill, often under curiously rigged circumstances. The surgeon develops a new style of surgery by experiment, perhaps cultivating his dexterity and accelerating his speed by operating on animals and cadavers until he is ready to attempt the operation on a living man. And his competence will continue to improve *in* practicing surgery on human patients, as long as his own health, vigor, and alertness —his own learning powers—remain on this side of decline and senility. The same kind of movement toward excellence and complex capacity occurs, of course, not just among surgeons, but among all professional people, artisans, laboratory and service technicians, and administrators and executives.

The relation of technological imperatives to science raises questions that are very difficult to analyze and solve. Operationalism, a widely accepted theory in the philosophy of science, holds that the meaning of scientific sentences is precisely the operations which they prescribe. The meaning of a scientific statement is the procedure, the method of attainment of a sensible result.

In academic science classes, where old knowledge is taught but no new knowledge discovered, the emphasis is ordinarily on facts and hypotheses; but from our perspective, more attention ought to be given to learning through *real* experiments (the result being uncertain), and to the development of *new* procedures and maxims and *new* intellectual, manual, and machine techniques.

The relation of technical imperatives to action is no simpler than their relation to science and knowledge. We must "know"—incorporate and make our own—many imperatives, and especially such as begin with negative antecedent clauses, just to live and avoid hurt. "If you don't want to fall, don't lean too far out." "If you don't want to stumble, watch your step." To maintain life and growth, some members or other of society must learn imperatives connected with securing food supply and preparing it, and others must learn imperatives about the manufacture of clothing, shelter, medicine, drink, writing implements, weapons, vehicles. The discovery, statement, and inculcation—transmission—of such imperatives make up a big share of the work of every culture. Under civilized circumstances, such imperatives take on expanded and intricate forms: Engineers' handbooks and building codes, the traditions of masonry, carpentry, plastering, sheet metal work, electric wiring; the manufacture of brick, lathe, siding, gypsum products, wallpaper, and paint; and so on almost endlessly. All trades and industries are composed, essentially, of carefully wrought imperatives of skill. The division of labor is the division of task, skill, and know-how.

Not the least exigent set of imperatives of skill has to do with the organization of human activities. These are skills that specifically apply to people: the skills of mothers in training their children, the command skills of teachers and foremen, the persuasive skills of salesmen, the leadership skills of platoon leaders, captains of industry, labor leaders, statesmen, and heads of research projects. All these kinds of social skill—that in so many of us remain only rudimentary—are a part of the imperative structure of our culture.

Malinowski speaks in this connection of "the language of concerted action";[4] and precisely this language, with the views and powers it expresses, gives to each culture its special tone and flavor. In reality social traditions and ways of organizing people cannot be entirely distinguished from methods of production, distribution, and consumption of goods and services.[5] Changes in methods of doing things, moreover, often result in changed social relations; and changes in social relations often are followed by changes in working methods.

Enough about technical imperatives; we proceed now to the second classification of imperatives in the Kantian analysis.

## COUNSELS OF PRUDENCE

The opinion is widespread that the general welfare and the attainment of personal happiness are clear and distinct goals—in sharp contrast to every *moral* objective. This opinion is fallacious.

[4] See Robert T. Harris and Jarrett, *Language and Informal Logic,* New York: Longmans, Green & Co., 1956, p. 288; and see Bronislaw Malinowski, *Coral Gardens and Their Magic,* New York: American Book Company, 1935, Vol. II, p. 7.

[5] In our own culture, the head of a large engineering firm is likely to be an engineer. More typically, however, the heads of corporations and other enterprises are lawyers, former sales managers, or anyway experts in social relations.

Kant said that "happiness is not an ideal of reason but of the imagination." The over-arching imperative of happiness is formally identical with the universal imperative of skill, namely, that "whoever wills the end also wills the indispensable means that are in his power." The major difference between these universal imperatives seems to lie not in their form but in the fact that we can assume, within limits, that everyone seeks his own happiness, while we obviously cannot assume that everyone wants to build a bridge, make a cake, or do the endless number of things statable in technical imperatives. Happiness is everyone's goal.

Unfortunately, however, happiness conceived as a universal goal is only conceived *formally*. To foretell concretely of what our individual happiness will consist requires the greatest experience and the highest wisdom. Perhaps we should go farther and say that to predict accurately what kinds of experience and success will give us precisely the *greatest net satisfaction* in the present and future is beyond all human wisdom. Our sensibility changes: What pleases the child no longer pleases the teen-ager, and what pleases the teen-ager will not gratify the man of middle-age or delight an old woman. As Kant himself remarks, the elements belonging to the concept of happiness "must all be taken from experience, but at the same time require an absolute whole, a maximum of well-being in the present and every future state." [6]

Consider also that even if we were clear about the content of our greatest happiness, there would remain the further problem of learning the indispensable means. To aim effectively even at our personal happiness, we are required not only to judge our present and future sensibility, including our conscientious feelings, but also to judge the utility of all plausible means. Since our happiness will certainly depend on the loyalty and dependability of other persons, and on their future power of pleasing us, they too must be judged. And predicting the future conduct and interest of other people is not easier than predicting our own.[7] Is Kant then unduly pessimistic in denying that even the most penetrating human being can

> construct for himself a definite conception of what he really wants? If he wills riches, with what worry, envy and persecution is he not apt to burden himself because of it? If he wills knowledge and in-

[6] Be it on earth or in heaven!

[7] In southeastern Asia, where our dating culture is not accepted and not even understood, the parents choose mates for their sons and daughters, and the mother of a boy will sometimes test his intended bride for a year or more—her neatness and her cooking, but also her disposition—before giving final approval to the match. Divorce rates are low. But no system of testing brides or other personnel is infallible.

sight, that may merely make his eyes sharper to see as the more terrible the unavoidable evils which are still hidden from him, or else burden his avidity that already troubles him enough with further desires. If he desires a long life, what guarantee is there that it will not be a long misery? If he at least wants health, how often has not the discomfort of the body prevented dissipations to which an unimpaired health may have tempted him, and so forth. In short he is unable to determine with complete certainty, according to any principle, what will make him truly happy because it would take omniscience to do so. It is therefore impossible to act according to definite principles in order to be happy, but one must act in accordance with empirical counsels, for example, of diet, economy, courtesy, restraint and the like, of which experience teaches that they on the average best promote well-being. It follows from this that the 'imperatives' of prudence *cannot* command at all in the strict sense of the word . . . that they are to be considered counsels rather than precepts of reason. . . .[8]

We may find Kant's stoicism a bit quaint; and perhaps many of us settle with little discomfort, intellectual or otherwise, for a life built on probabilities anyway. We don't expect or demand complete certainty. Nevertheless, Kant is correct in finding that happiness and the good life are obscure and difficult goals to specify, unless we understand them only in a highly formal sense.

### *(1) More About Prudence*

Since college students and others often think that the individual's own maximum pleasure is the only life goal that makes any sense, we shall mention that this position is known among philosophers as *ethical individual hedonism.*[9] It is frequently contrasted with *social hedonism,* or the notion that the legitimate objective is the pleasure of all, or of the greatest possible number of men.

Hedonism is also to be contrasted with the famous position of Aristotle, eudaemonism, a name derived from a Greek word for happiness. The eudaemonist thinks of happiness not so much as pleasure—which is something likely, however, to be super-added—

[8] Immanuel Kant, *The Fundamental Principles of the Metaphysic of Ethics, loc. cit.,* pp. 34–35.

[9] Many college students are impressed also with the position known as *psychological individual hedonism,* which is not an ethical but a psychological position. It affirms that all men everywhere in fact do seek their own pleasure. It is not widely accepted by philosophers, because it overlooks that, *e.g.,* when men seek drink, it is drink that they seek and not their own pleasure. The difficulty with the view is less that it overlooks our higher nature than that it overlooks our passionate nature. Only the perfectly rational, economic man is a pure psychological hedonist, and no such man exists.

but as free fulfillment of function, the maturation and exercise of well-oriented capacities and powers. Aristotle thought of man as an animal distinguished from, and elevated above, other animals by his power to reason. A life of happiness, accordingly, is a life that secures satisfaction of our animal needs but which in addition consists in deliberate action and intellectual contemplation.[10]

The wisdom of the ancients very largely concerned itself with the attainment of happiness or of pleasure or of both. "What ought I to do to secure an enduring state of well-being?" surely is one of the profoundest human questions, practically speaking, and, once asked, one of the most insistent. If in modern times many of us have lost the nerve or the judgment to ask it, so much the worse for us. We are too tame or smug.

The entire view that either happiness or pleasure is the *end* of man has been challenged in recent times, or has at least been weighed against another possible view. Freud's thinking at one stage led him to consider the possibility that not life and happiness are the final goal of the human psyche, but rather:

> If we are to take it as a truth that knows no exception that everything living dies for *internal* reasons—becomes inorganic once again—then we shall be compelled to say that *'the aim of all life is death'* and, looking backwards, that *'inanimate things existed before living ones.'* [11]

If such a death drive is perchance an integral element in our mental and emotional life, then certainly it ought to be given recognition and taken into account. A kind of preoccupation with death, with our having to face death, is characteristic of the times. Witness the successful films of Ingemar Bergman and the vogue of existentialist literature.

## (2) *How Measure My Own Good?*

What is the right way to *measure* my own good? In answer to this question, Western ethics has given three major answers.[12] (1) The Cynics repudiated prudence, saying that it lacked sanction. What I

[10] President Kennedy expressed his personal philosophy more or less in these terms.

[11] Sigmund Freud, "Beyond the Pleasure Principle." In: *The Standard Edition of the Complete Psychological Works of Sigmund Freud,* ed. and trans., James Strachey. London: The Hogarth Press and the Institute of Psycho-Analysis, 1955. V. 18, p. 38. Reprinted by permission. The idea is here expressed only for its own sake and is quoted out of context.

[12] C. I. Lewis, *The Ground and Nature of the Right,* New York: Columbia University Press, 1955, pp. 73–74.

ought to do, they said, is grasp immediate values regardless; take the cash and let the credit go; be merry today for tomorrow I die. (2) Jeremy Bentham and any literal followers of his hedonic calculus have recognized the prudential sanction but have held that in calculating pleasures I ought specially to make a discount from them, if they are remote in time. The farther off in the future a gratification lies, the less worth it has for me today.—Now most of us would agree that the probability of actual occurrence should be part of the measure, but we would reject mere propinquity or remoteness in time as a factor in itself. (3) I want an adequate income now but I ought in reason today to want an adequate income ten years from now just as much. The third answer states that the prudent aim is precisely this one that maximizes the balance of my good over bad, weighing the future on a par with the present, but taking all the probabilities into account.

When the likelihood of my even having any future gets small, as just before the battle, then I may reasonably make a big discount of the future in favor of the present. The improbability of my own future existence sanctions the discount. But isn't the *ordinary* meaning of prudence (*i.e.,* if we don't puff it up) precisely the securing and controlling of my own future? The avoiding of ever becoming a battle casualty? The prudential aim is not the *noblest* aim there is but requires us, even in hot or cold war, to maximize our security. By definition, kamikaze, hara-kiri (seppuki), and last fling sorts of operation are not prudent—whatever other adjectives may apply.

The public may or may not be aware that it's so, but recklessness is much more common than cowardice. It is difficult to control. In Marine aviation we used to say that a pilot would be worth something against the enemy if only we could get him back safe from his first two or three combat missions. On the first missions, he was unseasoned but all too likely to be an "eager beaver." Neither cowardice nor recklessness [13] is an element of effective courage; but prudence *is.* Prudence is significant not only economically and politically, but also militarily. It is not itself noble, but it helps produce effective heroes.

One ought to respect himself and his own interests, both present and future.

## ARE THERE MORAL IMPERATIVES?

We naturally expect to find such a question answered affirmatively in a book about social ethics. It will be here. The reader may beware.

[13] Recklessness and overconfidence are not identical with daring.

He is not reading a fundamentalist's Bible but only a secular text, one that invites criticism. That the thought in a book should rise above the intellectual caliber of its author is as unlikely as that a river should rise above its source.[14]

There have appeared many book-length attacks against the existence of moral imperatives both in ancient and again in modern times. Much of Kant's work represents an attempt to counter earlier attacks on morality and to exhibit just what distinctively *moral* imperatives are, what their meaning is, in distinction from other kinds of imperatives.

To account for most of the current scepticism about morality and about moral principle and moral imperatives is not very difficult. And the misinterpretation of moral principle will be seen not to be the monopoly of sceptics, but to be shared by many strong supporters of "morality," especially of "dogmatic morality" and "traditional morality."

Those who doubt the existence of any really *moral* conduct usually do so because they accept individual or cultural relativism. Individual relativism is the doctrine that what is right for one individual, or considered by him to be right, is not so for another. Cultural relativism is the doctrine which states that what actions are right and what wrong are determined by the society or culture, and that such determinations vary from culture to culture. But that beliefs concerning what is right and wrong do vary from individual to individual and from culture to culture is an empirical fact that hardly warrants dispute. If acquiring this insight entailed discarding morality, there would be no option.

From the practical standpoint of choice, however, although both individual and cultural relativism may offer valuable leads, they won't do our deciding for us. The practical question, *what ought I to do,* remains with us. Given all the material circumstances, including the psychological and cultural circumstances, how ought I to choose, what ought I to do? That I have certain attitudinal sets is a very poor excuse for not doing what I ought. That the culture accepts certain kinds of acts as right is often the source of issues rather than their resolution. In deciding and acting I ought to take *everything* into account; the question of the existence of moral imperatives is simply the question whether there are considerations to be taken into account beyond those represented in technical and prudential imperatives.

[14] In paraphrase of a statement by George R. Stewart.

## (1) Is Conscience an Anachronism?

There is, according to Freud and Ernest Jones, no instinct impelling man toward higher ethical aims.[15] Conscience can be accounted for naturalistically.[16] It is related largely to narcissism and "ego ideal" and constitutes one of those essential traits of character that are laid down by the age of three.[17] From Freud's surely legitimate perspective, conscientiousness and guilt are psychological phenomena and can and should be understood as such. The more we can know about the psychology of morality the better. Freud himself discovered that a morality can turn against itself, that we may have "criminals from a sense of guilt." [18]

Psychoanalysts are not the only deflators of morality, conscience, and the sense of guilt. William James criticized Americans' moralism and over-conscientiousness. He preached "the gospel of relaxation" and thought the overstrenuous were only too likely, just at the moment of crisis, to hurry off on a moral holiday. Mark Twain disparaged puritanism, *e.g.*, in the story "Was It Heaven or Was It Hell?" in which two straight-laced spinsters were constrained to tell several lies.

In Anthony Trollope's novel, *The Prime Minister,* the wise old Duke of St. Bungay was advising the Duke of Omnium, the Prime Minister:

> "Psha;—nonsense!" said the old Duke getting up. "There is such a thing as a conscience with so fine an edge that it will allow a man to do nothing. You've got to serve your country."

A conscience can be so rigorous that it accentuates a man's lack of wit and detracts from his personality, so fine that it incapacitates him for his post.[19] It can be inhibiting and tension-producing. In social relations, an uncompromising conscience often proves irritating or even insulting; it sometimes obstructs serious business. "The strict sense of duty" may only make for sentimentality, hypocrisy, fanaticism.[20]

[15] Ernest Jones, *The Life and Work of Sigmund Freud,* New York: Basic Books, Inc., 1955, Vol. 3, p. 307.

[16] *Ibid.,* Vol. 3, p. 437

[17] *Ibid.,* Vol. 2, p. 306.

[18] *Ibid.,* Vol. 2, p. 373. There are related cases that fall short of criminality: A man scolds his wife because of his own inadequacies. Another feels guilty because he does not work harder and becomes hypercritical of anyone who "interrupts" him.

[19] In Washington, white collar people say that "you should have an official conscience," *i.e.,* do your official duty and follow orders, but keep your own conscience in a state of rest.

[20] Not to mention chauvinism, tartufism, ultra-montanism.

These are all cases, however, of deviation or exaggeration. Their existence and even their high frequency do not really take anything away from the import of conscience. Compare our attitude toward love. Love is associated with perversion, frustration, blindness, envy, and crime; yet all the same we don't turn against it. We blame such corruptions on human fault and go right on praising love as before. (Perhaps we could, like Lucretius, give up sentimental love and still sing paeans to Venus; certainly there are kinds and degrees of conscience that we could manage without.) Whoever cannot agreeably contemplate a world without love should weigh on the same scales a world without conscience. We are members one of another and depend on one another's conscience. That a man can commit crime from a sense of guilt should bring home to every individual the extreme importance of a wholesome state of conscience. Conscience can be misguided, corrupt, excessive; but it cannot be avoided. It seems highly unlikely, during the lifetime of our species, to become anachronistic.

### (2) *False Moralities*

Much that passes for morality is no more and no better than tradition grown irrelevant and inhibition born in frightful and eccentric experiences of childhood. But what have these *ersatz* moralities and these subjections to tradition or childhood heritage to do with the serious ethical problems of men? If a distant comparison be permitted, then let it be said that no seasoned businessman fails in such a gross way to distinguish the false from the real. A businessman who did would go bankrupt. Yet perhaps half the ethics courses in Christendom terminate in the finding that morality and ethics are meaningless.[21] This finding rests on confusing false morality with all the morality there is. It is as if one were to decide, after an experience with fools' gold, that it's the only kind of gold there is. You couldn't convince the officers at Fort Knox, nor successful gold miners. Nor could you convince men who have to make right decisions affecting other persons that there is no ethics and no real moral problem.

William James once said, "I cannot understand the willingness to act, no matter how we feel, without the belief that acts are really good and bad." Our young people of the present, living on a planet where so much depends on the explicit decision of men, can hardly fail to agree with him. Thoughtful college students will rise above

[21] Compare the Preface to George P. Grant, *Philosophy in the Mass Age*. New York: Hill and Wang, 1960.

such academic scepticism.[22] For they are vitally concerned to achieve right decision and right action at all levels of human affairs. But such rising above, in the sphere of decision and action, constitutes real morality: Rising above mere academicism, above psychologism, above mere tradition, above one's early experience with father, mother and sibling, in order to make sure that one's acts and attitudes really are appropriate and good.

We adults do not differ markedly from boys and girls in our faltering sense of reality, in our wavering between a fantastic gullibility [23] and a false scepticism. When recently I was on a so-called "snipe hunt" with a number of younger campers, one of the counselors shouted that he heard a bear in the brush. As the counselor had expected, the boys ran back almost frantically to our campfire. But then we heard five of the boys declare that they had actually *seen* the bear. But some other boys, or the very same boys, were so sceptical a few days later when presented with a genuine Chippewa Indian guide, that they thought we had painted and dressed up the stable boy. Men are forever mistaking wrongness for rightness, apparent rightness for the real: It's the grown-ups' "snipe hunt." One could not exhaust the ways in which uncontrolled imagination has been spent in moral woods and thickets. Scepticism often proves but one more way of getting lost, a less frequent and hence more startling way than dogmatism.

A few contemporary ways of going wrong that may suggest why there is still a demand for moral insight are:

(1) To mistake the real need of staying in the saddle for too much concession: Every executive—and every person—has now and again to make concessions or lose his power.

(2) Conversely, to grant a concession from principle when one is really only too lazy or too cowardly to stick by his guns.

(3) To refuse responsibility in the false hope that "George will take care of it."

[22] "What is sad about these young people is that our educational institutions cannot be ready to meet their needs. Our educational institutions at all levels are still largely formed by what is most banal in our society. They have lost what was best in the old European education. They are spiritually formed by the narrow practicality of techniques; they are immediately governed by ill-educated capitalists of narrow interest. But this very failure of our educational institutions is part of that alienation which will drive the best of our students to philosophy and theology. And these young people are the evidence that in our society profound philosophical thought is arising. They herald what may yet be, surprisingly, the dawn of the age of reason in North America." *Ibid.*, pp. 24–25. Reprinted by permission.

[23] John Dewey said that men do not see that a man is bad, they see a bad man.

(4) To accent the morally trivial at the expense of the morally crucial.

Perhaps this fourth way of leaving the track is commonest. The degradation of other people and violation of their right to work out their own lives are properly venal sins. Yet the people who loudly decry drinking, smoking, cardplaying, and dancing are sometimes the very same people who raid the lives of innocents. Those who call out, "Morality, morality!" at every turn have brought the moral life into undeserved disrepute, the more so because they make their laments in a tone that does resemble moral anguish. If philosophers acknowledge that such hypocrisy exemplifies morality, no wonder they are sceptical.

### (3) *Real Morality*

What then is the meaning of morality? Are there any imperatives really and distinctively moral?

A man who does his best to act right acts morally. When a man aims at the greatest objective balance of good over bad—giving due weight but only due weight to his personal interest—he acts from moral principle. He is disinterested in that he aims at the highest good and looks on conflicting interests of his own as so many distractions to be avoided. He is impartial in that he counts himself for one but not for more than one. *A moral agent seeks the realization of value in an outgoing way.*

We have found that there are imperative ways of achieving various technical ends. We have found that some ways of seeking personal happiness are more plausible than others. The question as to further and distinctively moral imperatives is the question whether we know any further imperatives and constraints in deciding and acting. If we recognize claims to consider the interests of other members of our family, of friends, of fellow citizens, or perhaps of a yet wider fellowship, then we recognize a *moral* obligation that constrains our will, that can limit and reorient our own claims. Since such constraint is universally felt and since it gives indispensable support to society and direction to legislation, an attempt to establish or "prove" its existence would be superfluous.

Moral imperatives are the final imperatives. It is always relevant to ask of a technical imperative, "Will it work? Does its antecedent clause express my purpose?" But it is also relevant to ask of a technical imperative, "Am I morally justified in adopting it, in following it?" We also ought to ask of our counsels of prudence, "Are we justified in seeking our happiness by such means?" "Are we being fair to other persons and other interests?" But there are no imperatives above the moral ones; there are no other kinds of imperative in terms of which we can warrant the ultimate moral ones.[24] Since moral imperatives have this peculiar status, Kant speaks of them as categorical. They express and represent a kind of obligation that is *sui generis*, that is final, and that is immediately and directly given to us as creatures of reason.

### PROFESSIONAL STANDARDS

The surgeon and the physician follow imperatives of skill in cutting and removing, in prescribing medicines, diet, and so on. These imperatives depend on knowledge of anatomy, physiology, diseases, medicines, instruments, and so on.

Professional people follow a further set of imperatives generally spoken of as "professional standards." Because of the intimate relationship between client and physician, lawyer, or accountant, because of the dependence of the client on him, and because of the importance of high standards to the entire profession and, in the end, to the entire public, tradition requires that professional skills be practiced on a level that is above the merely economic one. Technical competence, relation to the client, setting fees, manner of advertising, and the like, are matters of general concern. Accepted standards are accordingly maintained and enforced by the profession and often by statute as well. When pressure is exerted to change such standards, major battles often ensue.[25]

In the case of auditors, the interest of distant investors and lenders is at stake. The general standards of the profession supplement the reputation for integrity and competence of the individual auditing firm.

Three of the "Rules of Professional Conduct" of the American Institute of Accountants are:

> No. 2 A member or associate shall not allow any person to practice in his name who is not in partnership with him or in his employ.

[24] The rather widespread conviction that moral imperatives are justified by religion rests on a misunderstanding of the relation between religion and morals. Religion in the morally acceptable sense of the word certainly may support the highest moral cause. What passes for religion may also be blind and aggressive. One should always ask, "*What* religion?" "*What* morality?" In no case, however, does religion as such supply the warrant for moral imperatives, even if the highest religious insight often is equally moral insight.

[25] The first physicians who used X-Ray were called "quacks." Consider also the struggle over psychiatric, epecially psychoanalytic medicine, and the current struggle over investment counseling by certified public accountants.

No. 3 Commissions, brokerage, or other participation in the fees or profits of professional work shall not be allowed directly or indirectly to the laity by a member or associate. . . .

No. 5 In expressing an opinion on representations in financial statements which he has examined, a member or associate may be held guilty of an act discreditable to the profession if

a) he fails to disclose a material fact known to him which is not disclosed in the financial statements but disclosure of which is necessary to make the financial statements not misleading ; or

b) he fails to report any material misstatement known to him to appear in the financial statement; or

c) he is materially negligent in the conduct of his examination or in making his report thereon; or

d) he fails to acquire sufficient information to warrant expression of an opinion, or his exceptions are sufficiently material to negative the expression of an opinion; or

e) he fails to direct attention to any material departure from generally accepted accounting principles or to disclose any material omission of generally accepted auditing procedure applicable in the circumstances.

There are sixteen of these "Rules of Professional Conduct," and they serve as a guide to Certified Public Accountants, both members and nonmembers of the Institute. The Rules are supplemented by numbered opinions of the Institute's Committee on Professional Ethics.[26]

To distinguish morality from technique and prudence in professional standards is virtually impossible—and perhaps hardly worthwhile. In any case, the moral thread runs through the pattern. That interest is present (and that professional people make money) should not be allowed to obscure the point. As a matter of fact, the practical interest often is subsequent on the acceptance of a moral value. This is not to deny, of course, that unfair advantage may be made of professional calling and status.

### BRIEF SUMMARY AND TRANSITION

If men are to enjoy life to the full, they must find and understand themselves. They should want to be as clear as possible what their values are. Value judgment and even sensibility itself can be im-

[26] See John L. Carey, *Professional Ethics of Certified Public Accountants.* New York: American Institute of Accountants, 270 Madison Avenue, 1956. Obviously, the capitalistic system greatly depends on the maintenance of professional standards of accounting and auditing. Reprinted by permission.

proved. Social values are values jointly held. These also can be clarified by experience and reflection.

In order that goods may be produced, services provided, and values created and enjoyed, men have to be organized. Their wants must be harmonized and brought into focus, their work oriented toward the attainment of goals. The present generation has been fascinated by means of controlling society, or segments of it, and especially by use of devices that take hold of subrational facets of personality. A libertarian can accept all the findings of irrationalism in human decision and conduct and yet remain a libertarian.

If there is liberty, there is individual responsibility. If liberty is to be a living institution, individual responsibility must be widely accepted. To whatever extent men have the choice, they do well to obey rational imperatives rather than mere custom or brute coercion.

# PART II

# Liberty

# 4

# MILL AND THE SOCIAL UTILITY OF LIBERTY

## I

Between liberty and other social values there is high tension. In our own age, the desire for liberty often conflicts with the desire for security. Only yesterday it conflicted with economic security, and today with *national* security. People want liberty, but they also want the organization necessary to the output of goods. People want liberty, but they also fear an external enemy and internal subversion. To many the liberty of others seems to imply letting them criticize everything and letting them do anything, so that national ideology, the political-economic order, and holy religion are by it brought to the block.

We are fortunately in possession of a powerful heritage of liberty that has been built up for us by daring and intelligent men over several centuries. The meaning, value, and condition of our freedom are much disputed; and sometimes only tradition unaided seems to prevent its permanent destruction. Parliamentary government, democracy, and individualism, but also civil, political, and social liberty have been hotly challenged in our times. The innocent have called them cruel and inhuman institutions; the sceptical and the weary, the fanatical and the villainous have called them too strenuous for the likes of mortal man. But liberty has not been proved impractical, fugitive, or illusory. It has withstood attack both in the scholar's study and on the battlefield.

Liberty *may* be "only the late fruit of our declining capitalist civilization . . . ," [1] as Berlin writes in *Two Concepts of Liberty.* It is true that this cherished ideal is a recent conception. From that, however, as Berlin also remarks, no sceptical conclusions follow. The stubborn growth of liberty into one of our most sacred values, despite powerful attacks from many quarters, suggests that it has even more value and strength in practice than have yet been claimed for it.

We propose to look at some questions about the meaning of liberty, the grounds on which it has been defended and attacked, and its role in society today. We shall eventually consider meanings attributed to it by three of its chief proponents (two of whom are widely accused of having really sold it down the river). We begin with John Stuart Mill (1806–73), the latest of the three, for reasons of simplicity in exposition, but also because there exists a consensus that he, at least, really favored and defended liberty in a proper sense of the word—a consensus that happens to include both conservatives and progressives.

Mill's classic, *On Liberty,* was written in 1854, with the help of his wife, and published in 1859. Later, in his *Autobiography,* Mill spoke of his *Liberty* as

> a kind of philosophic text-book of a single truth, which the changes progressively taking place in modern society tend to bring out into ever stronger relief: the importance, to man and society, of a large variety in types of character, and of giving full freedom to human nature to expand itself in innumerable and conflicting directions.[2]

Mill aimed to bring out the importance of liberty, its value and utility to modern man. He fought for conformity by each person to his own sensibility and growth pattern, his own talent and strength and practical judgment. He fought against every preconceived notion as to what a man ought to be or become; he opposed on principle every monistic model for the creation of human character and life.

[1] Sir Isaiah Berlin, *Two Concepts of Liberty.* London: Oxford University Press, 1958, p. 57.

[2] John Stuart Mill, *Autobiography.* London: Oxford University Press, 1924, p. 215.

Mill had a plurality of purposes in mind. He wanted to inspire citizens of the new democracies with love of liberty. He wanted to insist that liberty means *the right to do what I want in my own way.* He wanted to go beyond liberty of conscience and speech to free choice of career, of mode of living, and of association. And he aimed to show that liberty was not, like license and privilege,[3] good only for individuals, but that it was equally good and wholesome for society. He defended liberty chiefly by underlining its social utility.

Mill has been accused of confusing two distinct notions, negative and positive liberty. I am free in the negative sense " to the degree to which no human being interferes with my activity." [4] But to be free in the positive sense means to be master over one's self, to be in control of one's own feeling and acting.[5] Mill thought that negative liberty could not be maintained in a democratic society unless its members practiced positive liberty. Unless its members are civilized and practice self-control, no democracy can preserve liberty.

### TOLERATION

Negative liberty—the basic right not to be molested or interfered with—is a right that makes up one side of a coin, the other side of which is the obligation to tolerate, to respect persons, not to trespass on others' property. Unless the vast majority freely acknowledges the obligation and police power restrains the rest, individuals will not long enjoy the social right of free choice.

Mill was vitally interested in the kinds of social circumstances and processes that would favor (or disfavor) liberty. Mill accordingly wrote about the damage to society of curbing and pruning individuals and about the benefit to society of respecting the sphere of the individual and encouraging individuality. He studied and gave emphasis to the conditions under which liberty would prevail and flourish and society reap its blessings.

Mill thought that it's good to be one's own man and one's own self; some have said that he was trying to introduce the aristocratic principle into the democracies. But the question he most frequently raises is: What is good for society on the whole? Where lies the greatest social utility, the greatest happiness of the greatest number? And he answers that it is good for society on the whole that toleration be institutionalized, personal choice respected, and individuality encouraged and cultivated.

[3] If they are in any sense good.

[4] Berlin, *op. cit.,* p. 7.

[5] The extent to which self-mastery implies self-abnegation, self-realization, and rationality suggests a cluster of questions.

## A PARADOX

Every argument for toleration is characterized by an apparent paradox: We are urged to put up with people, institutions, and standards that we plainly disapprove of. Whitehead once expressed the paradox this way:

> There is no tolerance unless there is something to tolerate, and that, in practice, is likely to mean something which most people would consider intolerable.[6]

Most conservatives and progressives lose patience with bids for tolerance and claims to liberty, when these collide with their own serious political habits and principles or strongly-felt moral standards. Naturally demands for administrative efficiency, for solidarity, for equality, all may strain a point. Liberty is construed as "license" by those who fight for standpatism and by some who fight for political, economic, or legal reform, for higher moral standards, or for the intensification of religious experience. When political extremists control the government, the last thing they wish to hear is criticism of their actions and policies.

The miracle of liberty, however, not unlike the living miracle of the persisting existence of the Church, lies just here: Liberty *does* exist. Challenges, deviations, innovations *are* permitted. They are even sometimes encouraged, as instances of free expression and conduct, at the same moment that, as concrete acts, they are frowned upon.

Can this miracle to any extent be justified and accounted for? Is it a good miracle? Ought a society deliberately to set up the tensions inherent in toleration? Why should a society not rather demand the peace of universal agreement? Is the liberty granted heretical individuals worth its social cost?

## THE SOCIAL PSYCHOLOGY OF TOLERATION

Mill was willing to contend with recalcitrant material. He tried to make an opening for spontaneity, though no one knew better than he, that "Originality is the one thing which unoriginal minds cannot feel the use of." [7]

He pointed up the utility of such freedom as existed and urged extension of the principle in the interest of further utility. Social utility can be understood, even if originality cannot.

[6] *Dialogues of Alfred North Whitehead.* A Mentor Book, p. 76.
[7] Mill, *On Liberty,* Everyman Edition, p. 123.

Mill saw that we had reached, in the great civilized and industrialized nations, a very complex state of human character. Many of us have grown up, or matured: That means, we have passed beyond expecting—and perhaps even wanting—to get our every wish and will. Our everyday private lives and even more our political and economic careers are based, in a highly civilized way, on the recognition that we cannot any of us succeed in imposing our ideals and standards,and our best-laid plans, on every Tom, Dick, and Harry. Emotionally as well as intellectually, we have recognized that we cannot hope completely to extirpate all competing criteria and perspectives. Except when touched on some extraordinary sensitivity, most of us expect and like it that way. The radical of himself will move too fast, the conservative too slow. When we don't like it, as Professor Leys has pointed out, the principle itself tends to restrain us. The principle and all the impartial spectators, the outside parties, who continue in the circumstance to be more concerned about the principle than they are about us and our parochial concerns.

Such a mature attitude of mind ventures beyond the powers of comprehension of tyrants and totalitarians. Even to an authoritarian administrator (in the Indian service) like Sir James Fitzjames Stephen, the picture Mill painted looked like a political pastel. The very humanity of free men and free institutions will always bewilder certain domineering types of personality. But who is fragile, and who wields a hard punch? Are the rigid authoritarians able to find allies, to engender the deepest loyalties? Will their nervous system endure pinch and pressure, the strain of waiting? Will they patiently suffer through, keeping up a steady fight until, at last, they prevail in the final battle? And of equal importance, can they manage to avoid the needless battles, the losses that don't accomplish much? [8]

[8] Professor Hayek says, ". . . the ultimate decision about what is good and bad will be made not by individual human wisdom but by the decline of the groups that have adhered to the 'wrong' beliefs." He continues, ". . . Which individuals and which groups succeed and continue to exist depends as much on the goals that they pursue, the values that govern their action, as on the tools and capacities at their command. Whether a group will prosper or be extinguished depends as much on the ethical code it obeys, or the ideals of beauty or well-being that guide it, as on the degree to which it has learned or not learned to satisfy its material needs. . . . Nor can we be sure that under constantly changing conditions all the rules that have proved to be conducive to the attainment of a certain end will remain so. Though there is a presumption that any established social standard contributes in some manner to the preservation of civilization, our only way of confirming this is to ascertain whether it continues to prove itself in competition with other standards observed by other individuals or groups." F. A. Hayek, *The Constitution of Liberty*. Chicago: The University of Chicago Press, 1960, p. 36. Copyright 1960. Reprinted by permission.

A too-easy analogy with the case of individuals is misleading. Societies are not individuals. We may grant that one athlete can knock down seven scholars or that one bully can rule a whole alley. More important, we shall have to grant that one leader, one Fuehrer, can exercise power over persons of high station. Yet after dominating all those brilliant field-marshals and generals of the *Reichswehr* through years of struggle, Hitler debased their strategy and lost the war.

The libertarian is not going to lose the war. With more background and scope, he will not settle for any narrow definition of success. He will more readily grant, "It takes all kinds." The last perspective attained to may be just the one from which a victorious outcome becomes visible. Organized masses of people are a poor substitute for that one last man who invents a formula for winning.

In truth, the strongest leadership is neither narrow nor authoritarian. It is a commonplace that our more outstanding bankers, industrialists, labor leaders, and politicians are markedly tolerant personality types. Their alertness to alternatives and support of minority views attract loyalty from numerous quarters.

We have a few reactionaries of the domineering type who seem always to put their own views and interests first. They generally manage to sound moral, pious, and patriotic. They are not, according to C. L. Sulzberger, as extreme as those French reactionaries who won notoriety by selling out to Hitler.

## HEAT AND LIGHT

Moral issues are heated issues. When one morality must be sacrificed to another, then the sparks fly. The co-existence of various moral outlooks in America and Britain has led to the development of procedural safeguards of the public peace. Much of our libertarian tradition is the product of historical accident. Ways of dealing with heated issues that avoided extremes of overt conflict have been hit upon by imaginative courts, arbitrators, and statesmen; and, where successful, these ways have been retained as more or less well-established procedure.

Mill was keenly aware that he was urging people to put up with persons and events that they morally disapproved of, that stirred their *moral* ire. Let heretics unite, he said, and make a principle [9]

[9] "A *principle,*" since, as Mill pointed out by reference to Marcus Aurelius' persecution of the Christians, even Stoical broad-mindedness, apart from principle, will not prove consistent in practice.

of tolerating disagreement both in opinions and ways of life. Mill deliberately aimed to modify and bring up to date our very conception of *what morality consists in*. He tried to sink powerful ethical pylons beneath every specific moral outlook and moral code.

The mere intensity of feeling with which one's moral outlook is held is no valid test of its real ethical worth. Intensity of moral feeling may indicate no more than fanatical or pugnacious character or immaturity. If a morality is narrow and bigoted, it is after all only a false morality. Mill despised constrictive "middle-class morality" even more intensely than Marx despised "rural idiocy."

A man is really fortunate to have to ask himself sincere questions about his accepted moral beliefs and moral perspectives. Are my attitudes broad enough to encompass all desirable forms of human nature? Do they support or cut off the growth of others in character and judgment? Do they allow for social advance? Are my moral beliefs consistent with one another? Do they relate to needs of men, including those of men with whom I am actually or prospectively in contact? Or are my moral perspectives more appropriate to the time of Moses? Or perhaps to the United States during the Reconstruction? Is my moral indignation spent on wrong things, on what may once have been crimes but are now hardly misdemeanors? Is my moral code only camouflage hiding my inhumanity?

Mill foresaw the judgment of social scientists at mid-twentieth century. To quote but one, Harold Lasswell has said:

> It may be that the most notable outcome of modern research is in documenting the role played by norms of right and wrong (the rectitude value). Attention has been directed to the consequences that may follow when a sense of guilt is unconscious and carries childhood conflicts and misinterpretations into adult life. Modern research has shown the frequency with which unadmitted and unrecognized appraisals of the guilty self provoke defense against needed insight and understanding. A person trying to defend himself against self-indictment is commonly self-righteous, censorious, and aggressive. We encounter personalities of this kind in all walks of life. As managers they complicate industrial relations, which under modern conditions usually depend upon a wide, cooperative network. Such persons find it difficult to function smoothly among equals. When we look for the source of difficulty, we find that it lies in the readiness with which adverse appraisals of the self can be aroused, and against which 'defense measures' are taken. One of these is the common device of treating the other person as the guilty party. Such 'misplaced moralism' appears to be a pervasive element in American civilization, at least, and perhaps of European culture as a whole. It poses the ques-

tion how the demand to take life seriously can be transmitted from one generation to the next without becoming contaminated by hostilities masked as feelings of self-righteousness.[10]

Mill's liberalism may correctly be viewed as a set of ethical principles intended to undergird—or to circumscribe, or to orient—moral codes, intended to provide a standard by which the real rightness or wrongness of our moral feelings and attitudes may be tested. Mill foresaw that in the end only the most carefully oriented conscientious feelings can, in the modern democracies, prevent the advent of totalitarianism. He called for a major transvaluation of values and morals, for a strong and well-considered movement in the direction of libertarian principle.

The paradox of toleration was not, of course, an invention of Mill. It was Patrick Henry (perhaps with Voltaire) who said that, although he did not agree with a word his adversary said, yet he would die for his *right* to say it.

## LIBERTARIAN ETHICS

The upshot is that Mill invited us to make a clear, sharp distinction between merely acting morally and acting ethically. To act in accordance with rectitude values that are inadequately deliberated can be to commit needless and inhuman damage and destruction. To act in compliance with a false moral code may amount to nothing better than to act from feelings picked up in the alley or the church basement. We either do, or we do not, act out of serious consideration for the rights of persons and the interests of mankind collectively.

Ethical acts are acts that have been thought through to their ultimate effects on the feelings of human beings. Ethical acts are conscious acts. Neither a coincidence nor a reflex has moral worth. Just as the expression "work of art" is less a term of ordinary discourse than a term of reflective critics and aestheticians,[11] so the expression "ethical act" belongs to those who seriously ask, "What is right?" An ethical act may be more or less sophisticated, but it is never careless. In the mental constitution of an *ethical* agent one

[10] Harold D. Lasswell, "The Normative Impact of the Behavioral Sciences." *Ethics,* LXVII, No. 3 (April 1957), Part II, pp. 5–6. Reprinted by permission of The University of Chicago.

[11] Cf. Margaret Macdonald, "Works of art are esoteric objects" (p. 683), and " 'Work of art' is a cultural, not an everyday term" (p. 691). "Some Distinctive Features of Arguments Used in Criticism of the Arts," reprinted in Morris Weitz, Editor, *Problems in Aesthetics.* New York: The Macmillan Company, 1959.

counts on finding alertness, sensitivity, imaginative appreciation of real interests, good will, knowledge, effort, independence. If there is a touchstone of ethical action, it is not mechanical conformity with code, precedent, or feeling. The ethical man aims to protect rights, save interests, and achieve values.

Libertarianism does not imply the defense of any given ideology. Libertarianism is itself of higher logical type. It implies judgment on moralities themselves, in the interest of human rights and the attainment of value in human experience. Mill, James, and all clear-thinking libertarians have therefore favored the broad-gauged personality that is tolerant while retaining psychological security and that is tolerant while avoiding concealed aggressions. Mill's *Liberty* fosters the cultivation of such a personality type.

## II

### THE SOCIAL UTILITY OF FREE INSTITUTIONS

That such free states as Switzerland, Britain, and the United States have by far the oldest and the most stable governments is not a mere accident of history. That the free world has long held the initiative in industry, science, and art is also not a mere accident.

Not only is his own civil and social liberty desirable for and to each citizen, but so is his membership in a *society* that respects liberty. Mill held that liberal arrangements are beneficial to the state and to all society. The principle that "each ought to rule himself in his own way" is good for the society as such, just as it is good for the individual.

(a) Life in a free society is more meaningful.[12] In a stereotyped society, everyone lives in accordance with stereotypes. Blandness pervades. Concepts, principles, everything is accepted "as stated"; no one has any alternative perspective. There is a minimum of mutations. If anyone does or thinks anything out of the ordinary, it is by accident. Such a drab and stifling state of affairs Mill calls "mediocrity." Such a society may indeed be well administered and peaceable, but death itself is scarcely less static. As in the Mandarins' China, life in one century is like life in another.

"Well," one might retort to Mill, "What do I care what century I live in, or what place, so long as I have my friends, my loves, my rice wine?"

[12] A highly developed theory of meaning underlies Mill's views. His best statement of this is contained, oddly, not in chapter 2 of *On Liberty*, but in his early correspondence with Gustave d'Eichthal.

To this remark, however, Mill is not required to answer. For there are but few of us, in Western society and Russia—if anywhere—who can honestly say that we would settle for that static order of "pedantocracy." We choose rather a world of fascinating persons, of progress, of adventure. A free society offers opportunity for men to find work to their liking, to develop skills as they may choose, to improve processes, to make of themselves collectively a realm of artists, craftsmen, traders, technicians, scientists, and professional experts. Such is the free world, with its richness of products, of personalities, of modes of living.

In a free society there are of course more open conflicts: persons and policies exist with which we agree and parties to which we belong, but there are also others that stand in opposition to our own. There is likely to be a vast multiplicity of tastes and aesthetic sensibilities, and my own sense of propriety may at times be irritated or shocked. New interests will appear and make new demands. There will be risk, and *I* may be the loser. The greatest social and political problem of all may well be the absence of some one absolute authority that can make final decisions and settle all disputes. But most of us estimate the advantages much higher than these "disadvantages." Individual orientation and social goals are both on the move, and hence subject to improvement; our lives are open to enrichment. Life is more meaningful than under static and absolutistic circumstances.

(b) The material products and values available in a free society are much more various and much better directed toward fulfillment of actual individual need. "Social value is definitely not confined to those things which are useful or gratifying to all of us alike." [13] The social values of things are values which they have for *some* of us.[14] The unregimented society allows men to specialize both as producers and consumers; one can produce what he wants, one can buy what he wants. Where society places in a commissar and his men the power of decision concerning what shall and what shall not be produced, "state goals" tend to replace individual demands for goods and services and to become the polestar of industrial production. In brief, consumers are better off in a free society.

(c) Access to information is more secure in the free society. In a really free society, scholar and scientist, journalist and broadcaster

[13] Clarence Irving Lewis, *The Right and the Good.* New York: Columbia University Press, 1955, p. 71.

[14] *Ibid.* Another expert on this topic is F. A. Hayek. See his *The Constitution of Liberty.* Chicago: University of Chicago Press, 1960, Ch. 2 and *passim.*

all come and go as they please, publish facts and discuss, criticize, and interpret opinion.

No people wants to hear the whole truth. The power of the Prince de Condé and his brother King Louis XIV was required to bring on stage Molière's *Tartufe,* a drama about religious hypocrisy. The strength of the Roman Catholic Church is required in Cuba to speak out against Communism and Castroism and in Louisiana to speak out against race prejudice. The truth does not always dawn brightly and happily on democratic peoples: *We* might prefer an occasional cartoon about Mao or a ten-word cable about mass starvation in China to a full report, carefully weighed, and based on close observation, about what the mainland Chinese have been doing since 1949. Our newly acquired habit of accepting partial truth may raise for us a greater danger than anything that Mao does or can do.

### ARE WE GETTING CASH VALUE?

The concrete tasks necessary to the exercise and upholding of liberty are unending. As institutions and circumstances change, the gap between ideal and actual has ever to be bridged and re-bridged.

The social utility of free speech and free press is only rarely and weakly questioned in these United States, yet there may be more than a little disparity between the utility we intend and the utility we realize. Let us look at some of the problems of realization through the eyes of Harry Ashmore. "Has Our Free Press Failed Us?" he asks. "Is the press—newspapers, magazines, radio and television—fulfilling its historic obligation to guard our democratic institutions?" [15] He quotes John Adams, who wrote after his experience as President:

> If there is ever to be an amelioration of the condition of mankind, philosophers, theologians, legislators, politicians and moralists will find that the regulation of the press is the most difficult, dangerous and important problem they have to resolve. Mankind cannot now be governed without it, nor at present with it.

The problem is complicated today by our having lost track of just *what* the press is. Legal exemption of the press from regulation rests on the First Amendment, and the exemption has been "applied to media that employ the electronic tube." These and certain other

[15] *The Saturday Evening Post,* October 29, 1960: "Adventures of the Mind" series. Quotations that follow reprinted by permission.

media, however, are not engaged solely in the business of communicating news; they are operating equally in the field of entertainment.

We have generally taken for granted that "to be free the press must be self-supporting." Mr. Ashmore finds, however, that a major part of the communications industry is not a public institution with rights and immunities but a private, profit-making enterprise presumably subject to regulation like other trades and industries. From the angle of *support,* "dancing girls attract more television viewers than commentaries on world affairs, and horoscopes have a higher readership than editorials." Many owners of media hence think they face "an impossible choice: No one can establish a priority between the duty to inform the public and the duty to survive."

The principal social utility of a free press lies in its power to bring home the news and to bring home to the reader the *meaning* of the news. Many critics, including persons themselves in the communications field, think that our press does not deliver.

When placed on the defensive, the proprietors "still try to sound like Tom Paine." They sometimes try to pass the buck to Government:

> The battle cry goes back to Locke and Adam Smith and John Milton and John Stuart Mill, and bears the American imprimatur of Thomas Jefferson. . . . It is, in short, the *laissez-faire* theory which in the beginning applied to virtually all the institutions of American life.

But the *laissez-faire* view seeks to overlook the revolution in technology: We no longer have the hand press.

When Hartford, Connecticut, had only 13,000 population, it had thirteen newspapers; but there is not now any great variety of offerings that reaches the broad public. Movable type itself seems to be on the decline, and such independent tradition as has survived the ascendancy of radio and television exists "in only the most diluted form." The personal responsibility of editor-owners has been replaced by corporate responsibility throughout the entire communications industry.[16] The trouble is not an absence of heroes. The new condition is the product of technology and economics.

Various means of modernization have been suggested that look toward a fuller realization of the social utilities of a really free and powerful press. Mr. Ashmore rejects the proposal of a publicly supported television network on the ground that, since public agencies are subject to just as many pressures as are advertisers, they will offer

[16] Except book publishing. The present trend toward merger and concentration, however, may spell the end of localizable responsibility even there.

just as bland a fare. An alternative proposal is that public responsibility be assumed on a voluntary basis, giving "equal time" on the air to political parties, and running "opposed line" columnists in the newspapers, *etc.* Mr. Ashmore makes short shrift of this notion, finding that it aims at a brand of objectivity which amounts to little more than "a retreat from unpleasant reality." Moreover,

> every practicing journalist knows that it is quite possible to give both sides without telling the truth, and that this can be a convenient way of consciously doing so.

All such proposals fail to promise the effective advocacy that a healthy society requires.

> The defense of the status quo is that the people are getting what they want—and if the proprietors need to put a moral gloss on the proposition they can always say, as they have been saying in Washington, that, after all, this is a democracy and what else do you expect? —We have got to insist that, in addition to what they want, the people have got to get what they need.

Yes, before we take any cookies, we need our spinach. Our minds, like our bodies, must get what they need. The free press was conceived as "the cutting edge of change," and "its sins of omission are surely a matter of public concern." But the press alone will not yet undertake reform, because it will not admit any need for reform.

Nevertheless, there is far "too little diversity, and there are too many total gaps of information and of advocacy."

> We must begin, I think, with recognition of a proposition the press rejects—that the inadequacy of mass communications in our threatened society is not a matter of internal concern for the press alone, but an issue of great urgency for the public at large. Beginning here we will at least raise the proper questions—which has always been the prerequisite of finding the proper answers.

### FALSE GENERAL PRESUMPTIONS

Socrates used to say that the ignorance of ignorance is worse than mere ignorance. To recognize that one does *not* know is at least to make a step in the direction of readiness to learn. To hold false convictions—the firmer the worse!—is to block access to true information.

Mill discussed "the ignorance of ignorance" under the title, "False General Presumptions." He noted that almost no one calls himself a bigot, but that there are bigots all the same. He also observed that truth does not always triumph over persecution. He could not see any justification for subjecting people who speak truth to persecution; but if we persecute anyone or any class for expressing their opinions, we are sure on one occasion and another to persecute those who are right. For in such value-infused areas as religion, politics, economics, and morals, are we infallible? Hardly! History alone, even without common sense, can demonstrate our fallibility, including most emphatically the fallibility of our great majorities. Even where the vast majority does hold a truth, it holds it the way a dog holds a rag doll, if no one is permitted to question it. A good society encourages people to tell the whole truth, as *they* see it. A good society hunts meaning and truth and reality, not witches. "Fair-mindedness," Mill said, "is the real morality of public discussion."

False presumptions block access to truth. Take a case that Mill pressed on Auguste Comte: Suppose a man claims to believe on biological grounds that women are inferior to men. Let us ask, what evidence would convince him otherwise? If there is no possible evidence that would convince him otherwise, his belief is a mere prejudice. The "biological grounds" serve only to conceal from him that he does not know what he means by "inferior," a word that belongs to the language of value, not to scientific biology.

The case is not atypical. Mill presses on us the thesis that until every human being has equal opportunity to attain to the largest and highest nature of which he is capable, society *cannot* know what is absolutely best: Who really are the best people? What are the finest human characteristics? Just what *is* maturity, ideally? Which paths lead to superiority of mind and feeling? The principle of equality of opportunity is the principle most likely to secure us knowledge, in distinction from mere opinion or guess, about social value. It is also the optimum principle for realizing social value itself: Let people grow in their own way in a fair competition for sunlight. If they can climb, pray let them do so. Then may they tell us what they've seen up there!

Equality of opportunity is the antithesis of a systematic stand on false presumption. To shut ourselves off from alternative perspectives slows the advance of our species. It costs us plenty, both in knowledge and in stature. But the only way to make sure of this fair competition, and to make sure of liberty "when the shoe pinches," is to make sure of them all the time.

## THE PSYCHOLOGY OF INTOLERANCE

As a matter of history, most slaves of any degree of intelligence have wanted their liberty and prayed day and night for manumission. The problem is, how has it come about that in our own time such peoples as the Germans and the Italians have, of their own volition, negated their freedom, given up their liberty? In America itself, we have seen McCarthyism and all the other sudden new pressures brought against civil and social liberty.

Mill was concerned to understand pressures against liberty, especially the popular pressures. He warned against totalitarianism, "the tyranny of the majority." Society's actual likings and dislikings should not be a law to individuals. Individuality is the supreme value; and full and consistent liberty is the condition of its realization. But there is no short cut, in the great democracies, to the establishment and preservation of liberty: The broad public has itself to be convinced of the validity and worth of the principle. Liberty and toleration must be incorporated in "the conscientious feelings of mankind."

Mill favored democracy, but, like de Tocqueville, he frowned on *totalitarian* democracy as the worst possible form of society.

> . . . the mind itself is bowed to the yoke: even in what people do for pleasure, conformity is the first thing thought of; they like in crowds; they exercise choice only among things commonly done: peculiarity of taste, eccentricity of conduct, are shunned equally with crimes: until by dint of not following their own nature they have no nature to follow: their human capacities are withered and starved: they become incapable of any strong wishes or native pleasures, and are generally without either opinions or feelings of home growth, or properly their own.[17]

Democratic peoples can all too quickly and easily fall into this state of disvalue. The deepest trouble besetting man in the twentieth century—a trouble that Mill foresaw—is his new disposition toward self-enslavement, a feeling and disposition that derive from a personal sense of no importance, of no potentiality and power, of *nothingness.* This "feast of unreason" is but a step from barbarism and brutality. The little step from self-disesteem to envy and hatred of others.

A British thinker and Labor Member of Parliament, E. F. M. Durbin, has said that the roots of (nontotalitarian) democracy "are emotional rather than intellectual. It is fundamentally a consequence of psychological health and the absence of neurosis." [18] Liberal democracy is of, by, and for good and free personalities. ". . . *Aggression* is the enemy of tolerance and *guilt* of the willingness to

[17] *On Liberty,* p. 119.

[18] E. F. M. Durbin, *The Politics of Democratic Socialism.* London: Routledge & Kegan Paul Ltd., 1940, p. 263.

accept political responsibility. Democracy cannot long survive the dominance, among a people, of either emotion.[19]

Mill himself hated acts injurious to other persons and encroachments on their rights, not to mention the dispositions that lead to them. He left us a little list:

> Encroachment on their rights; infliction on them of any loss or damage not justified by his own rights; falsehood or duplicity in dealing with them; unfair or ungenerous use of advantages over them; even selfish abstinence from defending them against injury—these are fit objects of moral reprobation, and, in grave cases, of moral retribution and punishment. And not only these acts, but the dispositions which lead to them, are properly immoral, and fit subjects of disapprobation which may rise to abhorrence. Cruelty of disposition; malice and ill-nature; that most anti-social and odious of all passions, envy; dissimulation and insincerity, irascibility on insufficient cause, and resentment disproportioned to the provocation; the love of domineering over others; the desire to engross more than one's share of advantages. . . . the pride which derives gratification from the abasement of others; the egotism which thinks self and its concerns more important than everything else, and decides all doubtful questions in its own favour;—these are moral vices, and constitute a bad and odious moral character.[20]

Self-respect and the desire to go one's own way and to be one's own self are the alpha and omega of sound feeling. They are the basis of good, as of strong, character.

> He who chooses his plan for himself, employs all his faculties. He must use observation to see, reasoning and judgment to foresee, activity to gather materials for decision, discrimination to decide, and when he has decided, firmness and self-control to hold to his deliberate decision. And these qualities he requires and exercises exactly in proportion as the part of his conduct which he determines according to his own judgment and feelings is a large one.[21]

The greatest social utility of free institutions lies in the sane, strong, and happy people that they produce, and the greatest inutility of unfree ones lies in the mad, sick, and unhappy tyrants and slaves that *they* produce. Referring to societies as well as to individuals, Erich Fromm has summarized:

> Mental health is characterized by the ability to love and to create, by the emergence from incestuous ties to clan and soil, by a sense

[19] *Ibid.* Italics added. Durbin thought also that "the passive acceptance of other people's aggression would be as profoundly neurotic as the manifestation of transformed aggression itself." (p. 69).

[20] *On Liberty*, p. 135.

[21] *Ibid.*, p. 117.

of identity based on one's experience of self as the subject and agent of one's powers, by the grasp of reality inside and outside of ourselves, that is, by the development of objectivity and reason.[22]

[22] Erich Fromm, *The Sane Society*. New York: Rinehart & Company, Inc., 1955, p. 69. (Italicized in the original.) Copyright © 1955. Reprinted by permission of Holt, Rinehart, and Winston, Inc.

# 5

# ROUSSEAU: RIGHTS AND PARTICIPATION

Rousseau's *Social Contract* was published two hundred years ago, a hundred years before Mill's *Liberty*. Most of us feel, however, that Rousseau was more radical than Mill. This feeling is deceptive, but it is true at least that Mill was a liberal, while Rousseau really took the democratic bit in his teeth. Rousseau (1712–1778) was prime mover of the American and French Revolutions: He was carefully studied (in French!) by Franklin, Jefferson, Madison, Hamilton, and others who signed the Declaration of Independence or who took the lead in persuading the states to adopt the Constitution. (A false rumor has been set afloat that nowadays our college youth swings to conservatism. Are conservative young Americans expected to favor Rousseau or not?)

Like Mill, and unlike Kant, Rousseau should be understood as philosopher *and* propagandist. Rousseau promulgated a doctrine of natural rights which he used to attack privilege and corruption in the civilization of the old régime. If Rousseau had no political or philosophical significance, he would be remembered for his rhetorical powers, his histrionics, and his romanticism. He was a mythmaker and a liar,[1] at least in the meaning of Plato.

[1] Many scholars think his *Confessions* report sins he never committed.

The natural rights theorists of the eighteenth century held that every man has a right to be free and a right to participate in the business of the state. These men and the Philosophical Radicals in England [2] spearheaded the rise of the great Western democracies. Of the natural rights theorists, Rousseau was the greatest. He was a Swiss from Geneva but spent most of his life in France or in the service of the French. He was sometimes Protestant, sometimes Catholic, and perhaps sometimes neither. He tells us that he rose from his seat at a dinner party of atheists to attest his simple faith in God. He was interested in religion, education, law, political theory, fiction, musical theory and notation; and he composed opera.

Rousseau and his revolutionary contemporaries insisted that inequalities, especially hereditary privilege and status, expressed and fostered aberrant society and corrupt man, that they were contrary to nature. For these thinkers, there was no valid question of tolerance *versus* intolerance, but there was a natural and moral right to liberty of conscience. Thus Tom Paine wrote:

> Toleration is not the opposite of Intolerance, but is the *counterfeit* of it. Both are despotisms. The one assumes itself the right of withholding liberty of conscience, and the other of granting it.
>
> Were a bill brought into any parliament, entitled 'An Act to tolerate or grant liberty to the Almighty to receive the worship of a Jew or a Turk' or 'to prohibit the Almighty from receiving it,' all men would startle and call it blasphemy. There would be an uproar. The presumption of toleration in religious matters would then present itself unmasked. (*Rights of Man.*) [3]

We all recognize, I suppose, a difference between being tolerated and being treated by others as equally a human being with themselves. Rousseau and Paine "found" that every man had from birth the right to be treated as a respectable member of our species. Their judgment was not influenced by the fact that most people in their own time and place were not so treated. They may be classified, consequently, and sometimes are classified, as fanatics. To this very day, neither in America nor the U.S.S.R., nor in England nor France, is there a consensus as to whether Rousseau was a fanatic

[2] Bentham, Horne Tooke, James and John Stuart Mill, Major J. Cartwright. See Elie Halévy, *The Growth of Philosophic Radicalism.* Boston: The Beacon Press (Paperback edition), 1955.

[3] Auguste Comte observed that liberty is not something conceded: it is something one takes. (La vraie liberté ne se concède pas: elle se prend). *Lettres Inédites De John Stuart Mill A Auguste Comte.* Paris: Alcan, 1899, p. 547.

or a proper enthusiast for the human race. That he hated arrogance is obvious; whether or not he fought arrogance with arrogance is a moot question. To what length may a man legitimately push his claim as a man, just *qua homo sapiens,* regardless of his social usefulness, regardless of the size of his role in the human comedy?

Actually, Rousseau has been widely misunderstood. He said that man is born free, but everywhere he is found in chains. But Rousseau did *not* object to chains: He just thought that the iron must be tempered to fit men born free. He thought that by birth and nature all men are free and equal and good; but they grow up and live in society under a variety of laws and conventions that affect their characters in different ways.

The fundamental problem of the *Social Contract* was, in Rousseau's own terms:

> To find a form of association that defends and protects with the entire force of the community the person and goods of each associate, and whereby each, uniting with all, still obeys only himself and remains as free as before.

The freedom one is to retain is not construed as the mere psychological *sense* of freedom or mastery; Rousseau expressly states that some believe themselves the masters of others while not ceasing to be more enslaved than they. The *feeling* is not to be trusted: One may feel free enough because he has never known real freedom, or feel masterful, because he has never known real mastership. Aristotle was dead right, Rousseau remarks, when he said that some are born for slavery and others for dominion, but he took the cause for the effect. Any man born *into* slavery is born *for* slavery. Slaves lose everything in their chains, even the desire to have the chains removed. If there are slaves by nature, it is because they have been slaves against nature. Force made the first slaves, their cowardice or laziness has kept them slaves.[4]

Rousseau, in brief, hates slavish natures and hates any system that creates slavish natures. Slavish natures are against nature. If men put up with slavery and other injustice, it is because they have been brought up under a system of custom and law that has disregarded their natural equality and liberty; they have been deformed.

The "romantic" idea of Mill, that human nature is not a machine, but a tree that requires to grow according to its inner forces, favors the analogy of society to the English forest and finds deformity in the pruned and clipped trees of the French formal garden. Rousseau's conception is somewhat less gothic. He gives less stress to natural

[4] *Social Contract,* Book I, Ch. II.

difference among men but gives much more stress to natural likeness. *All* men are alike born free. Deviation is often the result, precisely, of pruning, clipping, grafting. It is civilization that corrupts. The social roles that men are forced into make their "natures" compressed and degenerate; men grow—in the greenhouse of civilization—along lines that lead them away from the light of reason.

So for Rousseau absolutely everything depends on the characteristics of the social order. The social and political order is sacred; but it is not something natural, not something born to its present condition: It is only conventional.

Paradoxically, a social order is nothing more than a set of conventions, and yet it is essential. The right question for idealists to raise in political and social philosophy is, on *which* conventions, on *which* laws, shall the social order be founded. Granting the natural virtues and liberties and the innate dignity of man, what are the criteria of the social order? Rousseau would make the social structure and social process satisfy all our demands for consistency and rationality. Instead of dumbly accepting the corrupt and corrupting institutions that exist as a result of historical accidents,[5] the lord-and-serf mentalities, the "have" and "have-not" statuses, Rousseau would establish a new order that meets a double standard: (1) All citizens shall be brought to a perfect obedience, brought under absolute control of the order. (2) Yet all are to remain self-directing, brave, and free. The person and property of every associate is to be subjected to the absolute sovereignty of the whole; but each associate is still, united with all, to obey only *his own* interest and conscience.

At the head of his book, Rousseau states the problem in another way:

> I want to see if, in the civil order, there can be some legitimate and certain rule of administration, taking men as they are and laws as they can be. I shall try always to align, in this study, that which the law permits with that which interest prescribes, so that justice and utility do not get separated.[6]

## NATURAL RIGHTS

Mill rejected many of Rousseau's doctrines, especially the doctrine of natural rights—or "abstract rights," as Mill called them. Mill spoke of the "imaginary law of the imaginary being Nature," and Mill's mentor Jeremy Bentham called both natural law and natural

[5] Rousseau quotes the Marquis d'Argenson: "Scholarly researches on public right are often nothing but the history of ancient abuses."

[6] *Social Contract,* Book I.

rights "nonsense upon stilts." Twentieth-century criticism of Rousseau has been equally severe, almost all thinkers except Catholic apologists having rejected self-evidence, natural law, and natural rights. The logical positivists have found the concept of natural rights to be metaphysical and meaningless.

In view of frequent misinterpretation of Rousseau's view that rights attach to a man as a man, to learn some statements that he did NOT intend to make will save us time:

1. That all men are, were, and will be free in the civil state—(an established historical falsehood, a dream).
2. That men should prefer to live like barbarians, or that they should prefer to live in a state of nature rather than in society with organized government.
3. That all men have equal merit—(an immoral doctrine).
4. That men are born with rights attached to themselves like legs and arms.
5. That "men are born free" is an empirical proposition, that we can experience "men born free" by using our senses.
6. That it is a redundancy that men are free, *i.e.*, that if you know what a man is, you already know he is free.[7]

The conscience of Rousseau was disturbed by inequality and slavery. "Of right," he thought, "men are free, equal, brotherly." He expressed the growing conviction and the deep decision of men of his time that all men ought to have liberty under order, that they ought to be treated as equals before the law, that they ought to have equality of opportunity to advance their self-interest and to serve the community.

To see why Rousseau called these rights "natural" is not really so difficult. First, there is a sense in which liberty *is* natural, in which it is just a fact of life. Unless some powerful reason—or ruse—demands its postponement, people simply won't go without it. The modern totalitarian nations have all pretended to hold free elections and to maintain most of the apparatus of libertarian countries. They have called out "Freiheit, Freiheit," and feigned that they were increasing, not decreasing, liberty. They have tried to blame their invasions of liberty on some other country (and often enough on England and America).

Second, Rousseau wrote against a philosophical, if not even a popular, background of acceptance of natural law and natural right. His intellectual antecedents include Cicero, St. Thomas Aquinas, Locke, *etc.* The accepted Catholic philosophy involved a theory of

[7] Part of this list is owing to Margaret Macdonald.

natural law to which positive (*e.g.,* enacted) law was to be accommodated, if it was to be really right.

Third, and perhaps just as important, Rousseau wanted to speak of liberty, fraternity, and equality as natural, because to say they were was to advance the obvious and simple contrary of the position of his adversaries. There were bluebloods. Those who were noble, rich, and powerful by heredity had long been claiming their position as a natural right, as their born right. Rousseau wanted flatly to deny that their status and privilege were natural.

> "Kings have a divine right to rule"—false! All men are born equal. "The lower estates are the subjects of the first two estates!" —false! All men are born free.

Rousseau was a poor man, but he had many rich and noble friends. He knew the needs of the rich for cake, for luxuries, for style; but he also knew the needs of the poor for bread, for necessities, for life however somber. He sided with the poor. He wanted to make equality the legitimate, "natural" starting point of the race. Let inequalities be justified in detail, in each instance, or else be removed. He wanted to make liberty something universal, something parcelled out in equal portions. Let any special privilege or special liberty belonging to the aristocratic or priestly class be carefully scrutinized and legitimized or else be brought down to the common level.

Fourth, and the point differs only a shade from our first one above, the inequalities and subjugations of the *ancien régime* often really did carry an air of being factitious and unnatural. Nobles who had great estate and power were in their own persons weak and stupid and irresponsible. Noble friends of Rousseau knew this and supported his critical spirit. We know that, in the upshot, the Marquis de Lafayette was one of the original revolutionaries; that he was one should not amaze us any more than that Washington led the American Revolution while at the same time many of his compatriots in the Tidewater and Piedmont countries remained staunch Tories. The machinery of the old régime had gotten full of sand; it didn't work well, and it didn't work fairly. Rousseau spelled out the almost overwhelming sense of unfairness and frustration in France, much as Samuel Adams spelled out the unfairness and frustration of having the mother country tax, without representation, the American colonies. These larger facts, this larger sense of what is fair and what is workable, are often hard to come by, hard to express; but they affect the political and social picture, in the long run, more than the "beliefs" superficially held—even by a majority —at any given moment.

The attitude of Bernard Baruch will serve to illustrate the point. He says:

> . . . if one had the facts right, one could stand with confidence against the will or whims of those who were supposed to know best.
>
> Later in public life I found this rule equally valid and applicable. In every government assignment that was given me I would begin with a relentless search for the facts of the situation. President Wilson took to calling me "Dr. Facts." I strove to let the facts shape my recommendations. Many times, as in my long fight against inflation during World War Two and afterward, friends would come up to me and argue, "Bernie, why aren't you more reasonable? What you propose isn't politically possible."
>
> But even in such situations I held my ground, feeling that if the facts called for certain measures nothing less would suffice. I still believe that no President or Congress can make two and two equal anything but four.[8]

A British idealist neatly expresses the same point, referring to our facts as "the situation":

> For a man about to act, the situation is his master, his oracle, his god. Whether his action is to prove successful or not depends on whether he grasps the situation rightly or not. If he is a wise man, it is not until he has consulted his oracle, done everything in his power to find out what the situation is, that he will make even the most trivial plan. And if he neglects the situation, the situation will not neglect him. It is not one of those gods that leave an insult unpunished.[9]

Natural law and natural right theory have held out for a position of objectivity. They have held out for objectivity and held out for loyalty to all humanity. They therefore offered standards to which the old régime could not measure up. They can be turned against Marxism also, and against all the "isms" that deny every morality but class morality. Can Marx really have meant to say that there is *no* objectivity under capitalism? Or, to raise another sort of question, will the Afrikaners not really have it coming, really deserve what they get, if Negreos and Indians eventually take over Southern Africa?

[8] *My Own Story*, pp. 131–132. Copyright © 1957. Reprinted by permission of Holt, Rinehart, and Winston, Inc.

[9] R. G. Collingwood, *The Idea of History*. New York: Oxford University Press (A Galaxy Book), 1956, p. 316. Copyright 1956. Reprinted by permission.

Is there really no difference at all between a strike and a ball? Most men seem to have convictions about how they ought to be treated; and most men seem not to like *anyone* to be treated in violation of those convictions. Most men dislike and disapprove foul play and bad refereeing. Rousseau looked on the dignity of man and the rights of man as objective elements, intrinsic to the human game of tag.

### INEQUALITY AND INJURY, PRIDE AND REVOLUTION

Of the Europe of Rousseau's era, Thomas Jefferson wrote that it is a place,

> where the dignity of man is lost in arbitrary distinctions, where the human species is classed into several stages of degradation, where the many are crushed under the weight of the few, and where the order established can present to the contemplation of a thinking being no other picture than that of God Almighty and His angels, trampling under foot the host of the damned.[10]

Some years later Jefferson asked, in reference to the laborers of England, whether " 'the moral coercion of want' does not subject their wills as despotically to that of their employer, as . . . physical constraint the slave?"

And he said, "In England, happiness is the lot of the aristocracy only." [11]

Men who are reasonable, *i.e.,* not biased by class, race, or other prejudice, are appalled on sight by slavery, exploitation, discrimination, and special privilege. An actual universal agreement in favor of human rights was never postulated, not even by Rousseau. He knew that many aristocrats were blinded by class interest. But the plain man with his unclouded vision could see it; or, perhaps better, the plain man with his simple heart immediately felt it.

Rousseau represented the revolutionary wing, so to speak, within the larger Aristotelian party. He accepted the relevance of conceptions of nature to the social order, but he did not accept the Aristotelian interpretation of the natural order. Aristotle had said, in a famous passage:

[10] Letter to De Maurier, 1786. Quoted by Jerome Frank in "A Sketch of an Influence," in *Interpretations of Modern Legal Philosophies.* New York: Oxford University Press, 1947, pp. 214–215.

[11] Letter to T. Cooper, 1814. *Ibid.,* p. 214. Bentham's attack on natural law and natural right was an attack on Blackstone's interpretation of them. Jerome Frank says, "But Blackstone employed natural law to discourage all but minor criticisms of the English government, and to glorify its way. No wonder that Jefferson feared Blackstone's philosophy." *Ibid.,* p. 230.

> There must be a union of those who cannot exist without each other; namely, . . . of natural ruler and subject, that both may be preserved. For that which can foresee by the exercise of mind is by nature intended to be lord and master, and that which can with its body give effect to such foresight is a subject, and by nature a slave; hence, master and slave have the same interest. (*Politics,* Book I, Ch. 2. From *The Student's Oxford Aristotle.*)

Rousseau, himself the brilliant son of a common Geneva watchmaker, found that passage curious.

A question famously answered by Rousseau was not formulated by him but by the prize committee of the Academy of Dijon: *"What is the origin of inequality among men, and is it authorized by natural law?"* Rousseau replied that inequality was not natural, but that it was made legitimate by enactment of statute law and by the establishment of institutions of property. Inequality belongs to the superstructure of social life, and it requires justification; equality of men as men, born of woman, someday dying, is the basic fact.

The dignity of man and his essential equality lies in his capacity to have fair or unfair intentions towards his neighbors. It is realized only in fair acting, in respecting other men as essentially one's equals and brothers.

Rousseau's central problem is the problem of distinctively human co-operation, in contrast to mere gregarious behavior: the problem of co-operation that is intentional and deliberate and yet fair. We may grant a certain oversimplification in Rousseau's method of dealing with this problem: The problem itself and his perspectives on it still warrant our serious consideration.

If we quarrel with an animal, the animal, impelled by his instinctive nature, may harm us. No animal, however, can in Rousseau's sense *injure* us. No mere animal could from malice aforethought set out to kill a man (or another animal) as Cain set out to bring down Abel. By the same token, the quarrels of men in society can take on a character of personal and moral bitterness beyond any bitterness in nature. Our human problem of living and working together is thickened by the heat of egoism, cunning, and the sense of injury. As analytically distinguished by Rousseau from the social state,

> . . . in our primitive condition in the true state of nature, egoism did not exist; for as each man regarded himself as the only observer of his actions, the only being in the universe who took any interest in him, and the sole judge of his deserts, no feeling arising from comparisons he could not be led to make could take root in his soul; and for the same reason, he could know neither hatred nor the desire for revenge, since these passions can spring only from a sense of injury:

> and as it is the contempt or the intention to hurt, and not the harm done, which constitutes the injury, men who neither valued nor compared themselves could do one another much violence, when it suited them, without feeling any sense of injury. In a word, each man, regarding his fellows almost as he regarded animals of different species, might seize the prey of a weaker or yield up his own to a stronger, and yet consider these acts of violence as mere natural occurrences, without the slightest emotion of insolence or despite, or any other feeling than the joy or grief of success or failure.[12]

Rousseau's general thesis that intelligible social relations are an ingredient of many significant impulses found in the psychology of individuals has found support in recent anthropology. Dr. W. H. R. Rivers, the British ethnologist, has insisted that vengeance, for instance, must be explained in terms of the blood-feud, and not the blood-feud in terms of vengeance. Jealousy can be explained in terms of marriage and property customs, and not the latter in terms of jealousy.[13] Avarice cannot be understood in terms of some native passion to possess and hoard coin. To begin with, coin is not found in nature but is a product of manufacture, is the medium of exchange among civilized men. Avarice is only derivatively gratified by the sight of a higher and higher stack of coin; the essential madness relates to the increase of *social power*. Men want less to be rich than to be *richer than other men*.

Rousseau insisted, in effect, that egoism must be understood as a distinctly human impulse, a narcissistic product of our self-critical faculty functioning in the social environment. The one mirror in which we can see egoistic desire gratified is the opinion of other men. Bodily desires and their gratification pose no insuperable problems for us civilized men. But we demand also the esteem and respect of our fellowmen, and sometimes their subordination; we want through them our own self-respect and dignity, and sometimes we want power over other men. Mill, although a utilitarian, not only granted this general point, but added that the *principal* object of human pursuit is consideration esteem.

The desire for approval and applause, unlike desire for food and sleep, has no intrinsic limits. We concern ourselves here, accordingly, not only with the healthy drive towards justice and equality of membership in the human race, but also with the drive towards tyranny and despotic control. Nor is the real competition limited to the goals

[12] Rousseau, *The Origin of Inequality*. In *The Social Contract and Discourses*, Everyman Edition, p. 197, note 2. Reprinted by permission.

[13] W. H. R. Rivers, "Sociology and Psychology." In *Psychology and Ethnology*, London: Kegan Paul, 1926.

of "approval and applause." What the miser wants, for instance, is not so much the fickle respect and estimation of his fellows as reliable *power over* men and their work. The miser may even leave it a secret that he has so much power; approbation and hand clapping are purchasable on demand. Every democratic public has a strong "instinct" for, a special sensitivity to, these social (or sometimes antisocial) impulses. De Tocqueville, trying to explain the new American states to European aristocracy, once remarked that what the Americans demanded of the rich was not their money, but their pride. Pride and hunger are the twin causes of revolution.

## LIBERTY AND DIGNITY

The dignity of man does not flourish in an uninhabited forest, even if Rousseau's noble savage is at least free from social deformation. Dignity lives where self-respect has been secured, and that generally means where respect is freely granted by one's fellow men. Men do not so much wish to be free from other people, as to be free *among* them. True, men do want sometimes to be alone, to enjoy solitude; men like the feel of things their own, the certainty that home's an inviolable castle. "It is a quietness to a man's mind to live upon his own and to know his heir certain." It's nice to have and hold freely —or damn and dump.[14] But it's even nicer to be free to become rich, to enjoy equality of opportunity to seek pleasure, riches, estimation, power, and achievement, to be able to speak one's mind. An American student who recently returned from a year in Moscow said, "I went to Russia taking the U.S. for granted. I came back realizing that nothing is so precious as being able to say what you want whenever you want to." [15] And it is not a matter of talking freely in an uninhabited forest, but *to people* in the heart of congested cities.

Mill's dictum that "each ought to rule himself in his own way" assumes a different aspect in this context. It applies less to the sensual and more to the *social* interests of a man. Nor does the ideal of freedom to live as one wishes look like perhaps, "only the late fruit of our declining capitalist civilization." It looks more like an ideal that can be not only validly fought and died for, but actually and successfully preserved to futurity. To be free means to be respected for what one is: A man among one's fellows, with one's own

[14] When his yachting guest, a connoisseur of wines, did not enthusiastically compliment his recent import of Bordeaux, a certain Chicago millionaire ordered all twenty odd cases then and there thrown overboard.

[15] *Parade,* March 12, 1961, p. 18. (I would not quote him, were this not the universal experience of those who visit Russia for more than a month or two.)

character, volition, and pattern of growth. Freedom implies dignity—the dignity of an equal. To call this liberty "natural" does not seem to be either a mistake or an exaggeration. "The spirit of liberty has its deepmost roots in the biological impulsion toward optimal growth."[16] In the opinion of a contemporary philosopher, C. I. Lewis,—in reference to one right:

> Not only is the liberty of thought essential to personality, and one of those highest goods which set the goals of human life, but in addition to any such natural-right sanction there is an indispensable social utility in the preservation of individual freedom of dissent. There can be no item of learning, and nothing in any social consensus reached, which should not originate in individual minds, reflecting their diversities and that experimentalism which characterizes independent thinking. The social order is the main selecting and preserving agency. But without the freedom of private judgment—often dissident to tradition—there would be no intellectual innovation, and progress would dry up at the source.[17]

As Rousseau would have it, social utility and natural right are not divided.

### LIBERTY AND SOCIAL COERCION

Liberty is freedom from coercion, including rather pointedly in our day, social coercion and the tyranny of the majority. A man is not free when beset by robbers and cutthroats. Neither is a man free when incarcerated or when he can't send his child to school without being cut off from his job and income. Is a man free when he can't criticize his employer or his union's business manager?

Bentham was led to say that "Every law is an infraction of liberty."[18] Although we admire his semantic integrity, his frankness, we are still going to have a look at the other side of the coin. We must recognize not only that law and social coercion restrict liberty but also that they alone can grant and preserve it. Well-enforced protection of the law is prerequisite to a life of liberty as we know it. Neither law nor liberty is just an abstraction. Rights to do this, that, and the other thing are operational only where concrete social forces, stronger than every opposing force, support them. Individual liberty as we know it can only be exercised in a free country. The first ten Amendments to the United States Constitution, along

[16] Arnold Gesell, *Studies in Child Development*. New York: Harper & Brothers, 1948, p. 215.

[17] C. I. Lewis, *Our Social Inheritance*. Bloomington: Indiana University Press, 1957, pp. 105–106. Copyright 1957. Reprinted by permission.

[18] Quoted by Isaiah Berlin, *Two Concepts of Liberty*, p. 33.

with the Fourteenth, establish our liberties; but those liberties were effectuated by stubborn men who preferred death to bondage.

The great danger to liberty in the modern world is "a spirit of suspicious and intolerant mediocrity." [19] If that spirit is not to pervade our democratic life, strong men must stand by prepared to prevail against it.

Liberty is not a substance; it is rather a quality of a very special complex of relational properties, a quality of certain very carefully wrought societies. "To be free" means "to be permitted" and also "to be competent"—to do what I want in my own way. If there is to be liberty of this sort for a whole society of free men—a free society—strong men must want liberty and enforce libertarian principles.

### OUR SPECIAL AND GENERAL OBLIGATIONS TO ROUSSEAU

Our special obligation to Rousseau is universal suffrage: The established right of every adult to go to the polls and cast his vote on election day. The obligation is not all owing to Rousseau, but we may let him have some credit; and he can stand for the rest of those who, in the eighteenth and nineteenth centuries, worked for universal suffrage. This political ideal, or course, has not been completely realized; but it has been almost completely realized. Where we fall short of letting all adults vote—or stand—for political office, we can well let the name of Rousseau remind us of the end and the direction.

Our more general obligation is the whole trend toward democracy and equalitarianism: political democracy and political equality, opportunity for all to read, write, and count, opportunity to fill economic office, economic security for all. The view that all citizens should share in political and economic activities and rewards was held clearly and espoused forcefully by Rousseau. There is a sense in which Rousseau is still a step or two out in front of us.

[19] John Stuart Mill, "M. de Tocqueville on Democracy in America." *Dissertations and Discussions: Political, Philosophical, and Historical.* Boston: William V. Spencer, 1864, vol. II, p. 159. (Reprinted from the *Edinburgh Review,* October, 1840). ". . . The defects, to which the government of numbers, whether in the pure American or in the mixed English form, is most liable, are precisely those of a public as compared with an administration. Want of appreciation of distant objects and remote consequences; where an object is desired, want both of an adequate sense of practical difficulties, and of the sagacity necessary for eluding them; disregard of traditions, and of maxims sanctioned by experience; an undervaluing of the importance of fixed rules, when immediate purposes require a departure from them,—these are among the acknowledged dangers of popular government; and there is the still greater though less recognized, danger of being ruled by a spirit of suspicious and intolerant mediocrity." (Pp. 158–159.)

## IS THERE AN ANSWER?

Is there an answer to the problem of the *Social Contract* that we can hold acceptable? Can we place the force of the whole community in support of the person and goods of every citizen? Can we unite justice and utility? Can we have liberty *and* equality and fraternity?

The primary condition of the social contract is the total alienation from every associate of all his rights in favor of the community. Rousseau says that in giving himself to all, one gives himself to no one. The fundamental point is that *all* are wholly subjected to the sovereign authority and laws of the state. If any were in any way left outside, the contract would not be valid. That is to say, there cannot be any little states within the big state. There is one indivisible sovereignty.

Given the absolute sovereignty of the state, and universal participation in the suffrage, majority rule is binding on all. The general will is expressed initially in the express or tacit acceptance of the contract; it is expressed thereafter in majority rule, according to Rousseau.

For his doctrine of the general will, Rousseau has been much criticized, and precisely from the perspective of liberty. He himself raises the crucial question: How can a man be free and be forced to conform to acts of will that are not his own? How can minorities be free and be subject to laws to which they have not consented?

Rousseau's comment is that "the question is badly posed. The citizen (as such) *consents to all the laws,* even to those passed despite him, and even to those which punish him, if he dares commit a violation. The constant will of all the members of the state is the general will: Through it they are citizens and free." Rousseau appends a footnote reference to Genoa, which posted the word "Liberty" over its prisons and galleys: Rousseau applauds the practice, calling it good and just, since, "it is only the malefactors who prevent the citizen from being free. In a country in which all those people were galley slaves, one would enjoy the most perfect liberty." (Book IV, Chapter II).

We cannot accept Rousseau's "optimism" on this score. We do not see how Rousseau lays down any formula for distinguishing political opponents or business enemies from "malefactors." To think that perfect obedience means (in any way) perfect liberty strikes us as absurd. Why? Because opinions concerning right and good are fallible, and, hence, rebelliousness and angry determination to oppose those who hold power are sometimes essential to progress. Our own experience tells us that changing administrations every few years is a condition of making such changes regularly and by an accepted constitutional procedure. We don't just oppose hereditary stratification, we want new men and new parties to be able peaceably to rise to the top—in the interest of political, economic, and social transformation, and in the interest of introduction of new ideas and of new adaptations to world conditions, to changes in technology. Besides, our own country gained its independence initially by rebellion and revolution. So we can't be sold on mere obedience for the sake of obedience, and even less on obedience for the sake of liberty!

Yet universal or almost universal acceptance of the intention to obey the law is essential to the establishment of a libertarian order. The social contract must be voluntarily obeyed, or obedience forced, or offenders must be punished or isolated. This demand is reasonable and relates to the condition of man in society, not just to any given system of positive law. I quote from current discussion of criminal law:

> One has to agree with Professor Bodenheimer's view that punishment should convey to the offender the expression of public disapproval, and one cannot agree with Professor Weihofen that the revulsion which world public opinion felt against the Nazi gas chambers, for example, was just an immoral hatred which civilized people ought to learn to control. To assert this is tantamount to denying the existence of a sense of justice in the human soul, and it is exactly this sense of justice which allows the average human being to remain a law-abiding citizen. To reduce the collective feeling and demand for justice in humanity to an animal impulse for vindictiveness and vengeance would be oversimplifying things. The failure of the state to satisfy this collective feeling leads to widespread fear and insecurity. To the community the crime appears as a documentation of uncontrolled strength or power which, at any moment, may become directed against any one of them as the vindication of a right which the other members have agreed to surrender to the state. If the state fails, therefore, to repress lawless, individual action, the citizens may rightly claim that they have been released from the social contract, and that each is again free to do as he pleases. Hence the criminality increases as a result of the state's failure to do proportional justice. It is for these reasons that aversion to crime and to the criminal who personifies it is unavoidable; unless the social group maintains its reprobation of crime it cannot remain intact.[20]

[20] K. J. Newman, "Punishment and the Breakdown of the Legal Order: The Experience in East Pakistan." Nomos III: *Responsibility,* ed. Carl J. Friedrich. New York: The Liberal Arts Press, 1960, pp. 135–136 (From Part Two: Criminal Responsibility). Copyright 1960. Reprinted by permission.

Yes, retribution is obsolete; but no, you cannot maintain any kind of an order, least of all a libertarian order, if the social contract can be "freely" violated. Rousseau is right, that there must be a perfect (or very near perfect) obedience.

The mistake lies not in insisting on obedience, but in taking obedience to be a sufficient condition or assurance of the most perfect liberty. For it could be equally the condition of a quietly oppressive state with no liberty whatever. It is just the mark of order, of any order.

We are forced, then, to the realization that Rousseau has *not* thought through the problem of liberty. He has not satisfactorily answered the problem of the *Social Contract* from the perspective of liberty, even if he has answered it from the perspective of order.

There are a thousand and one opinions on Rousseau; if we may add the thousand and second, he should be given credit for having forecast the modern movements in the direction of democracy (even if he said, democracies are for gods, not men). He gave great impetus to the cause of egalitarianism, including specifically the cause of equalization of opportunity: His work is a source book for both the liberal and the totalitarian democracies. His great contribution to libertarianism is his insight that liberty is a quality that should be universally distributed. A society is not free, if one or a few law-abiding citizens enjoy liberty, but others do not. He represented the principle of equality in the libertarian movement, as he represented it everywhere, not only by his writing, but also by *being* Citizen Jean-Jacques of Geneva. The social contract is a contract among *all;* the liberty or privilege of the few cannot be withheld by them from among the issues and values to be covered by the contract.

The result, however, should not be less liberty, but more liberty, for all. On this matter, Rousseau is somewhat worse than obscure.

There are many questions that live for us today to which Rousseau returns no adequate answer. The question how to combine liberty with equality is but one of them. How shall we combine equality and liberty with excellence? Where shall we trade liberty for economic security, and where not? How shall minorities be protected from tyrannous majorities?—(for him, not a legitimate question; for us, a question not avoidable). How shall "malefactors" be protected, when they are not malefactors but political enemies? How shall the absolute sovereignty of the state be exercised, its laws enforced, by *men*—and yet be free from all biases of particular individuals? In particular, how shall administrators of big government and big business be given the power and discretion necessary to excellent, imaginative accomplishment, and yet be precluded from sacrificing human interests to efficiency or to other values dear to all of us but dearer to administrators than they are to the rest?

### PARTICIPATION

Just at this point in the game, Rousseau pitches us a perfect drop ball. For he allows that *no* good state can have great size. Unfortunately for us, we have no choice in the matter: our states are colossal.

The most significant question posed by Rousseau for us on the contemporary scene is: How can we possibly maintain the active and intelligent participation of all citizens in nations of vast population? The denial that it can be answered poses the extreme challenge. "The farther the social bond gets stretched, the more it gives; and in general a small state is stronger (proportionally) than a large one." [21]

This maxim is supported, Rousseau adds, by a thousand reasons. The greater the distance, the heavier the administration (as if it followed the principle of the lever). (We speak of the evil here, in terms, *e.g.,* of absentee ownership or management, or of "distant Washington.") The weight grows, the more layers of administration and levels of tax-levying power there are: The people pay small local taxes, higher regional taxes, and so on, until at last the supreme administration takes the most and leaves nothing. Moreover, the higher up the ultimate governing power, the slower it is to avoid vexations or to correct abuses.—There is no need to go into all the details. Rousseau imaginatively presents all the faults, the omissions, the remoteness, the silliness, of "government way up there," blind to the actual needs of persons and communities. Retrospectively, and hopefully, we could call him small, narrow, and unrealistic. But then the small, unrealistic people, going about their daily work, are just the ones who offer us broader-minded, farther-seeing, realistic people our greatest challenges. Them we must face every day in our offices and classes, not unlike a jockey facing the feeding and grooming problems of the race horse he will ride. No freedom could be greater, than freedom from these people; but it is not available in this world. And so Jean-Jacques, with his narrow, keen insight into the problems of distance and the limits of imagination,[22] does present us with the full challenge of the vast, heavily populated, self-stratifying, liberal democracy: How can we know our business and co-operate, *so many of us,* so different from one another, and never cut one another's throat?

[21] *Social Contract,* Book II, Chapter IX.
[22] These insights are developed in his major work on education, *Émile.*

Well, it should at once be admitted that all the speedy evasions and quick answers lead directly to totalitarianism: Propagandize, preach loyalty to the higher-ups, kill criticism, kill critics, obfuscate unresolved issues.

If there are any substantive answers, they are expensive and slow. They are answers like Education: The right education for each man and woman. Communication: Full, clear, confident communication from top to bottom and from bottom to top. Good will: Good will that overlooks freckles and moles; good will that aims at the highest values and not without universal human sympathy, as well as sympathy for individuals encountered face-to-face. Money: Money when it's needed. Participating means giving and receiving and democratically discussing, thinking, and acting. Either Rousseau was right about participation in large states, or we have to face his challenge head on.

Social scientists do try to meet his challenge head on.

We have travelled a long way since St. Augustine. He would not even let the poor, naughty little fellows, of whom God made so many, enter into heaven. Indeed, he consigned them all to hell.

We have gone so far with Rousseau as to grant that every man should be counted for one (and none for more than one). All shall vote, and all shall have enough to eat. This ambition has not been realized, but we keep getting nearer its fulfillment. Within this century, William James quoted "that valiant anarchistic writer Morrison I. Swift":

> After trudging through the snow from one end of the city to the other in the vain hope of securing employment, and with his wife and six children without food and ordered to leave their home in an upper east-side tenement-house because of non-payment of rent, John Corcoran, a clerk, to-day ended his life by drinking carbolic acid. Corcoran lost his position three weeks ago through illness,—*etc., etc.*[23]

We have moved beyond the inegalitarianism that allowed that man to die. Everyone can partake.

Social scientists hasten to point out, however, that although the vote of Mr. Hunt or Mr. Rockefeller or Cardinal Spellman counts the same as that of John Corcoran or Thomas Flaherty and although everyone gets fed, still there remains in most states a heavy electoral weighting in favor of the old rural areas and against the hungry new urban areas; there still remain a few colored folk who do not get into the voting booth; some bright, eager, poor boys have to hustle to get a first-class medical education (and if they get it, graduate with much cynicism); Harvard still has indifferent relations with the

[23] William James, *Pragmatism*. New York: Meridian Books, 1955, p. 31.

poor Boston and Cambridge Irish, though it's true the relations are improving.

Other social scientists are quick to point out that we have been having a hard time in our external relations. A near-sighted American Secretary of State is said to have breakfasted with three secretaries from Latin America without having addressed or recognized them. Are we having a poor time in foreign relations because of lack of excellence or simply from lack of democratic faith and trust? These two may be indistinguishable in the practice of democratic politics at home and abroad. Being smug is being dumb. The secretary of state who can't or the dean of students who won't manage to love all the states or all the students comes off less than first class.

Ideal and practice do not always coalesce. Of our poor Asian relations Keyes Beech wrote already in 1952: [24]

> What the United States needs most in Asia today is not so much guns and atom bombs but ideas that will match the dynamic appeal of Communism. . . .
>
> Today in the search for scapegoats, it is forgotten that. . . . Chiang Kai-shek, who broods over a lost cause from his island retreat on Formosa, expressed his contempt for western materialism and political democracy in his blueprint for China's reconstruction.[25]

[24] Copyright December 6, 1952, *The Chicago Daily News*. Reprinted by permission.

[25] "Lewis Gannett, later the distinguished critic and essayist, but then in China as a roving reporter, watched the American marines policing Shanghai's streets, and among the twenty foreign warships anchored in the Whangpoo off the city's International Settlement he counted thirteen flying the American flag, and he observed, "Americans are doing all sorts of nice things for China, but they are not doing the one thing the Chinese want most—they are not abandoning the special privileges which make the foreigners a class apart in all the twenty-one provinces of the republic." He went one day in 1926 to the young "Red general" who as friend and ally of the Russians and the Communists had become commander-in-chief of the Chinese nationalist armies, and this general told him; "Thinking men in China hate America more than they hate Japan. Japan talks to us in ultimatums; she says frankly that she wants special privileges. . . . We understand that and know how to meet it. The Americans come to us with smiling faces and friendly talk, but in the end your government acts just like the Japanese. And we, disarmed by your fair words, do not know how to meet such insincerity. That is what is behind the anti-Christian movement in China. Your missionaries write 'charity' over their doors, and I do not deny that many of them are good men who do good work. But in the end they make it easier for American policy to follow that of the other imperialist Powers. So because we have been deceived by your sympathetic talk, we end by hating you most. Why cannot America act independently? Why does she preach fine sermons, but in the end tag along with the others? Why can she not, like Russia, prove her friendliness by acts?" (*The Survey*, May 1, 1926, p. 181.) This young general's name was Chiang Kai-shek. . . .—Quoted from Harold R. Isaacs, *Scratches On Our Minds: American Images of China and India*. New York: The John Day Company. Copyright 1958 by Massachusetts Institute of Technology. Pages 202–203. Reprinted by permission.

> If you were in China five years ago, you did not need to be a prophet or a Communist to know that Chiang's corrupt, incompetent regime was on its way out. It was written on the faces of the Kuomintang leaders. It was written on the faces of the militant young students who got their education in the American universities of Peiping and disappeared into Red China to dedicate their lives to the Communist cause.

SUMMARY OF QUESTIONS IN THE ROUSSEAUEAN MOOD

Do we have a political-economic order that moves more and more in the direction of liberty, equality, and fraternity? Or do we have an order that is allowed to move in the direction of oligarchy and stratification? Do we have flatly contradictory tendencies toward equality on the one hand, toward excellence on the other, and in such a way that we either perform poorly or perform undemocratically?

Do we really share purposes or are we just held together by luck? Can I as an individual citizen honestly admit that I am happily beholden to the system, even when by majority (or court) ruling, it goes against my individual interest? Can I admit the same as an official, when it goes against my organizational interest?

Do the forms of government in our country allow people to find the experience necessary for larger and larger responsibility and higher and higher office? Are these forms assisting regional communities to function as communities, or are they blocking common projects and preventing the sharing of important purposes?

Is our business organization democratic and liberal, or are we democratic and liberal only at the polls?

On the world scene, do we represent the ambition of the people to rise, or do we stand behind ancient hierarchies and selfish interests?

Do we believe that all individuals, the world over, shall have opportunity to rise freely, to determine their own interests, to be treated with respect at home and abroad?

Do we believe in full liberty for those born rich or talented, for nationals of strong countries, or do we believe in maximum liberty for *all* men?

Have we fought Communism with slights, slurs, and sling shots, or have we done our best to maintain the evident day-to-day superiority of our own kind of democratic system?

# 6

# KANT AND MORAL AUTONOMY

Immanuel Kant (1724–1804) maintained that men ought to be free, because they are moral beings. To treat a man as if he did not have ends of his own, or in Kant's terms, as if he were not an end-in-himself, is morally wrong. Not to respect men for the autonomous beings that they are is irrational; it violates the humanity in them who are so treated, and it also violates the humanity in him who so treats them.

In the Kantian ethic, there is little insistence on individuality and even less on social utility. Natural right is reinterpreted. Although Kant went to school to Rousseau, he has little interest in understanding or defending rights or liberties on the basis of a social contract or nature or history. He thinks that attempts to do so can only end in dogmatism. Rousseau had also said, however, that for a man to renounce his liberty is to renounce his quality of being a man, the rights of humanity, and therefore even his obligations. "To remove all liberty from his will is to remove all morality from his actions." [1] The dignity of man *as man* had become implicated with the notion of liberty. Rousseau saw the tension between a man as an individual and as a member of the state. He was asking questions about the

[1] *Social Contract,* Garnier edition, pp. 239–240.

*validity* of claims made by the state. More and more, since Rousseau, the conscience of those who enjoy freedom has agonized in the presence of those who are unfree. As far as our imagination reaches, we are interested in liberty as something universal.

This position should be contrasted with the situation in classical times. In the Gorgias, Socrates could stand for the Good and yet be called a slave by Callicles, ". . . a slave, who indeed had better die than live; since when he is wronged and trampled upon, he is unable to help himself, *or any other about whom he cares.*" [2] Modern men have accepted Callicles' view on this particular point. The dignity of all men has been acknowledged. Men have assumed responsibility for the rights of man collectively, not just for their own rights; they have not considered themselves free, while "the rights of man" were trampled on. Liberty as a universal and *moral* idea has taken hold.

Kant was the first great analytical philosopher. He tried to exhibit and to describe clearly what is already implicit in human actions and attitudes. From his perspective, we cannot justify liberty by citing history or by introducing a myth about the state of nature. He accepted Rousseau's ethic but not his arguments nor his rhetoric. Kant's procedure was simply to turn a light on our moral obligations and then to focus our attention on them. Kant scorned mere toleration just as much as Tom Paine or Rousseau. The obligation to respect other men and their rights is objectively there. The task of philosophical ethics is just to provide the illumination.

There is a sense in which Kant was more interested in morality than in liberty. All the same, his system turned on the first implication of right acting, and this first implication is the autonomy of the will.[3] I shall try to show that Kant's notion of autonomy adds something important to what Mill and Rousseau have said about liberty and an order of freedom.

## THE FORM OF HUMAN INTENTIONS

Kant was not a behaviorist or pre-behaviorist. It is true that he was always fascinated by science. His first book, which made him famous, was an hypothesis about the genesis of the solar system.[4]

[2] My italics.

[3] Professor H. J. Paton says: "In the *Critique of Practical Reason* it is Formula III of the Categorical Imperative which takes 'pride of place.' " This is The Formula of Autonomy.

[4] Professor Harlow Shapley has expressed regret that Kant did not remain an astronomer.

He taught the first course ever offered in anthropology. But Kant was always even more fascinated by another order of questions, namely philosophical questions, and especially by questions in the metaphysic of ethics. How can we recognize that a certain proposition is knowedge? How can we recognize the beautiful? What are the standards up to which we ought to act? How can we be certain of those standards? In what relation ought we to stand to other men? What evidence is there of (philosophical) freedom of the will? To what civil and social liberty are men entitled, and what is the relation of this liberty to morality?

These are questions that bear on understanding, ethics, judgment, human sensibility and purpose, even if they do sometimes get involved with questions of fact and methods of science. Kant was much impressed with the external world that surrounds us; but he was obsessed with the world of experience within us, above all with that which he quaintly called "the moral law within." "Two things fill the mind," he said, "with ever new and increasing admiration and awe, the oftener and more steadily they are reflected on: the starry heavens above me and the moral law within me." [5]

Kant was interested in the nature of human action, in the needs, values, and postulates from which our decisions and acts derive. His interest was not restricted to moral action, as our presentation of his analysis of imperatives in Chapter 3 demonstrates. Unfortunately, however, he did not leave us a fully developed philosophy of action or of administration. In any case, he was convinced that there *is* a distinctly moral aspect to human living; and in this chapter we shall concern ourselves only with Kant's views on morality and moral values, and even with these only as they appear to bear on the premises of liberal democracy.

Kant called himself a "critical idealist." He put great faith in ideas and ideals; but he intended to be "critical," not dogmatic. He had grave doubts about metaphysics, as he did also about accepted moralities and casuistries. He did not, ordinarily, tell us what we ought to do or not do; he was not properly a rationalist; but he maintained a great faith in reason in human conduct just the same. The exercise of reason in our conduct is from Kant's perspective peculiarly inward, personal, and free. Yet he was convinced that an ideal community of men could arise only from the exercise of reason in the first person by free individuals. Kant was so reluctant, both by temperament and by philosophical conviction, to do any more than state the purely formal conditions of right action, that his

[5] *Critique of Practical Reason,* Beck translation, 1949, p. 258.

analysis may at times have served narrow sectarians, militarists, and others who "jump to their morals" and who therefore prefer formalism and prefer not to draw attention to just *which* actions it is right to perform. (For there are people willing enough to take advantage even of men's best intentions.) Kant happened not to concern himself with questions of values, in our sense, happened not to concern himself with "what things I should live *for*."

Kant wants to tell us what must be the broad characteristics of action, *if it is to be defensible*. As Professor Leys has put it, Kant gives us not a complete guide for life, but a guide for *action that may be challenged*. Kant held, moreover, that all moral action, be it individual or group action, although it may not be challenged and justified, is at least *justifiable* and competent to face up to any challenge by rational spectators and critics.

Kant's study is accordingly a formal, rationalistic analysis of the meaning of duty; but he by no means looks on the sense of duty as bound up with the prevailing or any other particular moral code.[6] Both as anthropologist and philosophical analyst, he was beyond any such naïveté. Kant's analysis is aimed rather at clarity of intention just in those cases of decision where the values are fluid and dependence on codified morality does not suffice. Kant ought, accordingly, specially to interest those who are aware of having to exercise discretion and make original decisions. The kinds of questions Kant raises do not allow of answers that base themselves solely on custom and what has been considered satisfactory in the past. They are relevant just when tradition is challenged. They apply where casuistry fails.

The Kantian ethic is therefore relevant to persons in positions of public responsibility and to persons who mould public opinion, relevant to persons who must weigh the merits of codes and customs the survival value of which is itself just the subject of decision. In contemporary terms, Kant's discussion is highly relevant to the ethical problems of our élite classes: to the decisions of statesmen, administrators, executives, educators, editorial supervisors.

Kant's disinclination to make concrete applications is therefore sound. Express applications could only illustrate, after all, and might be seriously misleading. If an ethics has to do with really original decisions, no exact models can be presented. And this is precisely the Kantian orientation.

The clear recognition that there are such decisions is one of the most powerful arguments for liberty. If men are to make ultimate or

[6] See Paul Schlipp, *Kant's Pre-Critical Ethics*, Evanston and Chicago: Northwestern University, 1938, p. 163.

even penultimate decisions that are both original and right, they will have to be free to do so.

### IMPARTIALITY AND OBJECTIVITY

The person who must decide ought to ask himself, Kant says, "Could I will that in every possible case that is exactly like this one, the decider should come to the same decision?" If so, go ahead. What Kant demands of us—and claims that moral duty demands—is complete impartiality in choosing, deciding, and acting. Notice the forward look; I can't look to past cases, because by definition there are none; or even if there were, we could not be certain of their identity with this one. Kant makes casuistry subjective, in that the agent must himself pass final judgment on his own decision; but the agent must do it with perfect objectivity! The broad character of casuistry is still retained, for the agent has to discover the maxim in his unique decision and ask himself if he could will the maxim into universal law. He must look on what is really only his unique decision as if it were a case, and he must judge it as if it were to be universally the case. Kant's first formula of the categorical imperative, of the one and only distinctively moral imperative, therefore is:

> Act only on that maxim through which you can at the same time will that it should become a universal law.

Closely related is the formula that Professor Paton refers to as "1a":

> Act as if the maxim of your action were to become through your will a universal law OF NATURE.

Kindly observe that neither the Golden Rule nor either of these two formulas gives any content to any maxim of human conduct. They concern themselves only with the form of our intentions. They command impartiality, universality, and no exception in favor of ourselves or of anyone. "Do unto others as you would have them do unto you" presupposes that we know materially how we want to be "done to." Kant's formulas presuppose that we have concrete impulses and (imperative) ways of acting to gratify them, and not just individual impulses and techniques, but collective ones, social impulses.

### REASON, A SUBSTITUTE FOR COERCION

Every moral economy assumes that some persons, or classes of persons, will assume responsibility and initiative for setting goals and seeing to it that the work gets done. Plato proposed, before ever turning ultimate political responsibility over to his leaders, to cultivate their courage and wisdom for fifty years. Democracies face the hardest challenge in respect to moral and political responsibilities, because they aim to distribute them throughout the entire population. Democracies require that, not just the members of some élite, but every segment of the population and almost every individual, shall act spontaneously and responsibly. Plato's experience with Athenian democracy gave him little confidence in "the people." In his ideal Republic, he favored a self-perpetuating aristocracy of merit.

If democracies succeed, however, their success outshines that of any other kind of order. An ideal democracy would bring out the best and strongest in every individual; its members would all be responsible citizens and would all have a fine moral quality. If democracies fail, however, their failure will be complete and total and may leave nothing good still standing.

As a democratic thinker, Kant believed in the universality, [or at least potential near-universality,] of practical reason. He thought that every individual has enough constructive imagination to build his own ideal of personal happiness, and he thought that every individual has enough sense to set limits to what he asks for himself. He looked on reason as a cohesive force that empowers us to share purposes, to respect one another, to work together for good. Rousseau had said, "The real world has its limits, the world of imagination is infinite: if not able to enlarge the one, let us control the other. . . ." (*Émile*). Kant looked on reason not only as the instrument that permits the individual to devise means to his goals and to measure one goal against another, but also as a substitute for social and physical coercion.

Animals are impelled by instinct, and many are gregarious by nature and organized in hives and colonies. Man is the political animal: He must *learn* to get along with his fellows by exercising his reason. Rationality demands that we adopt the perspectives of other men, that we treat others, like ourselves, with justice. We can work together to achieve intelligent projects of mutual benefit. Kant thinks that reason can displace both the whip and the political lie.

## CAN WE DO WHAT WE OUGHT?

Can we all take the perspectives of others? Can we all act sensibly? Can we all do what we ought? Kant stresses that when we are under obligation we can perform adequately. Duty and obligation imply power. Liberal democracy demands that we enlarge our faith in humanity, that we count on the moral worth and striving of everyone.

Every élite is inclined by its status and class smugness to look down on the capabilities of "the lower classes." But Kant tells us how he himself was once awed by the moral goodness of an ordinary, illiterate gardener. In our own day, whole nations are trying to lift themselves up by their moral bootstraps to the level of political democracy and autonomy. Needless to say, many have fallen and many more shall fall. Lack of good will and good sense leads to "Balkanization": falling apart into states too small and greedy, classes too small and greedy, families and individuals too small and greedy. But there is ground for hope.

An episode in the political career of Mill can serve to illustrate Kant's point, to exhibit a degree of warrant for his faith in man. Mill was "the first Labor M. P.," serving for Westminister from 1865 to 1868. During the campaign, an opposition placard was printed quoting Mill's "Thoughts on Parliamentary Reform" to the effect that "the working classes, though differing from those of some other countries, in being ashamed of lying, are yet generally liars." This placard was handed to Mill at a meeting, chiefly composed of working class people, and Mill was asked whether he had written and published it.

> I at once answered 'I did.' Scarcely were these words out of my mouth, when vehement applause resounded through the whole meeting. It was evident that the working people were so accustomed to expect equivocation and evasion from those who sought their suffrages, that when they found, instead of that, a direct avowal of what was likely to be disagreeable to them, instead of being affronted, they concluded at once that this was a person whom they could trust.[7]

There are latent possibilities for good in all men. If businessmen distrust laborers and laborers distrust businessmen "generally and on principle," this can be explained by reference to ignorance, inexperience, and a narrow class outlook. Where the stakes are perhaps life and death, the scales fall from our eyes. For this reason, say Sharp and Fox, "there is always a supply of [physical] courage when needed.

> In 1929 a hospital in Cleveland was destroyed by fire. The disaster was aggravated by the fact that the heat converted the X-ray films stored in the basement into great clouds of poison gas.

[7] *Autobiography*, p. 241.

> Among the heroines of the disaster was Gladys Gibson, telephone operator at the clinic who died [the same] night in a hospital. The telephone girl saw the cloud of yellow poison gas coming and knew it carried death, but she stayed at her switchboard, making heroic efforts to warn everyone in the clinic of their danger and to rally police, firemen, and ambulances. Finally she collapsed. Someone carried her out, dying.[8]
>
> Gladys, it may be argued, must have been a very exceptional young person. As a matter of fact she may have had, on the whole, a commonplace character.[9]

Commonplace character can be transcended.

One of the wonders of our kind of democracy is its power of drawing leaders from the whole mass of men and women. The democratization of responsibility can lead to a democratization of competence, leadership, and virtue. Rousseau, Kant, Jefferson, all foresaw the possibility. The adage that "responsibility implies power" can be made to hold true of the social ethos. We can find out what human nature is capable of, only if we allow it to develop and manifest itself. Many have said, "Women can't do it, negroes can't do it, Catholics can't do it, workers can't do it," *etc., etc.,* but never allowed of the conditions whereby one *could* find out who can and who can't do what. To make matters worse, we all find it tempting to accept that certain kinds of action are beyond us, or even beyond human nature altogether, if someone will but say so and let us clean off the hook of responsibility.

Kant was a moral idealist, and he thought that duty can lead us into great development and improvement. Where a sense of obligation discloses itself, corresponding capacity will soon make its appearance.

### RESPECT FOR HUMANITY

Kant put great emphasis on respect for others and for oneself. He was not in a hurry to say that we should love others. Love may be unduly possessive; it may be sentimental; and sometimes it is hypocritical. The Golden Rule presupposes that you do well unto yourself. We know that many people hate themselves and that many people despair of themselves. The Golden Rule supposes a certain

[8] Associated Press Dispatch.

[9] Frank Chapman Sharp and Philip G. Fox, *Business Ethics, Studies in Fair Competition.* New York: Appleton-Century-Crofts, Inc., 1937, pp 240–241. Copyright 1937. Reprinted by permission.

"normality," and Kant explicitly insists on this "normality." He gives a second formula of the *identical* Categorical Imperative:

> So act as to use humanity, both in your own person and in the person of every other, always at the same time as an end, never simply as a means.

Professor Paton, who translated this, calls this formula the "Formula of the End in Itself."

Kant does not say that we cannot use people as means. We can and must, given the division of labor, use many persons as means. The postman brings letters, the baker bakes our bread, the spiritual leader leads our spirit. But we are never to treat persons simply as means; we ought always to treat them *also* as ends. Men are ends in themselves in being the *subjects* of experience. All men, moreover, have moral ends of their own; all men stand under moral obligation. Men deserve respect because they are themselves purposive, rational, moral.

Kant's positive message for us is moral goodness. Only moral goodness can be prized by us—objectively—without reservation. Gifts of fortune, qualities of temperament like courage, talents like wit or intelligence, all these can be used to serve evil purposes. "It is impossible to conceive of anything anywhere in the world or even anywhere out of it that can without qualification be called good, except a Good Will." (*Fundamental Principles of the Metaphysic of Ethics,* p. 1)

Today, in New York City or Chicago, the individual may find himself as remote from the apparent sources of authority and power as a Russian serf a thousand miles from St. Petersburg. But the larger the numbers and the greater the "sociological" distance, the more important is law and the objective enforcement of law. In the large community of the present, only respect for principle can save us. If this respect is lost, as in Hitler's Germany, millions suffer. Within the domestic economy and in the world economy today, respect for persons functions more as a matter of principle than of concrete concern. Inside the family, love makes for integrity and fair treatment, but in the larger society, the principle of equitable treatment must be maintained *as principle.*

## AUTONOMY

The question of autonomy has to do with the so-called "philosophical freedom of the will." This has often been understood to have nothing whatever to do with toleration and individual liberty in society. Directly, it does not; but I am going to maintain (somewhat speculatively), that, indirectly, it does. From a Kantian point of view, it is important to an understanding of the conditions of civil and social liberty.

The third formula of the Categorical Imperative is the Formula of Autonomy: So act that your will can regard itself at the same time as making universal law through its maxim.[10] With this formulation, Kant wished to bring out the majestic character of moral action. In acting morally, I am the sovereign who makes the law. It is my own reason that legislates. Moral action is rational, but it is individual and spontaneous: Its source is within me. To decide and act morally is to decide and act *as if* one were making universal law through his own will.

Let us see why the word "autonomy" is used in this connection. Action in accordance with technical and prudential imperatives is rational; but, in the end, it is impelled by animal drives. We can go so far as to say that all action is impelled by animal drives. But morally justifiable action, however impelled, is justifiable because it meets a further standard. Compliance with this further standard is not impelled by any animal drive, according to Kant, but is motivated by sheer respect for rationality. A moral act exhibits mastery over oneself as an animal self and thus over nature as something given and determined by external causes. In a moral act I transcend myself as something determined by heredity and environment.

Moral action, then, implies self-mastery. It is the exercise of a distinctively human capacity to take into account the perspectives of all men, and to count oneself for one but not more than one. It exhibits my right and power to legislate over nature, including my own animal, or merely psychological, nature. Kant accordingly thinks that moral action establishes moral autonomy.

## IMPLICATIONS FOR INDIVIDUAL LIBERTY

To the extent that I am a moral agent, no one else has the right to tell me what to do. I am obliged to act with moral spontaneity; and that means I am not entitled to act in a certain way just because someone else thinks I should. As far as moral decision is concerned, I am and must be my own master. From a moral perspective, no one can be permitted to look on himself as a slave.

History has shown that once the Kantian perspective is accepted

[10] Professor Paton also gives Formula IIIa as follows, the Formula of the Kingdom of Ends: So act as if you were always through your maxims a law-making member in a universal kingdom of ends.

slavery in every form is morally defunct. We stand obliged to work toward a universal community of free men.

That we are obliged to respect the humanity in ourselves and in all men does not have to be proved, and indeed it cannot be proved. But it is a given fact in our moral experience. No one can rightfully legislate for my moral conscience, and I cannot rightfully command the conscience of any other person. In this respect, every human being is autonomous and sovereign.

Thus Kant substitutes for the social utility of liberty and for the natural or contractual character of liberty his own view of liberty and his own warrant: We are directly obliged by our own ethical character to respect every man as an autonomous moral agent.

If we wanted to put it so baldly and simply, we could say that the great Kantian "discovery" in ethics is that every man has a conscience, that every man ought to rule himself by the light of his own reason. We thereby lose "the right" to tell another what he should and should not do, so far as moral conscience is concerned. Where moral rightness is at stake, he is not just entitled, but obligated, to make his own decisions. And *our* obligation as citizens, as independent agents ourselves, is to see to it that society becomes more and more libertarian, that the moral wills of men are more and more free.

The great and awesome moral fact about every man is that *he can act from principle.* We are never entitled to violate this power to act from motives of justice. By the same token, the one great moral crime against humanity is the reduction of individual liberty. And there is no moral progress apart from the progressive liberation of man: That means, moving toward the ideal of every man *his own man,* every man responsible for his own choice of ends and means.

### THE LEFT HOOK

Thus Kant is no reductive leveller. He would raise everyone to the status of majesty, give everyone moral sovereignty.

Kant himself said:

> The inner principle of the world is freedom. The end, therefore, for which man is destined is to achieve his fullest perfection through his own freedom.[11]

[11] Kant, *Lectures on Ethics,* edited by Paul Menzer, translated by Louis Infield. London, 1930, p. 252. Quoted in Paul Schilpp, *Kant's Pre-Critical Ethics.* Evanston and Chicago: Northwestern University, 1938, p. 151. Copyright 1938. Reprinted by permission.

Professor Paton has written as follows concerning Kant's historical background:

> If, as Kant holds, the moral philosopher formulates, clarifies, and systematizes the moral principles already presupposed in moral judgments and moral actions, we may ask what is the historical background with reference to which Kant's own doctrines are to be understood.
>
> . . . perhaps we can say simply that the two greatest factors in Kant's historical background are, firstly, the Christian religion in its Protestant form [Kant's parents were Pietists], and, secondly, the influences which made for the American and French Revolutions. . . . His Formula of Universal Law, insisting as it does on the spirit as opposed to the letter of the moral law, is his version of the Christian doctrine that we are saved by faith and not by works. His Formula of the End in Itself is his way of expressing the Christian view that every individual human being has a unique and infinite value and should be treated as such. His Formula of the Kingdom of Ends as a Kingdom of Nature [Formula IIIa] is quite explicitly his rational form of recognizing a church invisible and visible, the Kingdom of God which has to be made manifest on earth.
>
> The influences behind the American and French Revolutions, which can be summed up as the "Enlightenment," may be regarded as a continuation of the Reformation, though the French Revolution was more bloody, and more violent against religion, because there the Reformation had been defeated. These influences are shown most markedly in Kant's passionate insistence upon freedom as the basis of all progress and all morality. The more direct and obvious influences come out, as is natural, in his political philosophy and especially in his hatred of despotism in any shape or form.[12]

Kant's kind of view fairly well ruled the moral thinking of the last century. The spirit of our own age has found Kant a somewhat less congenial mentor. The left hook Kant throws hits here: There are in so extremely formal an ethic no manifest intermediate principles. Despite Kant, to learn what our concrete duties are is not at all an easy task. Even given the best will in the world, and the fullest liberty of moral choice, grave problems remain. How are we to maintain our political institutions and our producing and distributing institutions at full efficiency and at the same time insist on the full, free consent of all participants? The manager must report to his stockholders, as well as to his employees and to the larger community. The legislator must answer to his constituents and to those

[12] H. J. Paton, *The Categorical Imperative*. London: Hutchinson's University Library, pp. 195–196. Reprinted by permission.

who pay his campaign bills, as well as to his own conscience. The artist is responsible to his public, to his art, and to himself. The Hollywood producer may want to release film of the highest quality, and something elevating, too; but his competitor is only too glad to cater to the democratic (!) mass, to the adolescent aesthetic of the paying public. The loyal citizen wants to integrate and raise the level of his metropolitan community; but "pious" rural districts control the legislature and block every reform, especially every effort in the direction of equitable and democratic reapportionment.

I think we could say that the majority of philosophers today find Kant's analysis of the quality of moral intention profound and substantially accurate, but they find much more difficult than Kant did any solution to the question, "What Shall I Do?" or "What Shall *We* Do?" The gap—or the left hook—is specially disturbing in reference to the question of liberty. How am I to protect my liberty, my moral right to independent judgment and action, in view of unavoidable social constraints, in view of what appear to be absolute social and governmental necessities? Just where does my responsibility to respect and protect the liberties of other persons begin and end?—Of course, Kant is right that we cannot look to reason for an answer and at the same time gag it with censorship. He gives us the formal qualifications of a sound goal, of *the* sound goal, of a free community, including a free and peaceable *world* community.[13] He is correct, only where there is the fullest mutual respect of reason and good intention, only where there is real and well-justified mutual trust, can world peace and liberty consistently co-exist. We must move in Kant's direction.

Unfortunately (so to speak), Kant was followed by the French Revolution, Terror, and Reaction, and, in philosophy, by Hegel and then by the great irrationalist movements of the nineteenth and twentieth centuries. We have not yet succeeded in filling the gaps, removing the concrete difficulties, enlarging the imagination and moral perspective of the masses and of the sundry élites, instilling a love of liberty that transcends and therefore can hold out against all the fears of nations and classes, and against their limitations, prejudices, and immediate graspings and grapplings. We have not succeeded in learning to prize liberty above and beyond our narrow moral codes, above and beyond our confined and sometimes distorted sense of right and wrong, even if we do prize it above death. We are in the position of whole-heartedly accepting liberty as one of our absolute values. But are we able to live with it from day to day?

[13] In his little book, *Zum Ewigen Frieden: Perpetual Peace.*

In a pretended debate on BBC between John Stuart Mill and Sir James Fitzjames Stephen, Mill remarked that a free society is one that is *not* like a regiment, *not* like a school. Stephen replied that men are more like children than philosophers. In other words, men cannot rule themselves in freedom, but must be disciplined like children. This is the stock objection against libertarian democracy: It requires too much maturity, a maturity that may be expected of philosophers but not of the general citizenry. The philosophers of freedom, according to Stephen, commit the scholar's fallacy. They make the mistake of seeing all mankind in their own image, but mankind in fact are so many thugs, or so many sheep, or, at best, so many children.

This question of the *reach* of humanity is not easily answered. Hegel thought that history meant a movement in the direction of the democratization of freedom. He was much more conservative and much more a gradualist than Kant, but he conceived of freedom as having been at first the prerogative of none but the monarch, or tyrant, then later on of a class—freedom of "some"—and then in modern times becoming the right of all. Liberty can belong to all, if there is universal enlightenment and self-control.

Unfortunately, our middle-class moral codes have greatly underemphasized the obligation to cultivate imagination and to learn to see through the eyes of others. One class wants to see the other only on its own terms. This sort of limitation is parodied in the old English ditty:

> She was poor but she was honest,
> Just the victim of a rich man's crime.

Kant said, innocence is a splendid thing, except that it has little lasting power. It is unthinkable today that adults should advance their irresponsibility by claiming innocence and ignorance.

A related fault is finding one's own, perhaps repressed, failings in others. "I am clean as a whistle, but thou . . . !" This is parodied in a popular London song, the chorus of which runs:

> The things I see I wouldn't tell,
> When I'm washing windows.

Sixty-odd verses *do* tell the naughty things he sees through those windows. This sort of hypocrisy can't ride tandem with liberty or moral splendor. In Kant's view, our moral obligation is to look for the best, not the worst, and thus to elicit moral self-sufficiency. Kant in fact pointed out that even hardened criminals are "human" enough to respond to the biographies of good men and to tales of great moral courage. The systematic cultivation of mutual distrust is degrading; it is an evil that every libertarian democracy must fight without flinching. The bitterest irony of history would be realized if today, when our moral opportunities and choices are far greater than they have ever been in the past, we were suddenly to decide that moral splendor is nothing but an illusion.

I think that we should agree with Mill and Berlin that liberty to do evil is a necessary part of freedom of choice. But the optimistic libertarian assumption is that free men will by and large *not* choose evil; the assumption is not really very "optimistic." If we don't make it, in the light of history, what alternative is open?

Men deciding and acting with liberty are not only more likely to make choices good for them than anyone else could make; they are also more likely to make responsible choices, choices by and large the most desirable from a social perspective.

Liberty means freedom of choice. Freedom of choice does not suggest irresponsibility; it suggests the end, the loss, of irresponsibility. We could take hold of the same stick by the other end: The acquisition of liberty implies the gain of freedom from irresponsibility.

Professor Lewis has said:

> Man is open to remorse for what he has brought about or what he has failed to do: he cannot respond as present feeling incites him merely but must face the future with concern and act with care. What he chooses to bring about, he must thereafter recognize as *his* doing which he never can disown. His freedom of choice is the necessity of decision and the responsibility for what is chosen and decided. This freedom and this responsibility, whether as privilege or as burden, are a part of his inheritance as human; and the acceptance and exercise of them are the vocation of man. Freedom of choice and responsibility for decision and for action belong to the individual in his individual living, and they belong to men together in their living together and acting together.[14]

Kant anticipated the actual situation of contemporary man, individual and collective. Nothing can save us but our own sense of responsibility, or, as Kant says, "the consciousness of freedom."

> The law of duty, through the positive worth which obedience to it makes us feel, finds easier access through the respect for ourselves in the consciousness of our freedom. If it is well established, so that

[14] *Our Social Inheritance,* p. 16. Copyright 1957. Reprinted by permission.

a man fears nothing more than to find himself on self-examination to be worthless and contemptible in his own eyes, every good moral disposition can be grafted on to this self-respect, for the consciousness of freedom is the best, indeed the only, guard that can keep ignoble and corrupting influences from bursting in upon the mind.[15]

[15] *Critique of Practical Reason,* trans. Lewis White Beck. Chicago: The University of Chicago Press, 1949, p. 258. Copyright 1949. Reprinted by permission.

PART III

# Fraternity: The Social Animal

# 7

# MAN AND NATURE

Many people think that men should rely on science instead of moral principles. Many think that as science advances, ethical discussion becomes dispensable; as the law becomes more positive in its development, and more scientific, it severs itself from ethics.

Since science has succeeded so well in determining what is what in respect to external nature, why can it not do the same in respect to human nature? And when it does do as well with human nature —in individual and social psychology, sociology, and in such newer studies as bionics—, why should we not place exclusive reliance on it in the determination of social policy and in the control of men?

This view appeals to many natural and social scientists and to some philosophers. The scientist unavoidably contrasts the efficiency and progressiveness of scientific research and subsequent technical application with the awkwardness of politics and law and with the stupidity of old-time moralism. The social scientist and scientific historian contrasts his own carefully based predictions and their measured caution with the manifestly foolish, now over-optimistic, now over-pessimistic, predictions of politicians and the public. The scientist is likely to look forward to a day when all human decision, at least all *important* human decision, can be made through the instrumentality and with the efficiency and reliability of science.

Wherever knowledge, intelligence, and results are accepted criteria, highest prestige belongs to the physical sciences and mathematics. Social scientists have often accepted the physical sciences as their model. "To be intelligent means to be scientific."

Despite so much prestige, nowhere has a majority of men actually adopted the position that society should place its complete, or even its more fundamental, reliance on science. Perhaps the Communist Russians have made the greatest pretense of doing so. But their conception of science is a nineteenth century one, so far as social science is concerned, and amounts really to a metaphysical interpretation. We shall look more closely at Communist perspectives in later chapters. Nowhere, in any case, has the ultimate political power, the power of final allocation of values been placed in the hands of scientists.[1] No public has shown itself ready to turn over final decision, in its very human affairs, to science and scientists.

This is not to say that we ought not to give the fullest support to science. The great hopes of mankind, and the great fears, both rest very much on the rapid development of scientific knowledge. Science should not, will not, and cannot be stopped or slowed down. We of the West see our very survival depending on it; and so equally do the Russians and the Chinese see theirs. No morally or politically responsible citizen will arrest this movement. The prestige of science is sacrosanct. We may note in passing, however, that the responsibility here mentioned is "moral" and "political."

In the nature of things, and not without the support of so much prestige, conceptions of the nature of the world and of man that arise in the scientific community play their role in everyone's imagination and affect, directly and indirectly, our moral attitudes and beliefs. Is man free or determined? Can mind and feeling be understood, in principle, as passive expressions of events that are really physiological, and so physical? Granting the fullest scientific knowledge, does there remain valid human choice? If both science and moral principle bear on choice, by what standard shall we determine their functions and ratios? Where does science begin, and where does it end; *i.e.,* what are the norms of scientific knowledge, when is science really science? Granting that physics is a science, is mathematics? Is psychology, psychoanalysis? Is government? Is there "policy science?" Is aesthetics a science? Is ethics itself?

[1] The likeliest exception I can think of is the management of Union Carbon and Carbide Company, a matter of corporate, not political, power.

NATURE, A THIRD PARTY TO HUMAN TRANSACTIONS

Let us look first, in a general way, at nature as constituting the stage on which the drama of human life is played.

*We* are born in and of the world: Our inception, a fertilized ovum; our terminus, ashes and dust. Human life is conducted among air, earth, fire, and water; it keeps itself, on Planet Three, in intimate relation to material things. Maintenance of life depends on nourishment and drink; procreation demands a second human body. No wonder then that men do not concentrate their complete attention on human relationships. Things natural and artifactual not only have their place in the sun, but in one way and another are an item in every human affair.

Ethics is concerned with relationships among men. There is, however, always this third party to human affairs, this physical stuff. It's like the dummy in bridge, the widow in cut-throat games. As Harold Lasswell has said, "We think of the social process as man pursuing *values* through *institutions* on resources."[2] The "resources" are relevant, essential; the realization of social goals calls for physical change (and physical change often generates social heat). The bone of contention turns out to be a bone of real marrow and calcium phosphate, some physical asset or property. Our pride gets expressed in our house and garden, our brougham or airplane, in the raiment and coiffure of our wife.

We are responsible in some sense—needless to say—for one or another degree of acquaintance with the laws of nature in *all* our commitments to action, for our actions are taken up into nature and carried farther in accordance with those laws. There are, moreover, no end of occasions when special knowledge affects the merit of decision. The world is as it is,[3] and to control it, we must have the accurate vision supplied by scientific knowledge. An ethics, a "sense of rectitude," that does not face up to scientific knowledge and technology is silly. The great ethicists have, of course, interested themselves in physical science. Socrates' first intellectual passion was the thought of Anaxagoras. One inevitably thinks also of Spinoza with his primary concern for the material basis of the good life. Even such a one-time preacher as Emerson, himself an idealist and practical moralist, wrote in his journal:

[2] *The World Revolution of our Time*. Hoover Institute Studies, Series A: General Studies, No. 1, August 1951. Stanford: Stanford University Press, p. 11. Underlining in original.

[3] However, "the power of physical facts to coerce belief does not reside in the bare phenomena. It proceeds from method, from the technique of research and calculation." John Dewey, *The Public and Its Problems*. p. 3.

> An idealist, if he have the sensibilities and habits of those whom I know, is very ungrateful. He craves and enjoys every chemical property, and every elemental force, loves pure air, water, light, caloric, wheat, flesh, salt, and sugar; the blood coursing in his own veins, and the grasp of friendly hands; and uses the meat he eats to preach against matter as malignant, and to praise mind, which he very hollowly and treacherously serves. Beware of hypocrisy.[4]

Since the world is outside us, including the bodies—and hence also the *feelings*—of other persons, our *acts* are acts only if they eventuate in some physical change or other. In social ethics, our primary attention is given to mental and volitional phenomena. But the fact remains that our minds and feelings are incarnate, embodied; and human willing is accordingly a legitimate subject matter, not only of psychology and the social sciences but also of the physical sciences. "The first phase of the physical consequences of commitment is always some movement of the doer's body." [5] This bodily doing of something is the act.

## THE EXPERIENCE OF SCIENCE AND SCIENTISTS

The observations and reasonings of natural science can teach us many things about the conduct of affairs, if we will but learn. The history and philosophy of science are rich in experience of value. Empirical scientific experience can teach us that the world is what it is.

The initial implausibility of a hypothesis may turn out to be but a block to truth. When those first Danes and Germans, and returning American students, came to America with the early, awkward, rather oversize Roentgen ray equipment of the nineties and the first decade of this century, American physicians thought that they were quacks. Yet today no physician, surgeon, dentist, or hospital staff can dispense with X-ray. The initial, apparent ridiculousness of X-ray concealed its vast utility.

Going back a little farther into history, but not much farther, we can learn a lesson of strength and weakness from out the era of witchcraft, demoniacal possession, and early modern medicine. The Bible contains the injunction, "Thou shalt not suffer a witch to live." Many a brave physician opposed witchcraft, if not openly, at least by not certifying this, that, and the other woman or child for torture. Homage has been paid Harvey and Gilbert. The power of casting

[4] *The Portable Emerson.* New York: The Viking Press, 1946, p. 606. Reprinted by permission of Houghton Mifflin Co.

[5] C. I. Lewis, *The Ground and Nature of the Right.* New York: Columbia University Press, 1955, p. 44.

out devils was once accepted as a leading proof of the divine origin of the Christian religion. It is *one* of the reasons why scientific—or even decent—treatment of the mentally ill began so late in Christendom. The *tortura insomniae* was once an accepted treatment for witches and for the possessed.

> Of all things in brain-disease, calm and regular sleep is most certainly beneficial; yet, under this practice, these half-crazed creatures were prevented, night after night and day after day, from sleeping or even resting. In this way temporary delusion became chronic insanity, mild cases became violent, torture and death ensued, and the 'ways of God to man' were justified.[6]

It was not the theologians alone, nor ignorant peasants, who were responsible for witch-hunting and for converting the mentally ill to insanity. They were indeed responsible.

> But the most contemptible creatures in all those centuries were the physicians who took sides with religious orthodoxy. While we have, on the side of truth, Flade sacrificing his life, Cornelius Agrippa his liberty, Wier and Loos their hopes of preferment, Bekker his position, and Thomasius his ease, reputation, and friends, we find, as allies of the other side, a troop of eminently respectable doctors mixing Scripture, metaphysics, and pretended observations to support the 'safe side' and to deprecate interference with the existing superstition, which seemed to them 'a very safe belief to be held by the common people.' [7]

We may learn from this, not to distrust every physician and scientist, but that objectivity, detachment, and strength of character are in order everywhere, including among scientists, physicians, and other professionals. Looking backward, those physicians who took sides with religious orthodoxy were most contemptible. There are occasions in life when professionals and experts cannot ethically side with common sense. Persons who do not have the strength to stand with nature and truth against fads and accepted views have no business entering on professional or scientific careers. The notion that science and art are matters of intelligence and information only, but not of character and nerve, is absurd. The attainment of objectivity does not any more imply detachment than it does integrity and courage.

Science can teach us a difference between practical certainty and smugness. Natural scientists have learned the hard way that our con-

[6] A. D. White, *A History of the Warfare of Science with Theology in Christendom*. New York: Dover Publications, Inc., 1960, vol. II, p. 119. (First publication in 1896.)

[7] *Ibid.*

clusions about the world are never theoretically certain, but only probable, albeit sometimes *highly* probable. From the uncertainty of the world and its events, it follows that the totality of the consequences of our acts never is predictable with perfect reliability. Excuses for actual outcomes can be valid. We should on this account be tolerant, both of others and of ourselves. At the same time, our total responsibility is shown to range over the whole field of empirical knowledge. We ought to act on the best estimates of consequences that we can make. A reasonable man will strive to learn all he can, in the time available, about the likely consequences of his actions. Nevertheless, likely consequences do not always become actual. A few persons have drawn thirteen spades at bridge, showing that unlikely single events do occur.

Our knowledge should not make us smug and certain, but neither should it make us weak and spineless.

## THE EXCITEMENT OVER SCIENCE

The other day I was privileged to discuss careers with a mathematician; he is the former head of a college physics department, now a research executive in industry. He was telling about what interested him when he was very young. He has always been fascinated by mathematics and physics. Now he is interested in bionics. Nature is always interesting. There is no danger of running out of problems.

Recently a boy in Indiana scored 785 in "quantity" on his college entrance examination; another boy, from farther north in Indiana, scored 800, an unanticipated perfect, in the linguistic part of the test. Both these boys look pretty good to Harvard College. Nobody is expected to get equal scores on both parts of the test. Some of us have more interest and more "bent" in mathematics or science, others in language or the humanities. Some boys and girls in Indiana don't absolutely excel in mathematics, science, language, or the humanities. They may excel in technology or farming or they may, unfortunately, not excel in anything. There should be room, however, for all who bravely try to do their best. In America, we should like to see all protected and respected and those who render valuable services rewarded.

The various interests we have may bias us in one or the other direction. Perhaps the danger of bias is less than the danger of insufficient interest. The average American television set is turned on six hours a day. The danger of bias is in any case real. The perfervid respect now paid, along with tax money, to science is in part a matter of fad, in part a matter of fear. To their credit, scientists have not encouraged this fear and fad. Most scientists are keenly aware that to enjoy full value, and to render full value, a man or woman needs an education and experience that range farther than ever sails the gallant ship of science. Or better stated: Most scientists will tell you, keep all your interests alive, no matter how important specialization and penetration. This advice is sound, not only because after all you are a human being with a multitude of needs and powers, but also because science itself drinks at many streams. (Young Claude Bernard conceived of himself as a dramatist; Schliemann was first a business man; Malthus was a minister.) Our country and our culture require science, statesmanship, keen expression, physical and moral courage, social and mechanical skills. Extreme competence in the natural sciences is one of our needs.

## THE POWER OF SCIENCE AND TECHNOLOGY

"Energy" is one of the key terms in the philosophies of Plato and Aristotle. In modern times, we tend to think of energy in connection with physics rather than with philosophy. However, modern comprehension of nature and utilization of power have a significant bearing on man's theoretical, practical, and moral life.

"Energy is the multiplier of human effort." [8] The total energy in the United States from mineral fuels and water power, in trillions of British Thermal Units, is estimated to have been 1,520 in 1871–75, and 36,636 in 1948.[9] Per capita consumption of energy, in quantities of coal or coal equivalents, was 7,834 kilograms in the United States in 1959. In mainland Asia (principally China) it was 511.[10]

Thinking of the Chinese and others not utilizing much power, Sir Charles Snow said, "Most of our fellow human beings . . . are underfed and die before their time. In the crudest terms, that is the social condition." [11] He also said, in opposition to certain "existentialist" writers whom he considers antisocial, if not immoral,

[8] An expression of Sir Harold Hartley.

[9] *Historical Statistics of the United States* 1789–1945, p. 155 and *Statistical Abstract of the United States* 1952, p. 477.

[10] United Nations, *Statistical Yearbook, 1960.* New York, 1960, pp. 274 and 276.

[11] C. P. Snow, *The Two Cultures and the Scientific Revolution* (London and New York: Cambridge University Press, 1959), p. 7.

> . . . one truth is straightforward. Industrialisation is the only hope of the poor. I use the word 'hope' in a crude and prosaic sense. I have not much use for the moral sensibility of anyone who is too refined to use it so. It is all very well for us, sitting pretty, to think that material standards of living don't matter all that much. It is all very well for one, as a personal choice, to reject industrialisation—do a modern Walden, if you like, and if you go without much food, see most of your children die in infancy, despise the comforts of literacy, accept twenty years off your own life, then I respect you for the strength of your aesthetic revulsion. But I don't respect you in the slightest if, even passively, you try to impose the same choice on others who are not free to choose.[12]

No doubt, we should seek to avoid the moral trap of belittling the importance to *others* of energy and industrialization, and to avoid the intellectual and practical trap of underrating their importance to ourselves. A high material standard of living and the knowledge that is power over nature are not to be sneered at.

On the other hand, our power over nature is neither an unmitigated evil nor an unmitigated good. The greater our knowledge and power respecting nature, the more we need control over ourselves as men and *over* our knowledge and our power. Knowledge, technique, power, all must be *turned* to good. Passing over the existentialists, we quote a statement of William James dating from 1906:

> One alternative now before man is . . . that the *being* of man may be crushed by his own powers, that his fixed nature as an organism may not prove adequate to stand the strain of the ever increasingly tremendous functions, almost divine creative functions, which his intellect will more and more enable him to wield. He may drown in his wealth like a child in a bath-tub, who has turned on the water and who cannot turn it off.[13]

In the best present meaning of the word, ethics is precisely studied in order to ensure that, in utilizing energy and manipulating natural forces, we do not lose control over ourselves, either severally or collectively, and perish in conflict.

## SCIENCE DOES NOT ELIMINATE CHOICE

The prestige of the physical sciences and technology is not unearned. A key difference between North America and northern Europe on the one hand and the rest of the world on the other is the difference

[12] *Ibid.*, p. 27. Copyright 1959. Reprinted by permission.

[13] William James, *Pragmatism* (New York: Longmans, Green and Co., Inc., 1907). Perma Book Edition, p. 123.

in energy utilization, largely a difference in the application of scientific knowledge. The result—that individual consumption in the States is eight times the world average and that here 6 per cent of the world's population enjoys nearly half of the world's income —poses a stirring challenge to the underdeveloped countries and manifestly affects our relations with, and our responsibilities toward, them.

Science does not cut down our opportunities to choose, and it does not reduce our responsibilities. Just as the man who has become President does not face fewer choices and decisions, but more and harder ones, so also the physician of great learning and knowledge has not less but more diagnostic possibilities and remedies to determine. The physicist who knows the most is also the one who sees the most alternatives and the most supporting arguments for each alternative. Max Planck once remarked that a whole generation is required to convince run-of-the-mill scientists of the merit of a revolutionary new theory. But the outstanding scientist is almost routinely entertaining and testing new ideas. Something similar may be said for the outstanding engineer. He is always hunting for short cuts, for new and more effective routes and vehicles to his destination. The greatest scientists and technicians are also characteristically always searching for new destinations, new combinations, new fields for discovery, new ways to resolve puzzles and conflicts.

Nature best serves us when we are obedient. We learn from nature by posing our questions and then accepting *her* answers, and our power lies in obedience to her dictates. Yet at the same time, knowledge that is power means not fewer choices, but more.

Prudent choice and realistic ethical decision will take into account the findings of physical science and of all science. The range of "utopian" choices may be restricted: There is left no expectation of help from fairy god-mothers, elves, and faith-healers. Scientific knowledge does mean, however, a broader range of effective choices and the acceptance of more real challenges and adventures. As will be seen, this assertion expressly applies to scientific knowledge of man, society, and decision.

As far as ethics is concerned, the more science, the more problems. The more power we have, and the more leisure and abundance, the greater the danger that we ruin ourselves. The more power we have, the more important it is that we use it intelligently.

Philosophy has been referred to as protector of the innocent. We are all unfortunately innocent when on the street and dressed in civilian clothes. Since the whole tendency of science and technology is to increase power without asking questions, to complicate the disease and refine the torture while developing a cure, to put an ever bigger stick, both a physical and a psychological stick, into whatever hands succeed in grasping it, philosophy and the strongest kind of practical deliberation have never been so much *needed,* however soft and low the voice that beckons. The danger that threatens is the danger we don't see: The *banality* of chugging along, increasing our knowledge, but *not* increasing our choices, *not* making our decisions.

### NATURE AS GUIDE

Nature has long been pointed to by thinkers as a guide for right conduct and as a model after which to establish institutions and social procedures. A current book of ethics ends with the admonition that, as always, nature is our guide.[14] The proponents of nature as guide range from the early materialists, hedonists, and Epicureans through Gassendi to Pepper in one tradition, and from Plato and Aristotle through the stoics to the idealists and Emerson in another and opposed tradition. The meanings associated with "nature" are manifestly not identical in these two traditions. In contrast to both, many contemporary thinkers would agree with John Stuart Mill that, "Conformity to nature has no connection whatever with right and wrong." And Mill meant flatly to reject *both* the naturalistic and the idealist conceptions of nature (and "the normal") as providing us with individual or social guidance toward morality.

### NATURE IN STOICISM AND IDEALISM

The less literal, more metaphorical, tradition is that of stoicism and idealism. This tradition has often proved capable of living with supernaturalism, and it should be distinguished from naturalism in the usual acceptation of the word.

Emerson often thought and wrote with this orientation, looking on Nature as that sun by which we may guide our lives. Nature, in this sense, is a star that appears to reason and that unreasoning people fail to see.

> Most persons do not see the sun. At least they have a very superficial seeing. The sun illuminates only the eye of the man, but shines into the eye and the heart of the child. The lover of nature is he

[14] Stephen C. Pepper, *Ethics* (New York: Appleton-Century-Crofts, Inc., 1960), p. 336. "As many of the ancient sages have reminded us, as well as the modern voice of science: Nature is our guide." The concluding sentence of the book.

whose inward and outward senses are still truly adjusted to each other. . . .[15]

Nature is our guide, but we must observe it with something more than our jaded adult vision. That a child may take the greatest delight in seeing and touching the world about him is a manifest fact, and not just an opinion of R. W. Emerson. Emerson means to say more than that, namely, that love of Nature and an experience of the *goodness* of Nature are native to human beings, who are themselves in and of Nature, and whose specific nature is a product of and a factor in Nature. Our capacity for clear seeing, when we have grown up, and with it our proper powers of living and venerating, is all too often disused, atrophied, shrunk, and perverted. The delightfulness known in childhood has been lost, and the vision that is native to our minds has become obscured by "the desire of riches, of pleasure, of power, and of praise."

> The problem of restoring to the world original and eternal beauty is solved by the redemption of the soul. The ruin or the blank that we see when we look at nature, is in our own eye. The axis of vision is not coincident with the axis of things, and so they appear not transparent but opaque.[16]

To the stoic and the idealist, Nature conveys less the "multitudinous detail of the phenomena," and more "the conception which might be formed of their manner of existence as a mental whole, by a mind possessing a complete knowledge of them." Nature, in this sense, denotes "the entire system of things, with the aggregate of all their properties." [17] The stoic aims to attain to the perspective of such a mind, aims at seeing things *sub specie aeternitatis*. The stoic, while admitting of his finitude and his animal body, nevertheless insists that his mind, and potentially all rational minds, are or may be in such a state of harmony and coincidence with nature as a systematic whole that he—and ideally all—can conduct their lives in a manner elevated and illuminated, and appropriate to a being capable of grasping the point of the whole of things. Typically, the stoic believes in the pointfulness of the cosmos. Or in a mood not identical but congenial, scientists of stoical cast may say with Max Planck, "And he whom good fortune has permitted to co-operate in the erection of the edifice of exact science, will find his satisfaction and inner happiness, with our great poet Goethe, in the

[15] Ralph Waldo Emerson, *Nature*. This essay was Emerson's first book, and, according to many scholars, his most important.

[16] *Ibid.*

[17] In the words of John Stuart Mill, in his essay "Nature," in *Three Essays on Religion* (London: Longmans, Green & Co., 1885).

knowledge that he has explored the explorable and quietly venerates the inexplorable."[18]

The Greek and Roman stoics believed that a divine fire, or reason, permeated all things. The good life was a life according to nature, the universe being governed by reason or providence. Human reason links man with the principle that controls the universe and raises him above the other animals. The ass is not born to be of any primary importance but to provide us with a back that is able to carry something.

> But you are a being of primary importance; you are a fragment of God; you have within you a part of Him. Why, then, are you ignorant of your own kinship? Why do you not know the sources from which you have sprung? Will you not bear in mind, whenever you eat, who you are that eat, and whom you are nourishing? Whenever you indulge in intercourse with women, who you are that do this? Whenever you mix in society, whenever you take physical exercise, whenever you converse . . You are bearing God about with you, you poor wretch, and know it not! Do you suppose I am speaking of some external God, made of silver or gold? It is within yourself that you bear Him, and do not perceive that you are defiling Him with impure thoughts and filthy actions. . . . O insensible of your own nature. . . .[19]

If nature can serve as a guide it is through the medium, then, of some divine or quasi-divine light in us.

In the idealist and critical ethics of Immanuel Kant, nature plays a precise role, but it is much more sophisticated and round-about than in Epictetus'. For Kant, the Idea of Nature as it functions in our comprehension of the universe as a whole in space and time serves to *typify* and symbolize that perfect kingdom which seems to be the ideal toward which the moral life is aimed. The heavenly city has an air of reality, because it is similar to the world we live in; but Kant is reluctant to affirm that it *is* real, or that we *know* it. However, it subsists as the postulated end of moral progress, or, if you please, as the notion of the kingdom of God on earth.

### SUPERNATURALISM

The position of Epictetus is but a short step indeed from supernaturalism. In many sophisticated circles that one may today fall

[18] Max Planck, "The Meaning and Limits of Exact Science," *Scientific Autobiography* (New York: Philosophical Library, 1949), pp. 119–120. Tr. by Frank Gaynor.

[19] *Discourses of Epictetus,* Loeb Library. Book II, Chapter 8.

into, supernaturalism is frowned upon as intellectually disrespectable. However, it has strong adherents, both churchmen and nonchurchmen. The supernaturalist denies that "naturalism is enough," in particular that naturalism can adequately motivate men to act right. Accordingly, Mr. James C. Worthy, formerly a vice-president of Sears, Roebuck and Company, and now the executive officer of an Illinois Republican organization:

> We need to define, much more clearly and emphatically than we have yet defined it, the intimate relationship between a man's religious faith and what he does in his business. . . . Especially do we need to establish explicitly understood Christian principles for the decision-makers of business. . . . As human beings subject to pride and vanity, these decision-makers need the humility that comes from conscious subordination to a higher will. As stewards of the welfare of others, they need the integrity that springs from a sense of responsibility to God and not merely to man. As frail vessels subject to the temptations of avarice, they need the guiding hand of a loving Father. They need, above all, a reinterpretation of Christian principles in terms of the totality of their experiences, which includes the demands and pressures to which they are subject in the conduct of their business affairs.[20]

The supernaturalist also questions whether naturalism can adequately explain all the phenomena that there are. Naturalism cannot answer why there is anything existent, why order is inbuilt in the universe. Max Planck believed in God and affirmed that the "whole world with all its treasures and horrors is subject to Him." [21]

Mysticism, pessimism, traditionalism, and ultramontanism are not integral to supernaturalism but are sometimes found associated with it. They are all despised together (*e.g.*, by Isaiah Berlin) in the position of Joseph de Maistre. Professor Berlin speaks of Maistre's "sardonic, almost cynical, disbelief in the improvement of society by rational means, by the enactment of good laws or the propagation of scientific knowledge." He speaks of Maistre's "deeply sceptical attitude towards all experts and all techniques, all high-minded professions of secular faith and efforts at social improvement by well-meaning but, alas, idealistic persons. . . ." [22]

[20] "Religion and Its Role in the World of Business," *The Chicago Theological Seminary Register,* Volume XLVIII, No. 3 (April 1958). Reprinted by permission.

[21] *Scientific Autobiography, loc. cit.,* p. 159. From a lecture delivered in May, 1937, entitled "Religion and Natural Science." Planck said that circumstances forced him to reflect on "all the unspeakable suffering and incessant destruction of life and property which have plagued mankind. . . ." (*Ibid.,* p. 118, from "The Meaning and Limits of Exact Science.")

[22] Isaiah Berlin, *The Hedgehog and the Fox.* New York: Mentor Books, 1957, p. 94. Copyright 1957. Reprinted by permission.

Both Tolstoy and Maistre think of what occurs as a thick, inextricably complex web of events, objects, characteristics, connected and divided by literally innumerable unidentifiable links—and gaps and sudden discontinuities too, visible and invisible. It is a view of reality which makes all clear, logical and scientific constructions—the well defined, symmetrical patterns of human reason—seem smooth, thin, empty, 'abstract' and totally ineffective as means either of description or of analysis of anything that lives, or has ever lived. Maistre attributes this to the incurable impotence of human powers of observation and of reasoning, at least when they function without the aid of the superhuman sources of knowledge—faith, revelation, tradition, above all the mystical vision of the great saints and doctors of the Church, their unanalysable, special sense of reality to which natural science, free criticism and the secular spirit are fatal.[23]

## NATURALISM

Near the heart of naturalism is the position that value is to be found in man and his interests and strivings, but that it is not to be found in the external universe. We quote a moderate and judicious naturalist, C. I. Lewis: A naturalistic conception of values repudiates the conception that with respect to intrinsic values,

> we are natively incompetent, or born in sin, and can discern them justly only by some insight thaumaturgically acquired, or through some intimation of a proper vocation of man which runs athwart his natural bent.

A naturalistic conception,

> holds that the natural bent of the natural man stands in no need of correction in order validly to be the touchstone of intrinsic value.[24]

Most contemporary naturalists would agree that the careful study of nature, including our own human nature, is precisely the correct course to follow, in order to achieve sound valuations, a sensible and middle road as against redemptionism and revelation on the one hand and relativism and skepticism on the other hand. Thus Professor Lewis continues, saying that such a naturalistic view,

> would recognize that while the natural man does not need any change of heart or any more than natural insight in order to make just

[23] *Ibid.*, p. 96.

[24] Clarence Irving Lewis, *An Analysis of Knowledge and Valuation* (La Salle, Illinois: The Open Court Publishing Company, 1946), p. 398. Copyright 1946. Reprinted by permission.

evaluations, still he does stand in need of all that can be learned from the experience of life in this natural world.[25]

Again quoting Mr. Lewis, but shifting our ground from value theory to ethics, he refers to his own ethical position as naturalistic in holding that,

> no act can be determined as right or wrong without reference to consequences of it as good or bad.[26]

Most American naturalists and supernaturalists will agree that respect for reason and respect for others are requisite to right social living. Man when avaricious and aggressive, brutal and unprincipled, is neither natural nor redeemed. The value experience of those who choose wrong, or who choose wrongly, is inadequate. A wider and deeper experience would lead them to choose to act reasonably and to maintain respect for other persons. The issue here between the naturalist and the supernaturalist is whether or not that broader and deeper experience, in order to be morally effective, need include correction by divine agency, by the guiding hand of a loving Father.

## EPICUREANISM

The position of naturalism has roots in the Cyrenaics, Epicurus, and Lucretius. Epicurus (B.C. 342?–270) held that pleasure is the only good, but that the way to *secure* a life of pleasure is by living moderately and abstinently, prudently curbing our desires lest they be frustrated or overindulged to the point of painfulness.

Epicureanism rests historically on a Democritean interpretation of nature, namely, that it consists ultimately of indestructible atoms in which motion inheres. Visible and all sensible phenomena, human beings and their activities, everything in the end consists of these seeds, these atoms in motion, by chance (or for Democritus, by necessity) falling into the multifarious concatenations that we experience and then again falling back out of them. The human soul is mortal; and when it has achieved its mortality, there is no pain. The fear of death is the greatest of human follies and superstitions. After death there is nothing, mind and soul and sensibility having disappeared with the dispersion of the atoms. As Lucretius, the great Latin poet who was a devout first-century B.C. adherent of Epicurus, wrote:

[25] *Ibid.*, pp. 398–399.

[26] Clarence Irving Lewis, *The Ground and Nature of the Right* (New York: Columbia University Press, 1955), p. 97.

The soul no less is shed abroad and dies
More quickly far, more quickly is dissolved
Back to its primal bodies, when withdrawn
From out man's members it has gone away.[27]

Disease and pain are both artificers of death. The manifest conclusion for human practice is that we should avoid pain, disease, and turbulence; live out our life as peaceably and independently as possible; and not fear death.

Therefore death to us
Is nothing, nor concerns us in the least,
Since nature of mind is mortal evermore.

. . . But if indeed do feel
The nature of mind and energy of soul,
After their severance from this body of ours,
Yet nothing 'tis to *us* who in the bonds
And wedlock of the soul and body live,
Through which we're fashioned to a single state.[28]

Lucretius is most concerned to establish (1) that the fear of death is needless and foolish, its grounds superstitious, (2) that the gods do not interfere in the events of the world, and (3) that love as a grand passion is destructive but avoidable. Going a level deeper, however, we would say with Cyril Bailey that Lucretius was motivated by a love of thought and of truth—that are still characteristic of naturalism—and by a desire to see his truth effectuated in human lives and in human society.

> And in this devotion to thought he finds the cure for the restless *ennui* which was the besetting misery of contemporary social life; the poet describes it with a fine scorn in the third book and concludes that, if only men could see the the true cause of their distress, one and all they would abandon the world and study to know the cause of things, since it is a question not of a single hour, but of all time that is to follow on their death.
>
> Lucretius speaks with scorn of those who attempt to find safety from their terrors by political or military power or personal wealth.
>
> From all these fears and disquietudes Lucretius finds his release in the philosophy of Epicurus, which by its demonstration of the material nature of the universe, atoms in infinite numbers, moving according to the laws of their own being in an infinite void, can save men from the fears of religion and give them the tranquil mind, which in its contemplation of the greatness of nature will rise above the conflicts and conquer the boredom of political and social life.

[27] Lucretius, *On the Nature of Things,* Book III. New York: E. P. Dutton & Co., Inc., 1957, p. 108. Tr. by William Ellery Leonard. Reprinted by permission.
[28] *Ibid.,* pp. 122–123. Italics added.

> To secure this end he explains Epicurus' philosophy in full as the true physical explanation of the universe and of human life. . . .[29]

Thus the greatness of nature and the wisdom of science are used as foils to counter all too human inclinations toward fear, ambition, and sexual passion. Nature can reveal to us—if we study squarely and diligently—how we ought to live and to relate ourselves to other persons, *viz.*, quietly, imperturbably, prudently, but not denying ourselves overmuch. As Freud once put it, "Blunt necessity, mute submission."

## MILL'S OPPOSITION TO NATURE AS GUIDE

That nature is, or is not, a proper guide for human conduct is neither psychologically nor logically obvious. The opposition of John Stuart Mill to nature as guide may at first seem to apply only to the stoical-idealist view, but this is by no means the case: [30]

> The phrases which ascribe perfection to the course of nature can only be considered as the exaggerations of poetic or devotional feeling, not intended to stand the test of a sober examination.
>
> For however offensive the proposition may appear to many religious persons, they should be willing to look in the face [of] the undeniable fact, that the order of nature, insofar as unmodified by man, is such as no being, whose attributes are justice and benevolence, would have made, with the intention that his rational creatures should follow it as an example.
>
> . . . the duty of man is the same in respect to his own nature as in respect to the nature of all other things, namely not to follow but to amend it.[31]

The duty of man is to *amend* his own nature and the nature of all other things. Mill's opposition to nature-as-guide is fierce: "Conformity to nature has no connection whatever with right and wrong. . . . There is hardly a bad action ever perpetrated which is not perfectly natural, and the motives to which are not perfectly natural feelings." [32] From his perspective, nature, including our own given nature, is there to be used, to be modified and metamorphosed to fulfill our highest *human* ambitions.

[29] Titi Lucreti Cari, *De Rerum Natura,* Libri Sex, edited, *etc.,* by Cyril Bailey. London: Oxford University Press, 1947, Vol. 1, pp. 14 and 15. Reprinted by permission.

[30] See *Auguste Comte and Positivism, passim.*

[31] "Nature," in *Three Essays on Religion.*

[32] From Mill's essay "Nature," *loc. cit.* I have objected earlier that Mill overshot the mark in "Nature: Emerson and Mill," *The Western Humanities Review,* VI, No. 1 (Winter 1951–52), where the above sentences of Mill are quoted on pp. 8 and 6, respectively. Mill rejected the precept *Naturam sequi,* and admitted only *Naturam observare.*

Mill particularly attained to his position in corresponding with, and in critical reading and studying of, Auguste Comte. Perhaps one should consider with Mill some of the blunders, even colossal mistakes, occasionally made in the name of science. (We ought not blame science for them!) For instance, Comte wrote to Mill:

> However imperfect biology may yet be in every respect, it seems able already to establish firmly the hierarchy of sexes. It seems able to show both anatomically and physiologically that, in the whole series of animal life, and especially in our own species, the female sex is constituted in a sort of state of radical infancy which renders it essentially inferior to the corresponding organic type.[33]

But, from Mill's point of view, such a "showing" is ridiculous in principle. The inferiority of women cannot be established in any such way; and, moreover, expressions like "radical infancy" and "inferior," as here used, are value expressions. They reveal more about Comte's personal prejudices than about the nature of things.

Perhaps the more frequent objection to nature-as-guide constitutes less "a complaint against nature" than it does a protest and caveat against the conclusiveness of every human *conception* of what nature is. Thus, many have protested against "scientific determinism." Does, or can, science show that all events are determined, that one total state of affairs in the world follows another with any kind of necessity? Or is the conviction of determinism only a failing of human nature, a failing that it is the duty of man to amend? William James said, "The *in*determinism . . . offends only the native absolutism of my intellect—an absolutism which, after all, perhaps, deserves to be snubbed and kept in check."

The British analyst, G. E. Moore, objected to nature-as-guide. ". . . the innermost hope and claim of metaphysical philosophers has nearly always been to discover in the ultimate nature of reality some source of ethics. . . . Moore would not have it."[34] Moore thought that the idealists were (for once) right, as against the empiricists, in insisting on thought and on objects of knowledge which we cannot *perceive*. "Good" may sometimes name a quality which cannot come under empirical observation.[35]

[33] *Lettres Inédites de John Stuart Mill à Auguste Comte Publiées avec les Réponses de Comte et une Introduction.* By L. Lévy-Bruhl. Paris: Alcan, 1899, p. 231. My own translation. Incidentally, one wonders if Comte was aware of the female black widow spider.

[34] G. A. Paul in *The Revolution in Philosophy,* Gilbert Ryle, *et al.,* p. 57.

[35] *Ibid.,* pp. 57–58. If, like Professor Ernest Nagel, we hold behaviorist scientific knowledge in great respect, we shall not desire to mix it up with value and ethical judgments; also, *vice versa.* Prof. Nagel has said: "It is surely not the case that we must ourselves undergo (whether actually or in imagination) other men's

Perhaps Mill was the first thinker liberated from "the naturalistic fallacy," the first man who, at least in his more serious works, did not violate what are now thought of as Moore's dicta. Philip Blair Rice anyway has cogently argued to this effect. He quotes, for instance, the following sentence from Mill's *Logic,* Book VI: "A proposition of which the predicate is expressed by the words *ought* or *should be,* is generically different from one which is expressed by *is* or *will be.*" As Rice remarked, "Mill's language itself has an up-to-the-minute ring." [36]

I should say that you cannot imply such a strict definition of scientific knowledge as is implied by Mr. Nagel and still expect that all human wisdom, or even a large proportion of the most important human wisdom, will fit inside it. It's like trying to squeeze an otherwise healthy tiger into a duffel bag. But the concepts of "truth" and "meaning" are tigers, too, and need space, and air to breathe. I should agree with Mill (1) that the correct statement of the conditions under which science best operates is not itself a scientific statement, (2) that the attainment of *truth* about the merit of social policies involves both truth with respect to the facts *and* optimum decision from both prudential and ethical perspectives, and (3) that all interests concerned must be represented in the processes by which the acceptability of policies is decided.[37]

As for the word "nature" itself, if it means everything that there

---

psychic experiences in order to know that they have them, or in order to predict their overt behaviors. But if this is so, the alleged 'privacy' or 'subjectivity' of mental states has no bearing on the acquisition of knowledge concerning the character, the determinants, and the consequences of other men's dispositions and actions. A historian does not have to be Hitler or even be capable of re-enacting in imagination Hitler's frenzied hatreds, to write competently of Hitler's career and historical significance. For knowledge is not a matter of having images, whether faint or vivid; it is not a reduplication of, or a substitute for, what is claimed to be known. Knowledge involves the discovery through processes of controlled inference that something is a sign of something else; it is statable in propositional form; and it is capable of being verified through sensory observations by anyone who is prepared to make the effort to do so." Ernest Nagel, "Concept and Theory Formation in the Social Sciences" (1952). Quoted from J. L. Jarrett and S. M. McMurrin, Editors, *Contemporary Philosophy.* New York: Henry Holt and Company, 1954, pp. 355–356. Reprinted by permission.

[36] Philip Blair Rice, *On the Knowledge of Good and Evil.* New York: Random House (1955), p. 95. John Stuart Mill, *A System of Logic,* Eighth Edition. London and New York: Longmans, Green and Co., new impression of 1947, pp. 619–620. In this passage, Mill is contrasting the propositions characteristic of all the practical arts with those of the sciences.

[37] *E.g.,* the relative inferiority or superiority of the human female is not going to be determined by those lovers of natural fact, the (male) biologists, alone—not, certainly, in the arena of social and political life, where women now have the franchise.

is and that occurs, then it means too much and cannot serve as the guide of human life. For as Mill said, the most atrocious things happen in nature. On the other hand, if "nature" means less than that, then what does it mean? Is it not just a concealment and camouflage, a sugar-coating (as in stoicism), for what is after all only a set of "all too human" ideals? Is it not surreptitiously used in an attempt to evade the fullest facts of existence? To reject both truth and responsibility? For, as Fromm has said, man "must proceed to develop his reason until he becomes the *master* of nature, and of himself." Perhaps it is a mistake even to attempt to divorce "natural" man from "spiritual" man; perhaps trying to grasp the character of man with only naturalistic concepts is oftentimes but a kind of "rigging." [38]

## WHAT IS A GUIDE?

A friend of mine recently took his family on a safari in Africa. The first arrangement that he made was for *a guide,* an arrangement absolutely essential for anyone not accustomed to hunting lion, tiger, rhinoceros, and other game indigenous to Africa. The guide rented adequate vehicles, tents, cooking utensils, and rifles; he bought the food, water, liquor, ammunition; he studied the maps, talked with other guides and hunters in order to obtain the latest information about the whereabouts of game, adding to his already amazing fund of knowledge of the country and its animal life. He gave advice about everything, and stood ready to protect my friend and his family, or to help them in the kill. However, it was my friend who used the vehicles and tents, ate the food, consumed the drink and medicine, made the safari, paid the guide and all the bills that he had incurred on his behalf, discharged the guide, brought home the

[38] Erich Fromm is himself a psychoanalyst and a Freudian. He says: "Psychoanalysis, in an attempt to establish psychology as a natural science, made the mistake of divorcing psychology from problems of philosophy and ethics. It ignored the fact that human personality cannot be understood unless we look at man in his totality, which includes his need to find an answer to the question of the meaning of his existence and to discover norms according to which he ought to live. Freud's 'homo psychologicus' is just as much an unrealistic construction as was the 'homo economicus' of classical economics. It is impossible to understand man and his emotional and mental disturbances without understanding the nature of value and moral conflicts. The progress of psychology lies not in the direction of divorcing an alleged 'natural' from an alleged 'spiritual' realm and focusing attention on the former, but in the return to the great tradition of humanistic ethics which looked at man in his physico-spiritual totality, believing that man's aim is to be *himself* and that the condition for attaining this goal is that man be *for himself.*" *Man for Himself: An Inquiry into the Psychology of Ethics,* pp. 6–7. Reprinted by permission of Holt, Rinehart, and Winston, Inc.

quarry, and hung the skins on the walls of his home in southern Ohio.

Yes, Nature is our guide. But man is boss. Man accepts, reforms, or rejects Nature. He observes or does not observe it, follows or disregards it. He values and cherishes, praises, loves, hates, scorns, injures, blames—all things that are not permitted Nature. Man employs and discharges, accepts the final responsiblity, pays the bills.

The emphatically human art of medicine observes the human body and studies its processes, seeks ever new knowledge of foods and pharmacology, of anatomy, physiology, allergies, synapses, neuroses and psychoses. It defines the state of health, and the multitudinous illnesses and injuries. It provides prescriptions, tourniquets, and surgical dressings, administers hospitals, controls the training of nurses, and signs the forms for Blue Shield.

The natural and social sciences study all nature, including man, individual and collective. They discover—besides the truth—phlogiston, spontaneous generation, the unchangeableness of species, the crystalline nature of the celestial spheres, the "certain" unrelatedness of mosquito and malaria, the incomparable curative power of leeches, the incurability of all insanity, the wholly "corpuscular," atomic nature of man. They serve—besides America, Man, and God—Hitler, Stalin, and Mammon. Fortunately, these human enterprises aimed at the critical knowledge and utilization of nature are systematically corrigible. As the observations of man become more exact, as his conceptions become more critical and sophisticated, as his logic and discipline increase in precision and relevance to his purposes, respectively, man's sciences come nearer the truth, increase in utility, and become an ever better guide *to* Nature, to the worlds of stars and men as they are now and shall be, and to the best modes of existence for mankind.

# 8

# HUMAN NATURE: SELF-IMAGES

How we look on human nature affects our conduct. We know that the U.S. Supreme Court was influenced substantively in its decisions in the nineties by ideas concerning the evolution of man through the struggle for existence. We know that a college dean of men is influenced in his policies and his actions by the confidence he has in student nature. We have been living through a period of suspicion in which the trend has been toward nobody trusting anybody. This attitude certainly has affected our federal legislation and administration and attitudes toward students and other thinkers. The longer-term thrust, however, has been toward confidence, optimism, and a larger view of human nature.

A foal stands up ten or fifteen minutes after it's born, while man is born in a condition of abject helplessness.

> The human infant, like a shipwrecked sailor cast ashore by the cruel waves, lies naked on the ground, speechless, lacking all aids to life, when nature has first tossed him with pangs of travail from his mother's womb upon the shores of the sunlit world.[1]

[1] Lucretius, *The Nature of the Universe,* translated by R. E. Latham. Harmondsworth: Penguin Books, Ltd., 1951. pp. 177–178. Reprinted by permission.

Yet man eventually rides the horse and domesticates the wolf. This eventual rulership and superiority over the rest of the animal kingdom is owing to our anatomical structure and physiological flexibility, to our standing on two feet and having our head in the air (as Plato says in the *Timaeus*), to our manual dexterity and phalangeal precision, but, above all, to our ability to think. The large human cerebrum with its specially intricate structure distinguishes us from the other animals. We have minds larger and more complex by far than any other creature. We are thus enabled, *inter alia,* to learn and to perform new (noninstinctive) operations of great complexity. We can have distinct yet remote goals and find our way to them. And we can freely propose and choose among varieties of such goals. We are equipped not only with sense organs and powers of observation, like other animals, but also with imagination and the real possibility of logical thinking.

The initial needs that drive men are, in themselves, blind. The newborn infant has a sucking instinct, but he must be guided to the source of supply. Children must later, when innate readiness to bite, chew, salivate, and swallow has matured, still be taught to use fork or chopsticks. While it is by innate and primitive needs, maturing at different ages, that man is driven, the blindness becomes dissipated. Men are constrained by nature, culture, and education to complicate their needs, to develop goals that relate to the initial needs, but in which the needs are actually lost from sight. The culture in which men live teaches them to act in such and such ways, ways that have been learned in the past to succeed comparatively well in attaining satisfaction. To a certain extent, intelligence and calculation determine ways of acting. We are social animals, and the images and ideas that we have are, for the most part, socially derived. Let us look at the basic elements of imagery, the images and self-images; and then we can better cope with conflicts of images of man and society as these relate to ethical problems.

## THE NERVOUS SYSTEM AND HUMAN BEHAVIOR

A brief but hard-packed quotation from the leading British physiologist will quickly give us the most recent conception of the relation between the mind, the nervous system, and behavior:

> . . . the nervous origin or counterpart of the urge to some particular kind of behavior will be a focus of disturbance in the brain, a new pattern of rhythmic oscillation, which is so constituted that it will continue to arouse one kind of activity after another [*e.g.,* in walking somewhere step by step, or in the various movements and

shifts of balance in lifting a weight] until it has been dissipated by the appearance of the particular afferent pattern which can neutralize it, and the neutralization will occur when the afferent pattern is the sensory counterpart of the behavior which was implicit in the disturbing pattern. The two patterns will then cancel out.

A formulation of this kind will apply only to relatively simple trends of behavior, scarcely to those in which a number of trials of different actions must be made before the solution is reached.[2]

## FREUD AND PERSISTENT IMPULSES

Prediction and planning, insofar as they are functions of the imagination, consist in projecting images and runs of images; the projected images are valued or disvalued and judged in terms of their feasibility and of their efficacy toward attainment of the goal. There exists a nervous counterpart and ordinarily also a muscular counterpart in the body. In preparing to act, there occur attitudinal and bodily *set*. Commitment is the actual "oomph of initiation," the beginning of physical doing, of the displacement of things by our hands.

One can hardly exaggerate the role in human thought and action of valuing and of value judgment. Freud describes the mind in terms of competing impulses:

> . . . the mind is an arena, a sort of a tumbling-ground, for the struggles of antagonistic impulses; or, to express it in non-dynamic terms, . . . the mind is made up of contradictions and pairs of opposites.

The gratification of one kind of impulse does not mean that its opposite has fallen dead and been forgotten. Both members of the pair are insistent.

> Evidence of one particular tendency does not in the least preclude its opposite; there is room for both of them. The material questions are: How do these opposites stand to one another and what effects proceed from one of them and what from the other? [3]

[2] E. D. Adrian, "The Mental and the Physical Origins of Behavior," reprinted in *The Yearbook of Psychoanalysis,* Volume 3, 1947. Reprinted by permission.

[3] Sigmund Freud, *A General Introduction to Psychoanalysis* (Permabook Edition), p. 80. One of Freud's illustrations is losing things. Our common sense disapproves of losing things, but nevertheless losing them may serve impulses of spite or of self-punishment. Knowing ourselves is a difficult enterprise, and it should be obvious that science is prerequisite to self-understanding: Mere introspection and self-observation and judgment do not suffice. "Being intelligent" is not equivalent to "being scientific"; but to be intelligent today, or to understand oneself, surely implies a modicum of scientific knowledge.

This is exactly what we ought to expect, for the impulses lie there because of our nature as *homo sapiens*. There is an immensity of vagueness, contradictoriness, and conflict in initial human nature: That is the "price" of our invaluable plasticity and of the opportunities singular to human life.

The Old Testament offers an interesting alternative view of why man must resort to his own faculties and why he must struggle to orient himself. Eating from the tree of knowledge of good and evil was not bad in itself.[4] "The sin was disobedience, the challenge to the authority of God, who was afraid that man, having already 'become as one of Us, to know good and evil,' could 'put forth his hand and take also of the tree of life and live forever.' "[5] Man is quasi-divine in knowing good and evil, but he has not been allowed to eat of the tree of immortal life. We men must catch as catch can. We have our own resources, having eaten from the tree of knowledge, and, unlike the other animals, we can shift for ourselves.[6] God has seen to it that we *must* shift for ourselves. In summary, man is born in a piteous state because it has become his lot to live by his own human resources, to make his own existence and mode of life, to find his own meanings; the piteous state is the payment jealously exacted by God and the nature of things of an animal species that would dare to become supra-natural.

In the long run man *cannot* live like the animals, *cannot* fall back lazily on mere tradition. Our culture and history, prehistory and organic evolution teach the same lesson:

> In the long run, exclusive adaptation to a peculiar environment does not pay. It imposes severe, and in the end perhaps fatal, restrictions on the possibilities of living and breeding. On a long view what is profitable is the capacity for adaptation to changing circumstances.[7]

[4] Knowledge of good and evil is a basic virtue in both Jewish and Christian ethics. "My people are destroyed by the lack of knowledge; because thou hast rejected knowledge, I will also reject thee." Hosea.

[5] Erich Fromm, *Man For Himself: An Inquiry into the Psychology of Ethics.* New York: Rinehart and Company, Inc, 1947, p. 12.

[6] The Platonic tradition is highly similar, although there is in it less emphasis on knowledge of right and wrong. The gods stole various arts and crafts for man, who was created last, and after a material shortage had developed. The great gift to man was reason. The other creatures had instincts by which to live, and in particular the gregarious instinct by which to live *together.* Men must live by reason, and in particular must live *together* by reason.

[7] V. Gordon Childe, *Man Makes Himself.* New York: The New American Library, 1951, pp. 24–25. Copyright 1951. Reprinted by permission of C. A. Watts & Co., Ltd.

Man is the creature who can be liberally educated; and the future success of mankind in controlling its fate depends on the retention and intensification of perspective, sensitivity, and adaptability.

Education is more than animal training and the transmission of images. For our species to function successfully it must continually pass on the store of learning, no mean task in itself, and an ever growing one; but it must also accomplish something by way of education that is even more difficult, namely, pass on the "liberal" attitude, the sensitivity to changing circumstances and to new values, the maneuverability, that have won us past victories and accomplishments.

That man's dominance over the animal kingdom and over nature (in specifiable, significant ways) is well established may be conceded. But the great contemporary area of confusion and doubt is precisely the area of social ethics. Can man control his *own* nature, his own future history? There has been backsliding. As Erich Fromm says:

> The contemporary human crisis has led to a retreat from the hopes and ideas of the Enlightenment under the auspices of which our political and economic progress had begun.
>
> [Man] reverts to a position which the Greek Enlightenment, Christianity, the Renaissance, and the eighteenth-century Enlightenment had already overcome.

Virtue *is* unfolding individuality, but in the modern authoritarian concept:

> To be virtuous signifies self-denial and obedience, suppression of individuality rather than its fullest realization.[8]

"Curiously enough," Professor Boulding says:

> It is often the most successful images that become the most dangerous. The image becomes institutionalized in the ceremonial and coercive institutions of society. . . . As the world moves on, the image does not.

Mr. Boulding mentions the Chinese image of the family, the hardened orthodoxy of Islam, and Marxism. He is too tactful to mention the fossilized images of capitalism and Americanism that many of us carry about in our heads; but he adds:

[8] Erich Fromm, *op. cit.*, pp. 4, 5, and 13. Copyright 1947. Reprinted by permission. As a matter of historical record, the Enlightenment and the advent of liberal democracy preceded the Industrial Revolution.

History is so full of these dead branches of the tree of knowledge that we may well wonder with some trepidation whether our own society will be exempt from what seems to be almost the universal law. There are signs in our own society of a lack of self-confidence in our political images and a desire to maintain them by violence and coercion. This, however, means the cessation of growth. Science is still young. One wonders also, however, whether this too is not a phase of growth which will come to an end. Science can only flourish in an atmosphere of freedom and uncoerciveness. By its very development, however, the scientific subculture cuts itself off from the society around it. Already there are ominous signs in our society of a revolt against science. . . .[9]

It is the vitality, not the particular direction of the tree of knowledge which makes for hope in the whole course of time. It always seems to have a growing shoot somewhere. If one shoot dies another takes over. In growth we trust! [10]

Retreat is strictly *verboten.* The only real possibility, the only live alternative to failure, is rapid advance.

It lies in the nature of the case that the greater the store of learning and the more effective the use which is made of it, the more numerous and the more rapid in rate will be those changes which causally depend upon it. If already the rate of social transformation and the complexities so introduced make us a little dizzy, still it seems quite possible that "we haven't seen anything yet." [11]

There is little doubt that modern life and the store of learning have made us a little dizzy. As G. H. Mead has stressed, the only environment to which the organism can react is one that its sensitivity reveals. But most men are almost completely insensitive to the intellectual, aesthetic, technical, and political and social accomplishments of our race. Perhaps the burden presented us by the genius of man is more than we can stand up under and tote. Great though our relative dexterity and cerebral power may be, perhaps they are not great enough for us to continue in existence. Is mankind at the yoke of a rocket ship without license and diploma? Have we too little brains and creative adaptability to live with humanity and its powers over nature? Must our species die of its own brain weight, as in *On the Beach?* Or perhaps persist in *physical* existence but cease its *hu-*

[9] Kenneth E. Boulding, *The Image.* Ann Arbor: The University of Michigan, 1956, pp. 79–80. Copyright 1956. Reprinted by permission.

[10] *Ibid.,* p. 81.

[11] C. I. Lewis, *Our Social Inheritance,* p. 40. Copyright 1957. Reprinted by permission.

*mane* existence as in *1984?* Other creatures have grown too big, and at last stood transfixed until kindly shrouded by, and buried under, new and more timely forms of life. The question is: Can man continue to live, to live together, to live up to himself?

### SCIENCE, MORALS, AND POWER

Whatever the last chapter of the biography of *homo sapiens* may relate, earlier but equally exciting ones tell us that in this late creature of Earth "life became aware of itself." [12] The animal "is lived," as Fromm puts it, through biological laws of nature. It is in harmony with nature in the sense that it is equipped to cope with the precise conditions it is to meet, as the seed of a plant is equipped by nature to use soil, climate, and so on, to which it is adapted. Man's life cannot "be lived." *Man* must live. Man "cannot go back to the prehuman state of harmony with nature; he must proceed to develop his reason until he becomes the master of nature, and of himself." (p. 24.) Man

> has fallen out of nature, as it were, and is still in it, he is partly divine, partly animal . . .
>
> The necessity to find ever-new solutions for the contradictions in his existence, to find ever-higher forms of unity with nature, his fellowmen and himself, is the source of all psychic forces which motivate man, of all his passions, affects and anxieties. (p. 25.)
>
> We are never free from two conflicting tendencies: One to emerge from the womb, from the animal form of existence into a more human existence, from bondage to freedom; another, to return to to the womb, to nature, to certainty and security. In the history of the individual, and of the race, the progressive tendency has proven stronger, yet the phenomena of mental illness and the regression of the human race to positions apparently relinquished generations ago, show the intense struggle which accompanies each new act of birth.[13]

In man even much more than life became aware of itself. The mind of man is logical and thus reflects the ultimate order of possibility-impossibility of all the universes. Man can see stars far beyond the range of his natural vision, employing finally electronic instruments that have nothing to do with vision. He can count the stars by sampling method (i.e., supplementing observation by devices of logic and mathematics). He can foretell the movements of planets

[12] Erich Fromm, *The Sane Society*. New York: Rinehart & Company, Inc., 1955, p. 23. For the subsequent remarks, see pp. 22–27.

[13] *Ibid.*, p. 27. Copyright 1955. Reprinted by permission.

and stars and galaxies by exercise of his powers of reflecting the dynamic nature of the physical universe. He can guess and stab at their origins and at their ultimate fate. Surely nothing is so marvelous as the mind of man except perhaps worlds reflected so brilliantly in it.

Moreover, man can make religious and metaphysical interpretations of the ultimate nature of things, and also critically or iconoclastically judge the merit of those interpretations and of the questions that elicit them.

We ought not to allow the awe-inspiring scientific and philosophic accomplishments of man to blind us to his stature as a moral agent. If we think in terms of outer space, man's practical life may by comparison seem wee and insignificant. But such a perspective is space-warped. Kant said correctly that *two* things should inspire us with awe: The starry night and a moral act. Nothing is more amazing than a man acting at once energetically and disinterestedly. Man is the one and only creature who asks himself "Why?" who requires that his behavior be justified.[14]

The primary hope of mankind lies no longer in natural science and technology but in man's moral potentialities. Many scientists, of course, are keenly aware of this fact; perhaps scientists are more aware of it than any other class of the world's population.[15] However, many *interpretations* of science have lent support to the notion that "only science counts," or that "there is no knowledge but scientific knowledge." As against such views, Michael Polanyi writes:

> Science can . . . no longer hope to survive on an island of positive facts, around which the rest of man's intellectual heritage sinks to the status of subjective emotionalism. It must claim that certain emotions are right; and if it can make good such a claim, it will not only save itself but sustain by its example the whole system of cultural life of which it forms a part.[16]

Science can, however, hardly "make good such a claim." Science as such can only concern itself with presumptive values, unless we stretch the term "science" so that it is equivalent to every exercise of intelligence, deliberation, and judgment. The choice of goals (in

[14] For discussion of the nature of practical questioning and reasoning, see E. M. Adams, "The Theoretical and the Practical," *The Review of Metaphysics,* Vol. XIII, No. 4, June, 1960, pp. 642–662, and references therein.

[15] The intelligentsia includes both of C. P. Snow's two cultures. Some critics of the intelligentsia are bitter: "There is nothing to compare in the wide and uninformed wisdom of the uneducated with the utter idiocy of the intelligentsia of the twentieth century in search of clues." E. O. Liepmann, "The Ass's Face," *The Nineteenth Century and After,* Vol. CXLV, January–June, 1949, pp. 121–122.

[16] Michael Polanyi, *Personal Knowledge,* Chicago: The University of Chicago Press, 1958, p. 134. (Quoted on p. 660 of Adams, *loc. cit.*) Copyright 1958. Reprinted by permission.

distinction from the *study* of such choice) is not ordinarily thought of as science. *Validation* of choices of goals is partly a matter of ethics and only partly a matter of science. The precise, very important role that science has played in this connection in recent times has been to show the effects on personalities and on societies of *failing* to respect human dignity and other basic values. Science can enlarge the alternatives; it can make empirical studies of consequences. It cannot justify choice, at the very moment of choice (which, from the perspective of science, is not "the moment of truth"). The reason why it cannot is this: The term "science" does and should represent the extreme in objectivity; it should have nothing to do with decision except decision concerning what is the case, what is true. Practical deliberation, including ethical deliberation, is not science; and to call it so is to run an undue risk of subverting the meaning of science and knowledge.

There is also a possibility of subverting the meaning of ethical deliberation and a related overoptimistic dependence on science, *i.e.*, undue hope that attitudes characteristic of the scientific community will prevail along with its results in knowledge. Mr. Boulding says:

> There are those, of course, who see salvation in the development of the social and behavioral sciences. I cannot, I regret, share this optimism. These sciences can all too easily play into the hands of the manipulators. It is by no means clear that self-consciousness in all things leads to survival, much less to heaven or to Utopia.[17]

The view of Professor Boulding warrants careful consideration. The scientific élite has power, but not by any means controlling political power. This lack of power is not especially objectionable: In a democracy one does not expect a scientific or any other élite to own control. Moreover, the scientific community is not monolithic; it is not organized; it presses in contrary directions. Some members of the scientific community do not mind taking test oaths or even imposing them on others. Some foreign-born members do, and some do not, understand our liberal democratic traditions. Generally speaking, our scientists do not want to end up race horses in the stables of political manipulators; they have seen what happened even to the very conservative scientists in Nazi Germany (like Max Planck).

## THE CONCEPT OF THE IMAGE

The concept of the image has proved useful in recent social thought. The image is the acquired, subjective picture of some part of the en-

[17] *The Image, loc. cit.*, pp. 80–81. Reprinted by permission.

vironment. We can speak sensibly of plants and even inorganic things responding to the environment; that they react to changes in the environment entails that they are in some way sensitive to it. Animals have amazing capacities for receiving messages and responding to them. These capacities are interestingly dispersed through the brain, so that, for instance, four-fifths of the cortex of a trained rat can be removed, and yet, after the initial shock, the rat will remember most of what it had learned. As Boulding says (p. 42), "The image clearly does not reside in any one place or location. It is a pattern which pervades the whole." If the muscles of a higher animal are artificially connected to a foreign nerve, they may nevertheless soon function as before, or in some satisfactory new way.

Actually, the wonders of the animal's image need not be sought in exceptional phenomena. The everyday functioning of homeostasis in higher animals is a wonder of feedback, of thermostat-like control. The temperature of the body, for instance, is kept up despite wide variation of the environing climate. One should also ponder the marvelous power to ingest food and "inform" it how to serve the organism's requirements for existence and growth. These are the most ordinary phenomena; but they involve the most detailed image of "what the organism is up to." Without too much stretching of language or imagination, we can say that the organism has a self-image. It knows its needs, what materials will serve them, and how to put them to use. Shall we say, the sapling already sees itself as a full-grown tree? The kitten plays with yarn so that the full-grown cat will be able to work at catching mice?

### CONFLICTING IMAGES

Here we are not particularly interested, however, in the images of saplings and kittens, but in the images of men. Men are not the only animals with eyes and ears for receiving information. "It is the capacity for organizing information into large and complex images which is the chief glory of our species." [18] The monkey may have the same third-dimensional space imagery that we have. Our image of time, however, must be different in kind: We have an image of the past and of the future that rests on language and record. Dogs may know what they like to eat, but they can't tell the cook to serve it again. Above all, man has more self-consciousness; and *what we are* relates closely to our *image* of *what we are* and to our *image* of *what*

[18] Boulding, *op. cit.*, p. 25.

*we intend to become* and of where we are going. Now, to come at once all the way: "Because of the extended time image and the extended relationship images, man is capable of 'rational behavior,' that is to say, his response is not to an immediate stimulus but to an image of the future filtered through an elaborate value system." [19] Perhaps to refer to such response generically as "rational" is unduly optimistic; but it is not exaggerating to say that man evaluates potentialities "according to his value system and chooses the 'best.' " [20]

A strange capacity of man is the capacity to develop his images internally, independently of messages from outside. This capacity leads to the greatest achievements in science and art, but it can also lead to schizophrenia and other pathological conditions. A man can picture to himself: himself, his various roles in society, other roles and other men in society, society as a complex of roles and functions, and this complex as something to be secured and conserved or equally as something to be changed and improved. These statements about man and his capacities are not themselves, of course, statements in ethics. It should be more than obvious, however, that the facts just narrated bear on the nature of human conflict and on the peculiar characteristics of *human* conflict, on its intensity and on its frequency. A multitude of creatures with goals that extend into the future—goals that express much imagination but less control—certainly stands in need of a vigorous ethics. The men on Planet Three are in their own way quite as frightening (and frightened) as the round, square, and octagonal, the green and pinko-grey primates dreamed up by cartoonists and novelists. Here in fact we have a multitude of "competing systems," competing images, competing goals. We have Chinese on one side of the planet hating Americans, and Americans on the other doing their utmost to deny the very existence of any men on the land beyond the little islands of Quemoy and Matsu (although there are 700 million there, and more to come). Here we have not only a long history of wars over "things," but of wars of religion and ideology, wars over hegemony, sovereignty, justice and injustice. We have caste, segregation, and ostracism. We deal with a creature which is at once divine and diabolical, *pace* all of us disposed to naturalist interpretation of man. However, to call man both divine and diabolical is perhaps but to call him human.

[19] *Ibid.*, pp. 25–26.

[20] I interpret Professor Boulding here to mean by "best" only "best according to a man's given value system."

And forward though I canna see,
I guess and fear.

How we respond to challenges, problems, and conflicts depends on our images of the environment, especially on our images of persons, and of relations of persons, in our environment. How we respond depends also on our image of self in the environment, on how we conceive our own role, our own strengths and weaknesses, our own location.

Our image of other peoples is clearly the product and projection of many forces. At best, it is consequent on direct contact established over lengthy periods; or it is the result of direct contact and of systematic studies employing scientific technique and obeying high standards of scholarship. Our experts at Harvard and Columbia know a great deal about the Russian people, how they live, what their accepted goals and actual attainments are, how their system works. Perhaps, above all, they know what they don't know; they are conscious of specific limits to their knowledge. Science and prolonged observation and communication provide the most accurate images of other peoples. Since these images along with accumulated knowledge are at the service of governmental agencies, they have a certain bearing on national policy and are not entirely ineffectual in the national interest.

To hold that such carefully wrought images are the only effective, or even the most effective, images on the national or international political stage would be naïve. The effective images that one country has of another are largely domestic creations, related tangentially to the realities. They are often great superstructures based on foundations of sand, supported by slender reeds of information. If, in the text following, we illustrate in terms of American images of other countries, it is not in order to demonstrate any special weakness in our images in contrast to those held by other peoples. In the nineteenth century, the educated Briton very likely had, generally speaking, a much more accurate image of the classical Greek and Roman than he had of the American, the Hindu, the Nigerian, or even of the French. The images of the American now held by Russians and Chinese are synthetic, partly deliberate, distortions; later on we may briefly concern ourselves with some of these. From the perspective of ethics, in any case, our interest in images is specialized. We are interested in conflicts among images, and in the bearing of imagery on conflicts.

Harold R. Isaacs has published a book about our images of

China and India, called *Scratches on Our Minds.*[21] Although there is nothing more explicit than a map or globe and nothing easier to learn from, Mr. Isaacs begins at once by pointing out that, according to an opinion poll conducted four months after Pearl Harbor, 60 per cent of a national sample of Americans could not locate either China or India on an outline map of the world. At the end of the war, there was still a majority of college-educated Americans unable to locate Singapore on such a map.[22]

The old Mercator maps centered the world on Greenwich and caused the "East" to appear far and vast; the new American school maps arrange the world around Peoria, Illinois, and make its shapes and directions confusingly different. The new world projections, in particular, split China and the U.S.S.R. so that these countries appear on either edge, not unified but still threatening.

Our information and misinformation about China extend back at least to Marco Polo. China has never been well known by many Americans, and yet it has always occupied a special place in our national mentality. There are two principal kinds of image. The first is of China being a land of philosophy and art, of ancient civilization, the source of writing, printing, and fireworks. (When I was a boy, many of our fireworks were imports from China and carried Chinese inscriptions. China will always smell of gunpowder to me.) The central point of this image is of Chinese greatness; and it attributes to the Chinese high intelligence, persistent industry, filial piety, peaceableness, and stoicism.[23]

The second set of images can be traced back to the non-Chinese Genghiz Khan and the fictional Fu Manchu, as the first set can be to Marco Polo, Charlie Chan, and Pearl Buck. The second set of images gives us—

> cruelty, barbarism, inhumanity; a faceless, impenetrable, overwhelming mass, irresistible if once loosed. Along this way we discover the devious and difficult heathen, the killers of girl infants, the binders of women's feet, the torturers of a thousand cuts, the headsmen, the Boxer Rebellion and the Yellow Peril, the nerveless indifference to pain, death, or to human disaster, the whole set of lurid, strange, and fearful images clustered around the notion of the awakening giant and brought vividly to life again by Mao Tse-Tung's "human sea" seen flooding down across the Yalu, massed barbarians now

[21] New York: The John Day Company. Copyright 1958 by Massachusetts Institute of Technology.

[22] *Ibid,* p. 37. Polls dated March 26, 1942 and May 2, 1945, in *Public Opinion, 1925–1946,* ed. by Hadley Cantril, Princeton, 1951.

[23] Attributes listed by Isaacs, *op. cit.,* p. 63.

armed not with broadswords but with artillery, tanks, and jet planes.[24]

American children know that a hole dug deep enough would come out in China. We have had business relations with China since 1784, when Robert Morris sent out the first American clipper, and the dream of 400 million customers appealed to the American business imagination as late as 1937. Other important points of contact have been established by missionaries from the U.S. to China and by the immigration of 300,000 Chinese (from 1854 to 1882), mostly to work building the Western railroads. "Our everyday existence is dotted with Chinese flecks familiar to adults and children alike." [25] There are in *Webster's* three columns of Chinese things: Chinese lanterns, Chinese lacquer, Chinese amaranth, azalea, hibiscus, peony, and wisteria. But there are also Chinatowns, Chinese restaurants (our grandfathers' youth was spent in Chinese restaurants) and Chinese dishes, Chinese mah-jongg, Chinese tong wars, "Chinese homers," and the China Lobby.

Among the more important and more emotional images, Isaacs finds a dramatic polarity.

> The Chinese are seen as a superior people and an inferior people; devilishly exasperating heathens and wonderfully attractive humanists; wise sages and sadistic executioners; thrifty and honorable men and sly and devious villains; comic opera soldiers and dangerous fighters. These and many other pairs occur and recur, with stresses and sources varying widely in time and place . . . they are often jumbled all together, with particular facets coming more clearly into view when struck by the moving lights of changing circumstances.[26]

Isaacs finds that a certain chronology establishes itself in the history of American images of China and the Chinese,which he summarizes in the following table:

1. The Age of Respect (Eighteenth Century)
2. The Age of Contempt (1840–1905)
3. The Age of Benevolence (1905–1937)
4. The Age of Admiration (1937–1944)
5. The Age of Disenchantment (1944–1949)
6. The Age of Hostility (1949– )

Of course, each of these ages "lives on into and through the other, and in all their many expressions they coexist, even now." [27]

[24] Isaacs, pp. 63–64. Reprinted by permission.
[25] *Ibid.*, p. 69.
[26] *Ibid.*, pp. 70–71. Reprinted by permission.
[27] *Ibid.*, p. 71.

Passing over the fascinating content of Mr. Isaacs' book, and moving directly into the recent past, we have the unfavorable impression of the Kuomintang régime on American troops sent to China during World War II. Graham Peck wrote in *Two Kinds of Time:*

> I think every American who came to Kuomintang territory on war duty has bitter memories of do-nothing attitudes, and of profiteering which ranged from the prices the U.S. Army had to pay for airfields to the prices GI's were charged in restaurants.[28]

A few months after Pearl Harbor, backing up Brig. General Magruder, the head of our military mission to China, Ambassador Gauss told his superiors in Washington:

> . . . the Chinese armies do not possess the supplies, equipment, or aggressive spirit for any major military offensives or expeditions, and . . . we should not expect from them more . . . whatever assurances or offers of greater cooperation may be forthcoming. . . . It is also true that China is not now making any all-out war effort on the military front . . . I agree that the American press has unwisely accepted and exaggerated Chinese propaganda reports of alleged military successes which . . . have little foundation in fact.[29]

Since the Communists have taken over, and the Kuomintang escaped to Taiwan, two major American positions have co-existed. A Gallup poll on August 13, 1954, asked, "Judging from what you have heard and read, what would you say are the main reasons China went Communist?" The principal replies stood in polar opposition to one another:

| | |
|---|---|
| Poverty, living conditions, ignorance of masses | 33 per cent |
| Corruption of Nationalist regime | 7 per cent |
| Russian pressure, propaganda | 33 per cent |
| U. S. policy, failure to support Chiang | 7 per cent |

Mr. Isaacs' panel of 181 comparative experts on China were asked, "What do you think was the main reason for the Communist conquest of power in China?" They answered: [30]

| | |
|---|---|
| Kuomintang corruption, failure to cope with the people's problems | 80 |
| Shrewd Communist tactics | 46 |
| American errors of policy or judgment | 32 |
| Russian help to the Communists | 10 |
| Treason in the U.S. Government | 7 |

[28] Quoted by Isaacs, *ibid.*, p. 179. Reprinted by permission.
[29] Quoted in Isaacs, p. 187. Reprinted by permission.
[30] Isaacs, p. 190. Reprinted by permission.

Even experts on the ground gave contradictory analyses about "the loss" of China to Mao's forces. Thus Joseph Alsop, representing the one major position, wrote:

> Throughout the fateful years in China, the American representatives there actively favored the Chinese communists. They also contributed to the weakness, both political and military, of the Nationalist Government. And in the end they came close to offering China up to the Communists, like a trussed bird on a platter. . . .[31]

And Graham Peck, representing the other major position, said:

> We did not err by trying to stabilize Chiang Kai-shek's relations with the increasingly powerful Communists, or by giving him too little material aid . . . We gave him too much, helping him ignore [the fact that] competition with the Communists—offering the Chinese people better conditions of life than the Communists could —was the one way a non-Communist China could survive.[32]

Americans have been hurt and surprised; having long assumed a certain feeling of responsibility for the Chinese, we now look on them as ingrates. Not only the Communists have "let us down," but the Kuomintang Chinese, too. For instance, to quote Isaacs on an incident in Taipeh:

> In May, 1957, an American soldier who had murdered a Chinese was acquitted, before an applauding American crowd, by an army court-martial. On May 24, in what was described as a spontaneous eruption of mob violence, a crowd of thousands of Chinese sacked the American embassy and information agency building, tore down the American flag and ripped it to shreds. Several Americans were injured. An army of 30,000 Chinese soldiers was moved into Taipeh to restore order. More than embassy cars and desks were toppled that day in Taipeh. In the breasts of the staunchest keepers of the dream, citadels were shaken. The Taipeh violence, said Senator William Knowland of California, was "shocking to me and to friends of Free China." The ungrateful wretches on Formosa were the most unbearably ungrateful and the most unbearably wretched of all.[33]

### THE BIG SCRATCH

The big dragon that has awakened, however, is the Red one. One of his first blasts was at Americans, who have been entirely ex-

[31] Isaacs, p. 192. From "Why We Lost China," *The Saturday Evening Post,* January 7, 1950. Reprinted by permission.

[32] Isaacs, p. 192. From *Two Kinds of Time,* p. 700. Copyright 1950. Reprinted by permission.

[33] Isaacs, pp. 208–209. Reprinted by permission.

cluded from China. In 1937, 13,300 Americans resided in China; in mid-1957 there were,

> as far as was definitely known, 23 Americans all told in all of China. . . . in trade, travel, news reporting, personal contact, the severance was nearly total, more complete than at any time since the first American traders and missionaries landed at Canton and, in modern comparable circumstances, more complete by far than the degree of separation that existed between Russia and the United States at any time, including the sixteen-year span between the Bolshevik revolution and the resumption of Russian-American diplomatic relations.[34]

Although this state of affairs is now changing, and new pressures from third countries act strongly against this total severance, the distortion of images on both sides of the Pacific has only been furthered, and imagination fills the gap in information. Mr. Isaacs says, only the larger image is visible here at all, and this is an image of anathema. The images "are etched not only in pain but in fear." He finds the anguish caused by rejected parentalism and otherwise damaged ego, but of course also by China's having become part of the Soviet power system.

How has America reacted? Clearly, one cannot give a simple answer to that question. Americans have reacted in many and various ways. Of special psychological interest, however, has been the ever-augmenting refusal to grant any attention to mainland China at all. For instance, in recent national elections, both Republican and Democratic presidential candidates have wanted to discuss China, but they have had to limit themselves to talking about Quemoy and Matsu, and at most, Formosa.

Unfortunately, this kind of blindness that originates in ignorance, reaction, frustration, and belligerence spreads its influence upward into the higher reaches of government and national policy making. Even if our political leaders are insightful and responsible, as they are, still they must face the domestic political realities. Even if political greatness consists in leading the public to face up to the whole truth, and to face up to it with judgment and moral and physical courage, yet one must bear in mind that political greatness is relative. It is relative to the public, and it is restricted by the commitments of previous administrations, and by the degree of enlightenment of power factions and groupings. The political greatness of the highest leadership is also relative to the quality of personnel presently employed in the civil service and elsewhere, *e.g.*, in State and Commerce positions abroad. The President and Congress do not act in

[34] Isaacs, p. 214. Reprinted by permission.

a vacuum; they cannot express themselves apologetically. They must act in view of a domestic situation that pointedly includes conflicting images of ourselves and of other peoples, and both realistic and unrealistic conceptions of what we ought to do as a people and what we ought to accomplish through our government. The government, after all, represents us; to *blame* the government is in a way only to deny our responsibility as citizens. Political leaders in a democracy, even great leaders, can only lead those who are positively prepared to follow. If the public will not face the realities, political leadership has to take that refusal into account in its programs.

Knowing the whole truth about mainland China cannot hurt us; *not* knowing it certainly can. The whole truth constitutes the only solid foundation for our foreign policy and for the building of civilian and military morale. After all, China is one of the great and powerful countries of the world, with a population now of more than 700 million people.[35] Although the per capita income is only about five dollars monthly, China is nonetheless an immense potential market. It is, moreover, a potential friend or enemy of ours; and it stands in extraordinarily complicated and fateful relations with the U.S.S.R. One can only say China has been too much a trumped-up *domestic* issue in the United States the past several years, and too little a subject of objective investigation and intelligence.

There are individuals and groups who think that truth and objectivity are damaging to morale. The fact is nothing is so risky and potentially destructive, from the perspective of morale and *esprit de corps,* as untruth and waves of hatred. General David M. Shoup, Marine Corps Commandant, told newsmen on his return from a Pacific area inspection tour, and after making plain that he did not want to comment on what other services did,

> "As far as the Marines are concerned, we try to teach them to be good citizens, to be good soldiers.
>
> "We don't attempt to build a big hate against anybody.
>
> "We just train them to be ready to fight whatever enemy the President may designate.
>
> "We don't have to develop hate. We don't just keep talking communism, communism, communism. I've made a hundred speeches and I've never mentioned communism.

[35] The population of China was about 400 million in 1937. The United Nations, *Demographic Yearbook, 1960,* New York, 1960, page 108, shows the population to have been (approximately) 583 million in 1953, 669 million in 1958.

"I don't think that to be a good fighter you have to hate somebody. A professional boxer doesn't hate his opponent. If he does, he doesn't fight as well."

Shoup said "twenty minutes after fighting stopped" in World War II American fighting men were helping their former enemies, the Japanese, on the battlefield.[36]

We have to recognize the existence of 700 million Chinese under a government of strength. We need to know all that we can about that country, its people, its system; and we need informed and reflective judgment about its strength and about our relations with it. Impetuous policy and decision, in such a circumstance, is a kind of quiet treason against our carefully wrought traditions, and a rejection of our responsibility to ourselves and posterity.

The old gross image of the Chinese has, of course, since the Eighth Army and the First Marine Division faced Chinese troops in Korea, been displaced. *The New York Times* military analyst, Hanson Baldwin, wrote in 1951:

> That the world no longer thinks of the Chinese in terms of pacifism is a measure of the change in China . . . The picture we once entertained of the somewhat benign, inscrutable but wise and civilized Chinese, too intelligent for war—an oversimplified caricature 20 years ago—has even less validity today. For the future China is in the hands of peasant stock, of patient men who have shown on many battlefields that they *will fight*. We have learned this, somewhat to our surprise and at heavy cost, in Korea.[37]

The Marine historian, Andrew Geer, wrote in 1952 of Chinese tactics:

> "Human sea" frontal assaults are rare and are ordered as a last resort when the necessity for victory dictates such a high cost. Newspapers have reported "human sea" attacks on United Nations positions on many occasions. Actually there have been few such attacks made by the Chinese forces in Korea. Such tactics were reported as an excuse for the defeat suffered by United Nations troops.[38]

Even General Douglas MacArthur, who presumably had committed the Eighth Army and the First Marine Division, but who

[36] A.P. Dispatch, October 28, 1961. Reprinted by permission of Associated Press Assn.

[37] "China as a Military Power," *Foreign Affairs,* Vol. 30, No. 1, October 1951, p. 51. Quoted by Isaacs, pp. 230–231. Reprinted by permission.

[38] Andrew Geer, *The New Breed,* New York, 1952, p. 221. Isaacs, p. 235. Copyright 1952. Reprinted by permission.

"made the discovery at first hand," told Congress on his return in 1951:

> The Chinese people have become militarized in their concepts and their ideals. They now constitute excellent soldiers, with competent staffs and commanders. This has produced a new and dominant power in Asia . . .[39]

Nevertheless, since 1951, our public has been cut off from intelligence, military and otherwise, about China. There is considerable evidence that our images, not only of mainland China and Nationalist China, but also of Cuba, Central and South America, Africa, U.S.S.R., Germany and elsewhere are not as exact as they should be for the establishment and execution of American foreign policy in our real interest. The special warrant for choosing China as an example of our imagery is triple: Our old special interest in China, the present and future importance of China on the world scene, and our present almost complete severance from China and from information about China.

Our images of other countries naturally reflect our own interests. We are interested in other countries as they relate to us and we relate to them. Not only is the kind of information that we gather, but even more the interpretation that we put on it, a reflection of our concerns. But what are our concerns? Do we intend to know all that we can, and to make superior judgments on our data? Do we intend to calculate our long-term interest and to act appropriately, in the light of our best judgment of our interest and of the facts? Or do we intend to express our biases and prejudices? To let our foreign policy be a reflection of opinion, feeling, frustration—with little reference either to our own needs or to the objective world situation? And what do we expect of our politicians and elected representatives: Shall we let them count on our vote, if only they appeal to our ignorance and intensify hate and fear of other races, other systems, and other powers? Or shall we let them count on our vote only if they are careful students of American interest, of world affairs, of the value problems and ethical problems that underlie contemporary development and conflict? Are we to be gullible in masses and waves, the instruments of politicians who are expert in arts of propaganda, or are we to make of ourselves an intelligent, informed, and demanding *public,* that insists on being soundly led in sound directions?

Against the background of our images of other peoples, let us now look briefly at some conflicting images of ourselves. Certainly, our self-image affects our images of other peoples.

[39] *The New York Times,* April 20, 1951. Isaacs, p. 238.

## IMAGES OF OURSELF AS A PEOPLE

Some of the main images of ourself as a people are the following:

(1) The American people are a result of libertarian democratic, egalitarian, traditions. We won our independence from a corrupt old world and established the first great constitutional government, with a bill of rights that protects every individual in his conscience, religious and moral, and that offers every individual an opportunity to attain intellectual, moral and economic independence. On the world scene, our country, according to this image, still stands for revolutionary liberty, constitutionalism, and democracy. This image is supported at home by our having served as a melting pot, by our having seen men rise from inauspicious beginnings to great stature, competence, and happiness. Unfortunately, the image is not, for various reasons, as widely accepted abroad as it used to be. The image presents us as trusting in God, ourselves, intelligence, information, education. It is associated with confidence in careful legal process and representative government. It counts heavily on the individual, his energy, his desire to know, his will to act sensibly. It is supported by such newspapers and journals as seriously aim to present objective news and to elicit considerate judgment based on manifold perspectives. It is supported by a constant stream of fiction, theater, and film, including television script, which shows the innocent protected and the guilty, however shrewd, eventually captured (as in the Perry Mason stories and *The Ox-Bow Incident*). We should not think of this set of images as adopted and propagated only by a few intellectuals. It is a major part of "the American story," and it is necessary to the free and progressive business society just as it is to the university and a free climate for ideas.

(2) The American people are the product of puritanism, Protestantism, of hard work and long suffering, of thrift and pioneer spirit and energy. Perhaps but few Americans hold this image today, but it not only is an image formerly widely held, but it is an image that relates both to (1) and to (3).

(3) America is the last bastion of capitalism, individualism, and sound morals. It must be a garrison state, in a world in which half the people are Communist, but in which also the British and Scandinavians are socialist (really the same thing?), so that here a mere 6 per cent of the world's population is the only

hope left for man's salvation. But even here, few can be trusted. Union goons are trying to rob business until it is all bankrupt, while their professional agitators press for socialist government on the political front. We ought to have a small foreign service, since Americans cannot be trusted to remain capitalist abroad, except a few exceptionally rich ones and maybe the U.S. Marines. Federal pressure for racial equality and the like is Communist inspired. Supporting this image are various factions, some of them "well-educated." A widely published set of views of fraternity and sorority alumni leaders, frustrated by demands for removal of racial and religious barriers, and otherwise, can be summarized in a few excerpts:

> . . . much of the pressure regarding membership practices is Communist inspired. It ties in with their plan of keeping racial tensions an issue and of destroying the unity of large organizations by dividing them into weak and separate units.
>
> We know that the Communists wish to destroy all fraternal groups; this fact has been fully stated in their own writings . . . A Russian textbook for their agents states: "If we could effectively kill the national pride and patriotism of just one generation we will have won that country." This same idea could be disastrous to fraternities.[40]
>
> Some ministers and college administrators are urging fraternities to completely disregard race, creed, and national origin when selecting new members [and oppose restrictive clauses and so-called discriminatory practices, and favor "local autonomy."] Can we do this and still retain the friendly associations which we have cherished and which have made the fraternity system such a fine and popular experience for so many young people? [41]

There is even a direct avowal and support of prejudice and bias, an outright attempt to accept these accusations and convert the terms from pejorative into honorific ones. Thus Charles P. Curtis, in *A Commonplace Book,* is quoted as follows:

> There are only two ways to be unprejudiced and impartial. One is to be completely indifferent. Bias and prejudices are attitudes to be kept in mind, not attitudes to be avoided.[42]

This is somewhat more cautiously stated by another fraternity leader:

> We have talked about this word "discrimination." We have seen how it has been taken and used and torn apart and revised and re-

[40] The Theta Journal.
[41] Charles P. Curtis, *A Commonplace Book.*
[42] *Ibid.*

defined so that it is now a dirty word instead of a strong, clean word, and the Communists have taken the word "brotherhood" and are trying to do the same thing with that word. And so they try to sell us the idea that there must be universal brotherhood, that everybody has the same kind of civil rights, that you can't give one group of people one thing and not have the same thing for everybody else, so we are just going to make you brothers whether you like it or not. But brotherhood, based on compulsion, is not brotherhood any more than government subsidy is charity.[43]

Yet another leader says:

> . . . The landmarks which distinguish a true fraternity, start with its selectivity. One does not adopt a baby without much thought, nor a teen-age boy without some misgivings. To choose a "brother" whom you will always be proud to present in your home, your clubs, your dental society, is quite a responsibility. But it is far more difficult than that. When we confer brotherhood upon him we are also making him the brother of every existing member of our whole fraternity. . . . The freedom to choose one's friends, sweethearts, and spouse, has not as yet been surrendered outside of the Iron Curtain countries. Freedom of choice in such matters is worth fighting for. . . .

Not all fraternity people support the kind of view that has just been presented: The Kappa national constitution has from the very beginning required admission into sisterhood of a certain quota of Jewish girls.

The practical question, and the effective pressure, that the fraternities have to face is: Can American universities and colleges associate *themselves* with restrictive practices in selection of membership on their campuses?

### OUR IDEAL OF BROTHERHOOD AND GROUP CHOICES

The basic problem of liberty involved here is the problem of freedom of association *versus* freedom of individuals. If it sounds strange to call certain fraternal practices "un-American," in any case many liberal-minded university and government people have become convinced that, *e.g.*, clauses restricting membership to Christian Caucasians contained in some fraternity constitutions and charters were discriminatory, undemocratic, and illiberal. The disposition to accept membership in accordance with strict criteria imposed by alumni not of a given chapter but of "national headquarters" has been frequently deplored as preventing local chapters from recognizing

[43] The Theta Journal. *Ibid.*

personal merit and accepting into full membership individuals who were respected, liked, and wanted. The opposition to fraternities generally has looked on these practices as institutionalized narrow-mindedness, if not downright bigotry. The opposition is strong *within* many fraternities, and it is surely *not* Communist inspired.

There are many persons who have felt that one proper American reaction to the challenge of Communism is the rejection and defeat at home of all institutionalized discrimination and bigotry. It is not a light burden, in the United Nations and in Washington, and on the world stage, to have to justify or excuse racial and religious discrimination and segregation. How do you explain segregation to the black ruler of an African state? How do you put to him the proposition that friendly associations cannot be retained in college fraternities, if race, creed, and national origin are disregarded? Will it not be tempting to him to vote with an anti-American bloc? What does the rich and deep value of "friendly association" mean to him, who knows that he could not possibly be included. It's a friendly association *against* him, from his perspective. Yet at home certainly, and probably in Moscow, Peking, and perhaps in Paris, he is accepted and even honored. From his perspective, it is almost inevitably interpreted as a matter of prejudice, prejudice that is prejudicial to him. It is from his angle a case of pinko-gray men, or women, in gray flannel suits, tight-lipped, tightly-locked brief case in hand, supported by a narrow prudence and loads of money.

Fortunately, this is not the image of us that is held by most foreigners, including neutralists; and it may not even have been adopted by a majority of Russians and Chinese, despite the impact of Communist propaganda. American love of liberty, American generosity and bravery and adventuresomeness are too well known. But the world outside has had to "discriminate" intelligently from among the variety of its images of America and Americans in order to hit on satisfactory and friendly ones.

My personal impression is that most American youth makes a very favorable imprint, when it visits abroad. I say this despite having seen German students recognize American stereotypes, remarking that all the girls say 'Isn't it grand? Isn't it wonderful?" trying to drink in European culture in unanalytic gulps. And I say it despite having seen American students shouting for Hitler and arguing for Hitler, to the great annoyance of native German students. Also, although many American businessmen have made a very bad impression abroad yet major executives and foreign trade experts, *e.g.*, at National Cash Register and Sears, Roebuck, have undertaken a major campaign to see to it that American business abroad creates a favorable image by being just, by maintaining the same high standards that prevail at home, and by encouraging the employment and promotion of indigenous personnel, executive and otherwise.

We are none of us absolutely above reform. Self-reform, particularly in the direction of fuller realization of equality of opportunity and recognition of virtue despite every external consideration, is as American as apple pie. On reflection, most American fraternity people will agree. Very likely, most have already reflected and already agreed.

# 9

# MAN AND MAN: CONFLICT AND CO-OPERATION

*"Helen, do you suppose anyone would mind if I took you to Troy?"*

## I CONFLICT

Youth is idealist, and it grows up to a rude awakening. The interests of adults turn out to be at a much lower level than a young person would expect. When my wife first began teaching in an elementary school, she thought that, when the teachers went out for a smoke, they would talk about phonic *versus* sight reading, how to transmit the most possible information in the shortest possible time, how to bring out the best in the pupils, and the like. Instead, they discussed the personal failings of the principal and his wife, the impossibility of teaching anything whatever to most of the pupils, their own pay, hours off, and retirement plans.

I once dined and spent a long evening with a famous Marine Corps brigadier general whom I much admire. For five hours he conversed about nothing but his alternative retirement plans: Would he move to China, where living is cheap? Or perhaps to North or South Carolina, where living is also cheap, and where he would be near Washington and Florida? Would he buy a farm, or a house in a small town, or would he rent? (He was wasting his time and thought, for in fact he went on to become a lieutenant general and eventually retired with a much higher income than he had reckoned on.)

### LEVELS OF CONFLICT

A young person can go on without limit becoming more and more disillusioned, as far as the conflict among, and the smallness of, older persons is concerned. It does not follow, however, that the world is full of "bad guys," or even of stupid ones. The smaller concerns of men deserve to be viewed from a mature perspective. As any old pioneer or tripper will prove to you, the little problems, puzzles, necessities, really deserve a big share of human time and energy. Despite Frank Lloyd Wright, "Give me the luxuries, and never mind the necessities."

Human interests and conflicts occur at all levels, at the highest and the lowest, and we should not be surprised that this is the case. For man is a many-leveled being. The sources of conflict are multifarious. The most banal one, the scarcity of goods needed to satisfy basic wants, is still with us in the affluent society. Most human beings still go to bed on an empty stomach—a bitter thought in plush North America, but true. The needs of institutions and nations for basic materials and manufactures often conflict: There exist material shortages and bottlenecks. Dogs fight over bones, and men fight over *Lebensraum;* many people still think that "dog eat dog" accurately describes the human spectacle. The crasser materialists have made sense of this opinion, by assuming that man himself is only what he eats—*"Man ist was er isst,"* said Feuerbach. Thought is secreted by the brain as bile is secreted by the liver. That great Englishman, Thomas Hobbes (1588–1679) thought that ratiocination was a moving about of atoms, was corpuscles popping into one another. The life of man is "nasty, brutish, and short," he said. The pugnacity and belligerence of men are built into their physical nature, their brain, and their condition. Idealists sometimes have moody reflections about mankind, too, thus Plato, "The people is a beast!" (Republic, 493, and 588–589). And the word "beast" implies predacious claws, canine teeth for tearing, and the worst sort of habits.

The scarcity of goods is a "normal" source of conflict. We don't frequently fight for air, because there is plenty to go around. But we fight bitterly over money and the fairness of bills submitted. Marauding nations take possession of the harvest, or even of the land itself, as the Viking Normans took over Britain. The real battle these days is more likely to be over sources of regularly recurring supply than over mere stockpiles or the crops of one season.

Assurance of national life and welfare necessitates the possession and maintenance of strongholds. The struggle for goods thus leads to war over waterways, like the Suez and Panama Canals and the Dardanelles, and strong points like Gibraltar and Quebec. The position of power is desirable, and it is unique in the sense that it can't belong to the strong as well as to the weak. Gibraltar can't at once belong to Britain and to Spain. The position of power assures not only control of goods but also of men. And power gratifies, both in nations and individuals, a deep psychological need; power and position give confidence and self-esteem. Surely there is a sense in which conflict, including conflict of a psychological order, is native and primeval. Distrust of foreigners, of the tribe on the other side of the hill, of men in lower or higher subgroups, of classes of different economic status, is nearly universal. Man's natural state, according to Hobbes, is the state of war.

Men fight also over means, over ways of doing something, over ways of living together. The national home-builders will erect prefabs, while the horizontal unions and traditional contractors stand by their crafts and support traditional and statutory codes. All professors aim to increase the fund of knowledge, but they may dispute over who shall get the research grant and how it shall be spent. All parents want their children properly educated, but shall it be by progressive schooling or by an emphasis on the basic curriculum? As Dewey has stressed, to attain—or even to define—ends, we must get at the means, at the intermediate and auxiliary ends.

Men invent honors, systems of status, and orders of precedence and protocol. By their very nature, these social awards and decorations are always in short supply. Not everyone can be President, and not everyone can sit on his right hand at dinner. If there are goods aplenty, still there are not top positions for everyone. In all Sears, Roebuck and Company there are only some fifteen officers.

## COMPETITION

We normally speak of the struggle for money and prizes, not as conflict, but as competition. By and large, "competition" is a "good word," an honorific word, in our Western vocabulary, although it is pejorative among Communists. History, in this connection, is on our side. The brutal Romans' passion was competition to the death. The Anglo-Saxons competed for kingships. The English "shop-keepers" have accepted institutionalized competition for centuries—and they have always really been less a nation of shop-keepers than the Germans. In America, we love competitive sports, but also competition for money, for political posts and power, and for social position. We understand and appreciate a batting average of only

.385, because we know that the pitcher is working against the batter. By the same token, none of us expects to win every battle over policy, over legislation; we don't expect more than a few men to receive the Congressional Medal of Honor, or the Order of the Garter. Not all ideas can win out and get adopted in social practice. And not every employee can have a key to the executive washroom.

We believe that competition can be ordered and put to social use. Although everything is fair in love and war, competition can be regulated and kept decent. At times we put our faith in deliberate control of competition, in umpires and referees, and at other times in automatic control, in the market and effects of price fluctuation.

At the highest level, we enjoy so-called professional competition. The surgeon in Boston wants to perform a certain kind of heart operation ahead of the surgeon in Philadelphia. It is not so much a matter of publicity and recognition, perhaps, as of simply being the first. The professor would be proud to hold the chair that had been occupied by G. E. Moore, Wittgenstein, and John Wisdom, or to wear the same academic title as Isaac Newton. The philanthropist is proud to have his name associated with new steps toward the conquest of cancer or with new concepts of economic activity: "I footed the bill for that one." Sometimes the pleasure of being first to benefit humanity in a certain way makes any financial reward seem unworthy; thus, the discoverers of insulin refused to take out a patent.

There is no way of accurately estimating or stating the exact social utility of professional competition. Certainly much scientific and artistic progress is incited by it, not only in the West, but also in twentieth century Russia, where professional and artistic honors have been heaped upon Pavlov, Shostakovich, and Prokofiev.

To a certain extent, *ordered* competition means a shift of public attention away from the competitors to the judges, umpires, referees, and time-keepers. Our society is much concerned to produce fair judges, not only to occupy and administer the law courts, but also to judge sports, art competitions, and the relative merits of candidates for academic degrees. "Who shall be made a member of the Fair Trade Commission?" can be a question of warm political and economic concern.[1]

## PARTIES TO CONFLICT

No one assumes that all conflict is good, but everyone knows that a great deal of it takes place.

[1] I have borrowed in this section from lectures on social ethics by C. I. Lewis.

Conflict may be among individuals. Among certain American Indian tribes, and in the world of Jack London, when conflict between two men passed a certain degree of intensity, they went off with knives, or were sent off, in the expectation that only one of them would return alive. In some boys' clubs, boys who don't get along well together are given an express opportunity to fight it out, not to the death, but until one will call "quits." [2] In our culture, for the most part, battling among individuals is channeled and regulated. The interest of groups in maintaining tranquillity is paramount, and individual members are not allowed to fight to the bitter end. Society is interested in talent and service; and it's sentimental, so it won't allow unrestricted fighting. Moreover, if there is too much battling within a group, the group as a whole may lose out to another group that reserves its belligerence for outsiders.[3]

Conflict may occur among groups, subgroups, corporations. Competition among companies may result in the more efficient production and distribution of goods and services, in invention, in better usage of labor. But it may also result in waste, the lowering of standards of quality, "job-hopping" and executive "musical chairs." Conflicting interests within a corporation may do battle in sad disregard of the profit and loss statement. Opposing factions in a church may all but pull down the steeple.

Consequently, a good part of administration is, not so much keeping entire peace and smiling on all parties, but directing friction and static into useful channels, and assuring that basic loyalty is always to the group as a whole. Production and success come first. At the national level, there is an unwritten but widely supported policy of channeling politically—or economically—the opposing interests of agriculture *versus* business and labor; of labor *versus* business; of temporal *versus* spiritual powers; of North *versus* South, and East *versus* West. Many great disputes get themselves settled in the marketplace, and others get themselves settled in the mad scramble that closes every session of the legislature. Not everyone can win, but nearly everyone can—on reflection—feel that he has been treated fair.[4]

Conflicts also occur among whole societies, and our own century

[2] I refrain from judging the merit of this practice. I'm not sure that it should be judged "in general." I am sure that in some military academies the practice is exaggerated and abused, and fighting for position is shrouded in terror.

[3] However, there was always fighting aplenty within the famous Black Sheep Squadron of World War II.

[4] Where limited numbers of licenses and franchises are granted, as television channels by the Federal Communications Commission, not everyone ends up feeling that he has been treated fair.

is unfortunately a century of such conflicts, of great and global wars. We have transcended the destructive patterns of individual and family feud and revenge only to tumble into patterns of international destruction marked by use of fire-throwing, bacteriological warfare, and atom and hydrogen bombs. In an era that is otherwise one of integrity and responsibility, international agreements are scraps of paper and devices of infamy. In war truth is the first casualty.

### THE INEVITABILITY OF CONFLICT

Leaving the discussion of conflict *within* the individual personality to psychologists, biographers, and novelists, we shall try to cope briefly with that old chestnut, the inevitability of social conflict. In general, we might say that conflict is held by Western thinkers to be inevitable, forever and forever, and that the significant issue for them is how to direct it to good purpose. And we might say that, in general, among the slightly less sophisticated, hardened, and independent thinkers in the U.S.S.R., and everywhere in the Marxist tradition, conflict is held to be inevitable also, not forever and forever, but just until the establishment of the Communist international on earth.

Those who put very great faith in persons and movements are likely to question the reality and unavoidability of conflict. I recall how National Socialist acquaintances in Germany made light of every social economic, and political problem, including international ones, affirming confidently, "Hitler will easily take care of that." He did.

A similar refrain is sometimes heard from the American right and from the American left. "Pack the Court, and don't strain at a gnat." "Legislate its power away from the Court, and then nothing will stand in the way of the national security." "Impeach all nine justices."

Even inside universities' ivy-covered walls there is real conflict. Who shall speak to young minds? Which department shall gain in registration, in personnel, in budget-power? How very much would certain *outsiders* like to control these institutions, to control the development of young minds to their heart's desire. But no faction has unlimited power. Even members of the Board of Trustees can't run classes according to their will, can't get every friend's nephew admitted, can't fire Professor Smith or promote Professor Jones. Where boards do exert undue power, or zany multi-millionaire donors affect administration, the prestige of the institution soon shrinks, wiser donors withdraw, brighter students drop out, smarter professors won't get recruited.

Yet the denial of conflict is "a scholar's fallacy." Intellectuals solve their problems cooperatively. They are used to the solution of problems under laboratory—*i.e.,* artificial—conditions. But there is not much carry-over from the scholar's closet to the world of practical affairs. Solutions to the problems of scientists and scholars can wait for generations, wait for the intuitions of future genius. But social and moral problems are not like that; they can't wait; they must get decided on the run.

The denial of the reality of conflict poses a problem. Suppose we say to the man who denies it, "We disagree." How is he to reply to us? If he agrees with us, he has admitted of real conflict; but if he disagrees with us, he has himself initiated conflict. Consequently, those who deny the existence of real conflict usually try to run out into the future, affirming only that *someday* there will be no real conflict. One would be less sceptical about this "someday," if it could be clearly delineated, if it didn't bear the appearance of cloudy vagueness. The Marxist "someday" is not even a day of communism, but rather of peaceable anarchism, of lambs without bourgeois lions, of administrators who are selfless and omniscient, of plebs who are philosophers.

Most Western philosophers and political theorists, to the contrary, have accepted the reality and the inevitability of conflict of interest, temperament, personality, and position. They have accepted conflict as something indigenous to human affairs and tried to accommodate man and society to it.

Marx and Lenin themselves belong to this sceptical tradition, but Marx, especially, "hoped beyond it." One could say with some warrant that Lenin was the greatest sceptic at the Finland Station. Lenin equated progress with conflict: "Development is the struggle of opposites," he said, in the traditions of Hegel and von Humboldt.

The British tradition on this score goes back to Hobbes and beyond, but it reached its highest development, perhaps, in the Philosophical Radicals. To James Mill (1773–1836),[5]

> . . . the governments of his day appeared as groups of selfish people, intent on the safe-guarding of their privileges, and engrossed in the pursuit of their private advantage. . . . a benevolent aristocracy was, according to Mill's hedonism, psychologically impossible, and would in fact be a fraud upon the people.[6]

[5] W. H. Burston, "James Mill on the Aims of Education," *Cambridge Journal,* Volume VI, No. 2, November 1952, pp. 79–101.

[6] *Ibid.* Reprinted by permission.

The only protection against selfishness in officers of the state is representative government, with officers elected for terms of short, stated duration.

> Mill saw in . . . vested interests a striking confirmation of Plato's wisdom in arranging that those who had power in his ideal state should have neither privilege, private interests, nor property so that they would always rule in the interests of the many. And Mill anticipates Marx in his Commonplace Book by asserting that people who are privileged invariably rule in their own interests, even when they think they are serving the community, for they deceive themselves as to their true motives.[7]

Today, like James Mill's son, John Stuart, we would let our scepticism extend still much farther. If we are really concerned with value realization, why should we place our ultimate faith in the many, in the people? Which many? The great American middle-classes, with their TV shows and TV dinners? The masses of Germany who supported Hitler? The masses of U.S.S.R. who willy-nilly followed Stalin and then Khrushchev? No, we may better place our hope in the unborn multitudes of the future, and of course we are now speaking frankly about hope, not about warranted expectations.[8]

Can one go too far in the direction of scepticism? Can one overreach the mark and accept conflict beyond necessity? Some think that Hegel (1770–1831) did so.

> He insisted on the reality and necessity of conflicts and wars and revolutions, of the tragic waste and destruction in the world. He declared that every process is one of perpetual tension between two incompatible forces each straining against the other, and by this mutual conflict advancing their own development; this duel—which is sometimes concealed and sometimes open, and can be traced in all provinces of conscious activity as the struggle between so many rival physical, moral and intellectual forces and influences—grows in strength and sharpness until it turns into an open conflict, which culminates in a final collision, the violence of which destroys both the adversaries. This is the point at which the hitherto continuous development is broken, a sudden leap takes place to a new level, whereupon the tension between a new dyad of forces begins once more. Certain among those leaps, those, namely, which occur on a sufficiently large and noticeable scale, are termed political revolu-

[7] *Ibid.* Reprinted by permission.

[8] "The future, to our fathers an imperturbable witness, has lost much of its majesty." "The judgment of posterity was the supreme test. And each man moreover expected it to confirm him in his beliefs." Albert Dasnoy in *Encounter*.

tions. But, on a more trivial scale, they occur in every sphere of activity, in the arts and sciences, in the growth of physical organisms studied by biologists and in the atomic processes studied by chemists, and finally in ordinary argument between two opponents, when, after a conflict between two partial falsehoods, new truth is discovered, itself only relative, itself assaulted by a counter-truth (antithesis to its thesis), the destruction of each by the other leading once more to a synthesis—a process which continues without end. He called the process *dialectical.* The notion of struggle and of tension provides precisely that dynamic principle which is required to account for movement in history.[9]

But Hegel's fault is not in finding conflict nor even in finding it inevitable, but in approving it in and for itself (*an und fuer sich*). Conflict in itself is not good, but it can be turned to good use. Conflict in itself is not wise,[10] but it can be intelligently directed. The desire to win can be sublimated and reoriented in such a way that it serves a social purpose. Referees can be empowered to enforce fair play.

One of the chief problems of our day—one that we cannot really shrug off—is how to control conflict on the global level. In war, either hot or cold, each of the opposing forces, in aiming to destroy the other, always somehow manages to justify itself in its own eyes. The enemy has evil intentions, commits black atrocities, is decadent and corrupt. For its own part, while modestly disclaiming perfection, it insists on claiming good and just intentions, congruence with the real interest of future mankind and the support of God or History or both. Granting this psychology, how is global conflict of interest to be intelligently directed to good purpose?

## II CO-OPERATION

In contrast to that pejorative term, "conflict," "co-operation" is almost always used in an honorific sense. However, most of the antipathy toward togetherness can properly be directed against co-operation. Really, co-operation is neutral; by no means is it intrinsically good. As much conflict gets directed to good, so much co-operation gets directed to evil. Modern war is itself possible, in all its hypocrisy

[9] Isaiah Berlin, *Karl Marx, His Life and Environment.* London: Oxford University Press, 1948, pp. 54–55. Concerning Hegel, Chapter III, "The Philosophy of the Spirit." Reprinted by permission.

[10] A Washington correspondent says of the folly of foes of labor, "Every time there is sentiment to curb the racketeers in labor, the anti-labor foes outsmart themselves. Instead of going back to World War II, these elements try to go back to U. S. Grant."

and complex horror, only because of co-operation, because of modern industrial achievements and the mass psychology of the present —that loud joint whistling in the dark that all too likely precedes the holocaust.

Co-operativeness *cannot,* in any superficial sense, be a characteristic of the doer with his mighty impulse to a new deed, for he must always, as doer, "be grazing some piety or other." [11] If conflict is the wolf of moral mythology, co-operation is the cow.

Co-operation may occur among parties of unequal stature, status, or power. Co-operation among masters and slaves *is* a dyadic relation, and the master is dependent on the slave, but not as the slave is dependent on the master. The master depends on the slave for his victuals, their preparation and service, for his bed-making, his toilet, the care of his stable and horses. The slave depends on the master for his food, clothing, and shelter, for his thrashings, his mentality, and his morals. Like two kinds of timber, both necessary to the skeleton of a house, the master stands straight, the slave bent. In authoritarian marriages, also, there is co-operation among unequal parties. By necessity, the wife bears the children, but then she also has the unique responsibility for bringing them up, and she has to mould the household, the children, and her own personality, all to suit the loud demands of "the old man." The sons grow up filled with resentment, awaiting the day when they in turn can be boss and "take it out" on their own sweet families.

A system of wage slavery is another form of co-operation. The worker in one-time English and American mines, logging camps, and lumber mills worked hard during all daylight hours, made a small wage, and paid high prices for his necessities, bought at the company's commissary. This experience of "co-operation" stands in the background of the political radicalism of our older mining and logging areas.

At its best, co-operation by free contract serves both parties. Neither buyer nor seller loses by a good contract; both parties gain, and both act of their own volition. Clearly if one party only is acting from dire necessity, the contract is not really free; hence the emphasis in America on *free* labor and on *free* competition.

Co-operation can exist out of interest but without any contractual arrangement. Many major distributorships in the United States function without any formal contract, or operate on a year-to-year basis (*e.g.,* certain exclusive General Electric distributorships).

[11] Friedrich Nietzsche, *The Use and Abuse of History.* New York: The Liberal Arts Press, revised edition of 1957, p. 20. Tr. by Adrian Collins.

Joint interest and joint success sustain such co-operative arrangements. On a larger scale, the co-operation of the U.S. and British navies across the nineteenth and twentieth centuries has been of this sort, with the British Navy patrolling the Atlantic and the U.S. Navy the Pacific. Perhaps our day-to-day peace with the U.S.S.R. constitutes a passive co-operation of the same kind. At least, it has not proved in the interest of either party to date to commence open conflict; at times, the co-operation has extended to the point of allowing either nation to explain itself and advertise itself to the other nation's public.

As Plato already understood,[12] the division of labor presupposes co-operation. If society is to enjoy the advantages of specialization, and let one man make shoes, another grow corn, then there must be mutual trust and an acceptable system of exchange of products. J. S. Mill spoke of the joint work of seven sailors tugging on one line as simple co-operation, of the division of labor into specialties as complex co-operation. Our own *industrial* system is better characterized as one of complex co-operation than as a system of free enterprise, or of free competition.

Mill spoke of co-operation among equals as the ultimate in social relations. We can catch an occasional glimpse of this ideal at work in the co-operation of surgeons and physicians, in the co-operation of research professors striving to "crack" a problem, in the co-operation of author and editor to achieve excellence in a publication. We can now and again see it realized in a marriage. Mill looked on his own marriage to Harriet Taylor as an instance of co-operation among equals. Such co-operation may be characterized by equality of the participants, mutuality and mutual respect, and shared purpose of a high order.

## III INSTITUTIONS AND THE SOCIALIZED PERSONALITY

Institutions consist in attitudes of mind.[13] Institutions, in turn, mould us and make us what we are. The reality that makes us into the men and women that we are is not only a physical, but also a social reality. In her wartime book, *And Keep Your Powder Dry,* Margaret Mead wrote that an important problem is:

[12] ". . . if one man gives another what he has to give in exchange for what he can get, it is because each finds that to do so is for his own advantage." Plato, *The Republic.* New York & London: Oxford University Press, 1945, p. 56. Tr. F. M. Cornford.

[13] In the phrase of Earl Dean Howard.

Not the problem of what we have, where we are and how many of us are available to use how many machines and weapons, but the problem of what we are ourselves. When the statesman or the general utters the word 'total war,' either as a threat to his own people or a threat to the enemy, he means that, to all these other questions of materiel, geography, and sheer numbers, has been added another—the quality of a people; their national character. The youngest child, its physical stamina, its psychological security, may be a factor in the resistance, in the total effort of a whole people, for if great numbers of children die—or even refuse to eat—under the stress of total war, the courage and the energy of their parents will be by that much lessened and depleted. The old grandmother, bedridden and half blind, also becomes a factor. Does she insist upon others leaving more important tasks to care for her, or does she fall half out of bed urging her children and her grandchildren to get on with the business of life and never mind even leaving her a sleeping draught beside her bed? The simplest mountain farmer may live on a remote spot where a parachutist drops; whether or not he is a real representative of rugged individualism may turn the tide of battle. Upon the alertness of some unskilled laborer in a great aeroplane factory may depend the prevention of a major act of sabotage. The chairman of the Senate Committee who inaugurates the wrong investigation may play a greater role than the general who gives the wrong command.[14]

Most of us are today keenly aware, thanks to the influence of the social sciences, that "what we are ourselves" has largely been determined by the social environment,

that the language one speaks, the religion one professes, the code of ethics by which one judges, and is judged, one's taste for wine or beer or vodka, or one's preference for paprika or snails or French-fried dragon-flies can all be referred to the culture within which one is brought up.[15]

The attitudes of men constitute a major element of that total reality in which we live and have our being, of that reality in which we find our limitations and our opportunities. A mark of reality is *necessity,* our inability to wish it away; and (paraphrasing David Hume), natural and moral necessity aptly cement together, forming only one chain of argument between them.

A prisoner, who has neither money nor interest, discovers the impossibility of his escape, as well from the obstinacy of the gaoler, as

[14] Margaret Mead, *And Keep Your Powder Dry, An Anthropologist Looks At America.* New York: William Morrow and Company, 1942, pp. 16–17. Reprinted by permission.

[15] *Ibid.,* p. 19. Reprinted by permission.

> from the walls and bars with which he is surrounded; and in all attempts for his freedom chuses rather to work upon the stone and iron of the one, than upon the inflexible nature of the other. The same prisoner, when conducted to the scaffold, foresees his death as certainly from the constancy and fidelity of his guards as from the operation of the ax or wheel.[16]

Social relations and attitudes of mind take on an inflexibility that is fully comparable to physical necessity. The social and physical necessities are often so cemented together as to be all but indistinguishable.

> For is it more certain, that two flat pieces of marble will unite together, than two young savages of different sexes will copulate? Do the children arise from this copulation more uniformly, than does the parents' care for their safety and preservation? [17]

And many of our sentiments and attitudes of mind are directly related to our social position and to our work.

> The skin, pores, muscles, and nerves of a day-labourer are different from those of a man of quality: So are his sentiments, actions and manners. The different stations of life influence the whole fabric, external and internal; and these different stations arise necessarily, because uniformly, from the necessary and uniform principles of human nature. Man cannot live without society, and cannot be associated without government. Government makes a distinction of property, and establishes the different ranks of men. This produces industry, traffic, manufactures, law-suits, war, leagues, alliances, voyages, travels, cities, fleets, ports, and all those other actions and objects, which cause such a diversity, and at the same time maintain such an uniformity in human life.[18]

Perhaps Hume overemphasized the uniformity of human nature and the permanence of stations of life. On the other hand, many Rousseauists have tended to exaggerate the relativity of human personality to culture, and the malleability of human nature. "For malleability meant that norms and institutions—the assumed cause of man's nature rather than the effect—could be malleable too." [19]

Social reality is constituted of the at least relatively stable and institutionalized convictions of men.

[16] David Hume, *A Treatise of Human Nature: Being an Attempt to Introduce the Experimental Method of Reasoning into Moral Subjects.* London: 1739, Book II, Part III, Section I, "Of liberty and necessity."

[17] *Ibid.*

[18] *Ibid.*

[19] Erich Fromm, *Man For Himself, loc. cit.*, p. 21.

## THE NATURE AND ROLE OF CONVICTIONS

Intimate and essential relations hold between thinking and believing on one side and acting on the other. We build up our beliefs as a part of our total education, formal and informal, along with our acquaintanceship and skill. Beliefs are *general rules,* to be acted on not on any and every occasion, but on every *relevant* occasion. C. S. Peirce classified belief as one kind of habit. "Our convictions reached are," Professor Lewis says, ". . . permanently stored up against any future and pertinent occasion—unless or until something happens to alter them." [20] A conviction is thus a well-settled way of dealing with a certain kind of problem.

Our convictions may or may not be distinctly present to consciousness at the moment we act on them; our tendency is to relegate them to memory, to store them up as habits, and to act on them without any deliberate effort of recollection. We are responsible for all our actions in driving a car, but we are not conscious of them all. "Believing that there is an intersection, ahead, we follow a routine which *originally* represented decisions taken but has now become a matter of customary response—still good or not so good according to our previous and reflective decisions out of which this habit was allowed to develop." [21]

To ask whether our convictions are conscious is not the same as to ask whether they are rational. We may act rationally with but little awareness. Conversely, we may act with self-awareness but without deliberation. With this latter state of affairs in mind, Freud speaks of "the affective feature 'conviction.' " [22]

## G. H. MEAD

Convictions, or attitudes of mind, then, are the stuff of which societies and institutions are made. Institutions grow round human purposes. Every institution and every society has its existence in organized relations among the attitudes of mind of its members. The "formula in the acorn" that controls growth will prescribe rules and their enforcement, will provide roles, provide rituals for the expression of loyalty, provide for practical support and replenishment. Barring some extraordinary windstorm, an institution, like a tree, may continue in existence for generations even after it is quite hollow within. This is owing to the toughness of the loyalties that it has built.

[20] C. I. Lewis, *The Ground and Nature of the Right, loc. cit.,* p. 41.
[21] *Ibid.*
[22] From *Beyond the Pleasure Principle.*

One of the more astute analysts of the nature of institutions and of the relations between institutions and individual personalities was George Herbert Mead. Mead pointed to generalized social attitudes and to continuities of response. He said, "The institution represents a common response on the part of all members of the community to a particular situation." [23]

Institutions are frequently older than any of their living members. The upbringing of new members raises crucial practical problems for every institution, and interesting theoretical problems for the social scientist. The new member must be made to internalize in himself the social convictions that constitute the institution. This internalizing is a taking into himself of a generalized social attitude, an addressing himself to the group. By such procedures, the biological individual becomes a social self and a mind.

> The society in which we belong represents an organized set of responses to certain situations in which the individual is involved . . . in so far as the individual can take those organized responses over into his own nature, and call them out by means of the symbol in the social response, he has a mind in which mental processes can go on, a mind whose inner structure he has taken from the community to which he belongs.[24]

These minds then can and do turn back upon society, controlling it, criticizing, adapting, and amending it. Societies and institutions are, as a result, dynamic events and not absolutely fixed and final structures.

Some institutions require members to fit in or get out. But institutions can also be "flexible and progressive, fostering individuality rather than discouraging it." Appropriate social institutions are a condition of mature selves,

> for the individuals involved in the general social life-processes of which social institutions are organized manifestations can develop and possess fully mature selves or personalities only in so far as each one of them reflects or comprehends in his individual experience these organized social attitudes and activities which social institutions embody and represent.[25]

Had we time here to pursue Mead's ideas, we should add that "to be alive is to be socially involved," that without the social event, the

[23] G. H. Mead, *Mind, Self and Society* ed. Charles Morris. Chicago: University of Chicago Press, 1934, p. 261. I am obligated in this connection to Professor William C. Tremmel, The Kansas State Teachers College, Emporia, Kansas, and to the Emporia State Research Studies.

[24] *Ibid.,* p. 270. Reprinted by permission.

[25] *Ibid.,* p. 262. Reprinted by permission.

human animal could neither arise nor persist. We should add that man is essentially the role-taking animal, and add something about gesture, language, and the uses of childhood games in teaching role-playing and the distinction of "me" from "you," and "I" from "me." We should enjoy dwelling on the notion of "reflective intelligence" in this context; for some observers and critics have tended to underrate the importance and role of intelligence and wisdom in the creation of institutions and of human personality.

Everyone today will agree with Hume that "men always consider the sentiments of others in judgment of themselves," and almost everyone will agree with Mead that mind itself is socially derived. But, in an era of irrationalism, in a mass age, the rôle of intelligent judgment gets played down. In fact, way up at the center of every institutional web, there is at least one wise old spider who knows when the sun shines and when it rains, who determines policy with care and with wisdom grown of experience and thought. Convictions alone do not constitute a heathy institution; the convictions must be well oriented.

## IV POLITICAL CHOICE AND POLITICAL SCIENCE

Aristotle said that man is the political animal, and he followed up his chief treatise on ethics by a major work on politics. Political science has recently been defined as "the study of the authoritative allocation of values for a society," [26] suggesting anew a degree of overlap between political science and social ethics. Social ethics, however, is not concerned only with the arrangements that have the force of law but also raises questions about what a man ought to do about public matters, whether or not law requires. Social ethics takes up problems of a man's conscience as an individual and as a member of private associations.

The traditional subject matter of political science is power, the *authoritative* allocation of both instrumental and final values. One is wise not to underestimate the negative contribution of political science: It teaches with some accuracy which choices we do *not* have. Images of choices proposed by utopians are rejected by political scientists in the interest of realism, on the evidence of actual political behavior. Many choices described by utopians have ignored the facts of political life, *i.e.*, the extent of conflict and disagreement, the relative strength of various interests and loyalties, and the stub-

[26] David Easton, *The Political System.* New York: Alfred A. Knopf, 1953, p. 129.

born lag that is political habit. Socrates called the state "a great and noble steed who is tardy in his motions owing to his great size," a steed that must be "stirred to life." The political scientist can measure that tardiness (which is not owing only to size), predict the amounts of energy (money, organized effort) required to stir the animal into life, realistically certify when the animal is stone-dead.

We may frankly admit that many of the choices postulated by Plato and other utopians were not choices that anyone really faced or faces. Realism is, in the history of the human race, always one of the slowest and greatest achievements. His own realism compelled Plato to grant that political institutions and processes proposed by him could come into being only if somewhere, sometime, a king were a philosopher, or a philosopher a king. In other words, he saw *his* political problem, but he did not squarely face it. He hoped for a lucky chance that would bring his Republic into being. He was realistic enough to recognize that for all the precautions he suggested, the ideal nature of his state could not be indefinitely maintained, even if it did come into being and follow the dynamic program that he set forth for it. Of course Plato has had a great influence on Western political thought, and perhaps on history; it is not easy to find a better analysis of aristocracy than Plato's, and one may suspect that the irrealism and weakness in Plato is the irrealism and weakness characteristic of aristocracy everywhere.[27]

We may concede a similar "idealism" in the political and legal philosophy of Immanuel Kant. Kant defended Plato, asserting that nothing is more important than to recognize perfection in our models, archetypes, paradigms. Otherwise, for all we can know, our scale of values may be false, our orientation in error. Perhaps we should say, "It is fine, sir, to preach good will and perfectionism; but the political work of the world must be done by rulers and officers who either control, or report back to their all too human superiors, or inferiors, or publics." Kant does not fully realize the meaning and role of agency, of representatives' responsibility, in domestic and international affairs.

The perfectionist runs a great risk of missing such good as there is, because he gives preponderant attention to seeking the absolute best. Many observers find themselves frustrated, for instance, in presence of the worldliness of United Nations delegations. But if we

[27] Plato has also been cogently described as anti-political. "*The Republic* is, for the most part, the description of a society without conflict: hence, it describes a society that does not need government, law, or political activity." Wayne A. R. Leys, "Platonic, Pragmatic, and Political Responsibility." *Responsibility,* Nomos III, Carl J. Friedrich (Ed.). New York: The Liberal Arts Press, 1960, p. 72.

are trying to achieve a firm result, is not worldliness in order? The states represented are not angels, they are actual states with supposedly sovereign interests. Yet they may have a sincere interest in getting along with other states, an interest that can grow luxuriantly if watered by occasional success.

On the other hand, if we turn to a hard-headed philosophical realist and materialist, Thomas Hobbes, we find that he also preaches a kind of perfectionism; only now it is not the perfectionism of life and value, but the perfectionism of power itself. That old man would have us turn over all effective decision to the monarch, receiving in return a subjection—an abjection—that he calls peace. Hobbes also fails to establish a *political* order. He only mounts a well-armed guard to prevent the eruption of civil war and natural human brutishness. Modern political science does not relate itself more to Hobbes than to Plato or Kant.

Political science opposes both utopianism and such unimaginative realism as allows of no alternatives and no flexibilities. It aims to know the truth about politics, however abhorrent, but it is of course interested in political opportunities and desirable alternatives of end and means. It will not accept rigidity, severity, empty forms as ends-in-themselves.

### A SKETCH OF THE "NEGATIVE" CONTRIBUTION

A major contribution of the political scientists—and of other behavioral scientists—is their detailed exhibition of differences between accepted norms and the realities. As was said in relation to Kant, to be ethical means to have good intentions; but even if we have good intentions, there remains for us the difficult question, what in fact *are* the right actions to perform, in a given context? To anyone with the least disposition to science and in favor of clarity and adequacy of knowledge the further questions will arise: *Are* my actions having the consequences that I intend? *Are* they relevant to the actual human situation on which they operate? And in the complex world in which we live, the answers to such questions cannot be taken for granted by anyone of serious intent. Moreover, our normative standards themselves are always subject to review, since we have learned that norms and "rectitude values" may not work as supposed and indeed may not so much represent good intent as very inferior, perhaps unconscious, prejudice and selfishness. Thus the negative impact of the social sciences on our ethical positions and attitudes is two-fold. It consists in a revelation of the discrepancy between intended consequence and actual result, and secondly in the rise of questions about the relevance and concrete operation and goodness of our normative standards.

The social sciences can and do show the near impossibility of certain kinds of measures. Actual studies of voting behavior, for instance, may reveal the difficulties in the way of promoting change. In the campaign to elect his brother president, Robert Kennedy is said to have prevented the major expenditure of national party funds in Nebraska in face of the consistent Republican voting record of that state. By means of various scientific procedures, not only political parties, but also business corporations, are enabled to set realizable quotas, make comparatively sound judgments respecting expenditures, and to judge performance. I refer to Nebraska, of course, only in order to give a clear illustration: The excellent performance of a campaign manager depends on detailed decision in border-line cases; Mr. Kennedy might have made that decision without any effort at "scientific exactitude," but should an all-out national effort have been made in Illinois, in Michigan, in Ohio? The merit of opinion surveys and analyses using multiple and partial correlation should be obvious.

If one seeks important community decisions, to know where the power to make those decisions lies is essential to success. In Regional City, studied by Floyd Hunter and his associates, "most of the top personnel of the power group are rarely seen at meetings attended by the associational under-structure personnel. . . ." [28] Realistic efforts at action in Regional City will be based on the recognition of the actual power structure in its day-to-day operation, in its characteristically informal, back-room ways; they will *not* be misled by the superstructure of front organizations, chambers, and official agencies, nor will they be misled by popular opinion about democratic process. In the interest of democratic process itself, knowledge of the actual situation must be acquired by those whose intent is democratic. By no means is it merely a matter of preventing manipulation to the advantage of the relatively few; it is also a matter of strengthening lines of communication up and down the community. One of Mr. Hunter's principal findings is that the actual leaders of the community do not receive accurate pictures of the needs and demands of the majority of the population. He uses *power* "to describe the acts of men going about the business of moving other men to act in relation to themselves or in relation to organic or inorganic things." [29] To learn how power in this sense is

[28] Floyd Hunter, *Community Power Structure*. Chapel Hill: The University of North Carolina Press, 1953, p. 90.

[29] *Ibid.*, pp. 2–3.

wielded is manifestly something that cannot be learned from the pulp or the slick magazines. Such learning rests on carefully controlled observing and categorizing. If such studies are infused with values of the observer or with his proposals for reform, as Mr. Hunter clearly recognizes,[30] they run an inauspicious risk of becoming distorted.

### SCIENTIFIC KNOWLEDGE AND THE DESIRE TO PUNISH

The demand to be punitive and severe plays important rôles in political life. Granting that suffering can be an instrument of education serving to deter "the offender who has taken a calculated risk" and to acculturate the immature, Harold Lasswell says that it ought and can be,

> kept out of the arbitrary, free-wheeling category of an alleged end in itself. The scientific image of an act as an interaction has reduced the demand to impose suffering insofar as this demand depends upon the expectation that people have the capability of abstaining from an act regarded as offensive.[31]
>
> The demand to be punitive can itself be taken as an object of scientific investigation. The late Professor Svend Ranulf conducted a number of studies that established a connection between the rise of middle classes and more reliance upon criminal penalties. . . . [He] drew attention to the remarkable rise of penal legislation in ancient Athens when the urban middle classes were becoming more numerous, articulate, and assertive. Puritan England displayed the same phenomenon. "Crimes" multiplied; sanctions became more severe. . . . More people begin to ask why the middle classes are more justified than other classes in committing themselves in favor of the imposition of suffering.
>
> Behavioral studies tend to establish a link between personality systems and the demand for severity. . . . The demand for severity was favored by relatively rigid personalities predisposed to use obsessional or compulsive mechanisms as a means of keeping their destructive urges under control.
>
> Administrators of sanctions take public indignation into account and the likelihood that so-called 'leniency' will provoke public

[30] *Ibid.*, (*e.g.*) pp. 4–5. I should like to enter a *caveat:* One should not accept without proof that community-leaders are class-motivated. One should not generalize without due precaution: Regional City is strikingly unlike the better middle-western communities both in its power structure and in the interests of its decision makers. Political scientists (not Mr. Hunter) sometimes *bring* a gestalt of naked power to all their observations.

[31] Harold D. Lasswell, "The Normative Impact of the Behavioral Sciences." *Ethics*, Vol LXVII, No. 3 (April 1957) Part II, p. 19.

disorder. If the assertion is that public order will be endangered by failure to be severe, the hypothesis can be studied (an issue separable from deterrence).[32]

Political scientists are by no means the only social scientists who can pour light on the nature and the effects of severity, as, of course, Professor Lasswell, himself a political scientist, brings out. Severity not only has psychological and social psychological aspects, but also sociological aspects. Each demand for "severity" deserves study. It can be logical and politically sound in certain situations. The word is not univocal, and each widespread and interesting use of it calls for its own meaning analysis.

In notorious brawls, feuds, and murders in southern Illinois, Baker Brownell points out,

> . . . the officers of the law took little action or were ineffective. The law, in fact, was thin and timid. Its weakness was one important reason for the expansion of the trouble. For the principals . . . , as men of prominence and power in the community, were not easily controlled. . . . With no overlord to intervene in the rather loose, primitive democracy of such a situation, the concept of the law itself needs to have an unassailable objectivity and prestige, or law will fail.[33]

"Unassailable objectivity and prestige" are not identical with severity, needless to say, but that they are entirely unrelated is to be doubted. Mr. Brownell continues:

> The law was largely personal in its administration and remains personal through most of the troubles and killings even down to today. It could be warped, sometimes with humanity and good sense, sometimes with infinite corruption. In the bloody vendetta and later in the Klan wars, the coal wars, the bootlegger killings, the wildfowl slaughters, and other villainous episodes of the region the law was too often adjusted flexibly to the friendship, the kinship, or the economic and institutional interests of the administrators.[34]

The consequences of lack of law enforcement—especially if combined with bad law—may range from serious to catastrophic. For instance:

> The Ku Klux Klan became powerful in the Illinois wedge during the prohibition era. Its masked and insulting visitations to churches began, says Angle, in Marion in May 1923 and thereafter such visits,

[32] *Ibid.*, pp. 19–20. Reprinted by permission.

[33] Baker Brownell, *The Other Illinois*. New York: Duell, Sloan and Pearce, 1958, p. 82. Reprinted by permission.

[34] *Ibid.*, pp. 82–83. Reprinted by permission.

with a gift each time of twenty-five or thirty dollars, were not unusual. By the end of August the Klan numbered many thousands. And the ministers loved it. Not all, to be sure, but enough to disgrace the Protestant Church. They gave what blessings they could muster to the ritualized voodoo and bigotry and the sinister clowning of the men without faces.

They embraced the Klan because the Klan was on their side against the bootleggers, at least for the moment. . . . As certainly as night follows day the Klan led to murder and other villainies. The insolence and secrecy of these busy bodies made it inevitable, but the ministers swallowed it whole.

There was, of course, the other side. Town and county government was often rotten.[35]

Let us not unwisely place strictures on severity. Nevertheless, the paramount finding of social scientists regarding severities no doubt concerns their source in psychologies that we are not especially pleased to admit of. *Knowledge* of their source may, however, force salutary effects on our mentality and attitude.

If we contemplate the possibility of interplanetary voyaging, we expect to work within the frame of knowledge about gravitational fields. But when we hear that behavioral research shows that middle classes exhibit unconscious bias against upper or lower classes, or that they are addicted to punitive demands based upon unconscious sadism, our response to this knowledge may have rather different results. *If we are middle class,* we may ask whether we choose to possess and to express such perspectives in the future. Possibly our choice is to liquidate the current orientation, and we take the steps necessary to modify ourselves sufficiently to live up to the choice.[36]

Analysis may also lead us to modify our images and conceptual models. Thus, a more circumspect reflection on democracy may result in a modified image. Placing democratic ideology alongside the realities of community power structure, we may give up the fantasy of the people's self-rule as a system that can operate without leaders and followers, with chiefs but no Indians or *vice versa.* To say so does not imply conceding democracy. The meaning of democracy is rather that authority proceeds from below.

The higher roles are supposed to act on behalf of and to be responsible to the lower roles. What this means in practice is that the

[35] *Ibid.,* pp. 85–86. Reprinted by permission. Reference is included to Paul Angle, *Bloody Williamson.*

[36] Lasswell, "The Normative Impact . . . ," *loc. cit.* p. 38. "This means that anyone who observes us in the future may formulate different laws of the impact of the class factor on bias, since the relationship will itself be changed." (Italics added.) Reprinted by permission.

decisions of the higher roles have to be made by discussion. That is to say, hypothetical decisions are made and communicated to the lower roles. The lower roles react to these hypothetical decisions and as a result of these feedbacks the decisions are modified until substantial agreement is reached—the discussion proceeds until the high roles announce the decision which receives the approval of the lower ones or at least of a majority of them. There may be different conventions of what constitutes approval—majority rule is only one of these, and it does not constitute an essential part of the democratic process.[37]

. . . democratic structures in which there is no adequate leadership, that is, in which the feedback is destructive of the decision-making process on the part of higher roles, are . . . unstable.[38]

## A SKETCH OF THE "POSITIVE" CONTRIBUTION

We have already, gradually, moved over to positive contributions of social science to the realization of ethical conduct. If the negative contribution consists in showing impossibilities and near-impossibilities, as well as in pointing out discrepancies between good intent and actual bad practice, the positive contribution consists in showing what can be done about it, and especially in proposing realizable alternatives. Thus, Lasswell:

. . . while the behavioral sciences conform to the logic common to all science, the laws formulated at any given time may not continue to hold for future events. Our behavioral knowledge may appear to be partly falsified as prediction of the future, thanks to the contribution that it makes to insight; the process of insight may shape the sequence in which conduct unfolds through the future. Clearly, insight is a more important function of social knowledge than prediction.[39]

Professor Lasswell's selected list of procedures of insight and enlightenment includes, besides the free association of ideas in a social context, the taking of statistical surveys of opinion, the use of equivalencies in the carrying on of communication, the employment

[37] Kenneth E. Boulding, *The Image*. Ann Arbor: The University of Michigan Press, 1956, pp. 99–100. Although it happens to be convenient here to quote an economist, the interpretation of democracy presented is supported by many political scientists. Reprinted by permission.

[38] *Ibid.*, p. 101. Reprinted by permission.

[39] Lasswell, *op. cit.*, p. 38. Lasswell contrasts insight with understanding. Insight "depends upon the overcoming of anxiety barriers, upon enduring the anxieties generated when unconscious processes are admitted to conscious awareness." Insight "comes from the 'private anguish of the mind' during the pursuit of self-knowledge by methods of free association." Reprinted by permission. *Ibid.*, p. 37.

of methods of continuing consultation, and the keeping of a logbook. We shall quote part of an example of his involving a log, this being one of the simpler devices but also a device which in use leads both to increase of understanding and to new insight. The logbook is "adapted to the needs of the conscientious person who is trying to live up to his normative ideals." Lasswell describes how the president of a college used it.

> As a former teacher the president belonged to that amiable company of college presidents determined not to lose touch with students. When I met him, he was telling us how fine his relations were to the campus. We challenged some of his statements, and he eventually volunteered to try to carry a logbook. He made it as simple as possible. His equipment consisted of a packet of blank cards. He filled one out each day. Because the president was interested in his relations to the student body, he decided to put down an 'S' every time he talked to a student. . . . The president compiled quite a list of categories before he began recording. After a month he got curious about the results and asked his secretary to add up the figures. He was horrified to discover that in a month he had talked to no student, save on disciplinary matters, and rarely to any faculty member ranking below . . . dean or department chairman. Obviously, the president had a fantasy-image of the self that required correction. And the logbook procedure was capable of contributing data to the reassessment.[40]

## THE DE-DISTORTION OF OUR IMAGES

Another way in which social scientists create improvements in administration and in public reaction to enforcement procedures is by presenting a more accurate formulation of a problem. For instance, everyone is willing to admit that we live in an age of comparative lawlessness and of widespread lawlessness on the part of some among our young people. But what is "lawless"? Who is lawless? Just how shall the problem be specified, and what procedures against it are sensible or workable?

This is "the hoodlum era, the era of the switchblade and the zip gun, the flailing belt buckle, the slashing bicycle chain, the era of violence on the streets." [41]

> We are fast approaching the time when this nation will have over 2,000,000 persons who have appeared in juvenile courts. Although our child population has increased only 25 percent from 1948 to

[40] *Ibid.*, pp. 30–31 Reprinted by permission.
[41] Arthur Hoppe, *San Francisco Chronicle.*

1957, appearances before juvenile courts have increased almost 150 percent in the same period.[42]

The problem is world-wide. In Moscow, according to *The New York Times* and *Awake,* there is adolescent gang violence,

> in the large new housing projects near Moscow University and near the Leningrad Highway. In one project a colonel's son was asked by a gang to help rob his father's apartment. He refused. The teen-agers pinioned the boy, took a sledge hammer and broke both his legs. In an adjacent block two teen-age girls were raped in a week by another gang. Parents in the new buildings have formed their own volunteer groups to work with the youngsters and try to bring the situation under control. [42a]

The public perception of these problems is not clear and accurate, however, according to criminologist Lewis Yablonsky of the University of Massachusetts. He does not accept the picture "of a violent delinquent gang . . . in which there is a shrewd leader having several crafty lieutenants who plot a strategic attack on rival gangs for territorial rights." The image of the shrewdly organized gang is imposed by the public and perhaps by publicity seekers, who would make gangs of children as highly organized as a march of the Rebecca Lodge. The gangs tend in fact to be highly disorganized, Yablonsky reports, with ever-changing membership and with leaders who are emotionally disturbed. Often the gangs get into wars by chance rather than by design.

Yablonsky studied the widely headlined, "vicious Balkan gang" in New York. The individual youths were out that night for a variety of reasons. The gang did not even have a name until after the fracas and the arrest. "How did we get our name? Well, when we were in the police station, the cops kept askin' who we were. Jay was studying history in school—so he said how about the Balkans. So we told the cops—we're the Balkans—and that was it."

A frequent therapy, redirecting the mob's activities into constructive channels like baseball, may only serve to bring the boys together and organize their gang activity. Otherwise:

> Violent gangs are a loosely organized structure motivated by a core of a few severely emotionally disturbed gang leaders, who are self-appointed, borderline psychotics with delusions of grandeur or persecutions.

Yablonsky's recommendation is that the leaders be treated, not as "hoods," which is what they like, but as mentally ill, which is what

[42] Senator Thomas C. Hennings, Jr.

[42a] From *Awake,* published by Jehovahs Witnesses. Reprinted by permission.

they are. But treating them as "crazy" or "nutty" would also take away from their glory. The leaders who incite to violence should be treated psychiatrically in an institutional setting.[43]

There is also an amount of rumpus and ruckus on our college campuses. Efforts to associate the college fracas with delinquency or with communism are deplorable in their misunderstanding and lack of insight. William Guthrie, former Executive Dean of Student Relations at Ohio State University, President of the National Association of Student Personnel Administrators, recognizes the cost of student crusading but likes to see students fired up over causes. The waste, the foolishness, and the misunderstanding on the part of the community ought to be weighed against the alternatives, "apathy and privatism."

> The way of the dean of students is not easy—particularly in a time of world ferment and in the spring of the year. But explosions of misdirected energy do less harm than the intellectual decay of conformity. Ohio State, a school so large that it requires an intricate meshing of freedom with order, is well off with a dean who understands this problem.[44]

The habits of apathy, privatism, and conformity-regardless-of-right induce not only intellectual, but also moral, decay. College administrations should have the resources, the energy, and the maturity to elicit student initiative. Their ultimate concern is to provide leadership for the coming generation. Knowledge and insight increase the quality of administration, whether it be in juvenile court, on the campus, in the factory, or in our consulate in Hong Kong. If forcefully communicated, they raise the level of public discussion and decision. Insight into people and society means corrected images, new and more worthy perspectives, better vision.

The acceptance of social science is sometimes slow, *because* it requires insight, because acceptance implies a new look at one's own attitudes and emotional responses. What we have to learn from social science often concerns relations and events that we *already* know about. Perhaps it is distressing to have it all retold in another language and with the values reorganized, as, for instance, by Thorstein Veblen. As Boulding remarks, Veblen likely was no great economist, but he invented the undying phrase, "conspicuous consumption." The master of such restatement today is not a social

[43] From a report to the American Association for the Advancement of Science, as reported by Arthur J. Snider, Science Editor, in the *Chicago Daily News*, Dec. 27, 1960.

[44] F. P. Locke in the *Dayton Daily News*. Reprinted by permission.

scientist but an expert in philosophical optics, John Wisdom of Cambridge University. We have hardly begun to make a systematic study of insight, but certainly both the social sciences and philosophy are going to make major contributions to such study in the next years. We may reasonably hope for knowledge, at last, about insight.

Increments in our knowledge of man and society, and especially increased depth and range of perspective, enlarge the sphere of moral autonomy.

### MORAL PRINCIPLE

Knowledge and insight provided by the social sciences do not reduce the pointfulness of moral principle, but they change it. Libertarian and scientific standpoints do not demand that we give up moral principle, but they do demand that we really rise to the point of information. We are asked to concede rectitude values that only constitute fantasies of individual or social psychology. We are asked not to proclaim intentions that are at cross-purposes with our real bent, that are not really meant. We are asked not to proclaim moral principles that connect with no intermediate maxims and therefore have no bearing on our actual conduct. We are asked not to be logical and consistent at the expense of insight and understanding, not to live in the heroism of the past and charge the costs to a quixotic present.

The social sciences may even require, on occasion, that we,

> alter our primary or sanctioning norms as a result of exposure to the flow of intelligence. Acting as responsible citizens of society, or as specialized ethicists, religionists, scientists, or men of affairs, we shall perhaps make use of procedures designed to deepen insight and understanding.
>
> . . . the potential impact of the behavioral sciences is to give depth and scope to the interaction of norms and knowledge and to supplement the formulation of norms with the application of procedures capable of narrowing the gap between aspiration and actuality.[45]

The search for knowledge and the desire that it have impact even on our norms and aspirations are thus represented as integral to responsibility. The role of philosophers and ethicists will be found in the clarification of meaning and desire, in the understanding of responsibility itself and of its grounds. Many American and British philosophers join hands with the social scientists in insisting on the

[45] Lasswell, *op. cit.*, p. 38. Reprinted by permission.

acquisition and the effective use of knowledge. They are in this way true to their Socratic tradition.

Socrates paradoxically said that tyrants do what they do not really wish to do. All men choose to do good.

> He is saying that what they choose is different from what it would be if they were clearer-headed and better informed. Did Isaac willingly bless Jacob? Did Oedipus willingly kill his father? The answer to these riddles is the answer to the riddle that Socrates sets us in his paradox: and the answer is 'Yes and No.' Isaac willingly blessed the man whom he blessed, Oedipus willingly killed the man whom he killed: but if he had known more, Isaac would have withheld his blessing: Oedipus, if he had known more, would have stayed his hand.
>
> Socrates seems at first sight to be denying that the tyrants deliberately choose to do what they in fact deliberately choose to do. But his point is different.[46]

His point is that tyrants, although they may deliberately choose what they choose, do so in ignorance of the disvalues that accrue to themselves through their tyranny, and with exaggerated expectations of positive value. In a time of rapid increase of knowledge about the world and man, knowledge of values, wisdom concerning principles, and responsibility itself are at a premium. If *they* are not supremely valued, not fraternity, but fratricide, is the warranted expectation. The instruments of extinction are at hand. Man commands the extremes of choice: He can choose tyranny or extinction, or he can choose a rare and difficult blessedness in brotherhood.

In America, we need more science, more clarification, and greater moral responsibility and courage. To read that, according to our own scientists, "Russia is throwing much more scientific brainpower into her governmental problems than the Western nations" [47] is discouraging or challenging, depending on how we respond to the opinion. That (*e.g.*) the Ohio State Medical Association should approve a resolution commending the House Committee on Un-American Activities "on its diligence in the task of inquiring into threats to the existence and security of the government of the United States" is, in view of the habits of the Committee, just discouraging. Clearly, one of the alternatives that we face is the possibility of science in respect to means, but primitivism of the systematic hate and suspicion variety in respect to ends.

The assertion that this is a time for greatness is plain understate-

[46] Renford Bambrough, "Socratic Paradox." *The Philosophical Quarterly,* Vol. 10, No. 41 (October 1960), p. 299. Reprinted by permission.

[47] The reported consensus among scientists gathered at the M.I.T. Centennial.

ment. At the same time that our avowed enemy appeals with every new gadget of propaganda to world-wide masses that are only beginning to become aware of their shortages and frustrations, we are called upon to act responsibly and with knowledge and insight. If we can live up to our highest traditions, we can meet the challenge. We cannot meet the challenge by trying to beat the totalitarians of the right and the left at their own game. This choice also is ours.

# PART IV

# Equality: Social Orders and Meanings of "Equality"

# 10

# COMMUNISM

Communism is one of the most sensitive subjects in America today. It is also, however, one of the most important to us, and merely to hate it is not an adequate response. If understanding and insight should inform our decisions and actions, then we surely should want to learn all we can about Communism[1] in theory and practice, its relation to socialism, its contrasts and comparisons with capitalism.

We want our intelligence services to know the last secret detail that is relevant to governmental policies and acts. In a democracy, however, we citizens at large, by election and by direct and indirect pressures, are the final arbiters of foreign and domestic programs: Also we bear the ultimate responsibility. It is not, therefore, a matter of moral choice if we should attempt to understand communism: It is our duty.

This may sound somewhat strange, in view of all the efforts that have been made during the last years to use "communism" as a derogatory label in domestic politics; actually, that is an old story, and, as we shall see, one that plays into the Communists' hands. Despite all the red herrings that have been drawn across our path, we

[1] I capitalize "Communism," because I am speaking of Marxist and Bolshevik Communism—not of Platonic, primitive, religious, or other brands of communism.

proudly possess some of the greatest experts on Communist theory, history, and practice in the world. These experts [2] are researchers supported in their research by our major universities and by the armed forces. It cannot here be our aim to summarize their results. For the most part, our interest will be confined to the statement of a perspective on theoretical Communism from the standpoint of knowledge and moral choice. Nevertheless, since so little public attention has been given to the background of Marxism, a brief biography of Marx is included.

## KARL MARX (1818–1883)

*No thinker in the nineteenth century has had so direct, deliberate and powerful an influence upon mankind as Karl Marx.*[3]

Marx was born and reared in Trier, a small town far up the Mosel valley from Coblenz, almost to the borders of Luxembourg and France. In the years of his boyhood, his home town stood outside the main course of industrial development in Europe. His early years were happy, his relations with his father excellent. His father was a lawyer, a Jew who had accepted the Lutheran state religion of Prussia.

The second personal influence on his youth was Baron (Freiherr) von Westphalen, the Marx family's neighbor and friend. The baron opened his library to young Karl, took him for long walks, and cultivated his taste and nourished his self-confidence. Marx developed a passion for great literature, especially for Shakespeare, which stayed with him for life. Before his twenty-fifth birthday, Karl married the baron's daughter, Jenny von Westphalen. (Her brother became famous as a reactionary Prussian Minister of the Interior, from 1850 to 1858, in charge of all Prussian state police.)

In those early days in Trier, Karl Marx knew nothing of capitalism and industrialism. He was imbued with that liberal German upper-class culture which had been particularly influenced by Goethe and Schiller. His later scorn of the bourgeois—still the extreme pejorative in the vocabulary of Communism—may be understood as expressing not only the lack of confidence of some industrial

[2] No one knows as well as experts how much of their subject-matter is not known. It is not surprising, therefore, that Harrison Salisbury, himself an authority on Russia, has said, "There are no experts on Russia, only varying degrees of ignorance."

[3] Sir Isaiah Berlin, *Karl Marx.* London: Oxford University Press, 1948 (first published in 1939), p. 1.

laborers in the employer class, but, above all, the aristocrat's contempt for trade and philistinism.

After a college year at Bonn, Karl transferred to the University of Berlin. There he soon shifted from the study of law to the study of philosophy. In the 1830s, the philosophy of G. W. F. Hegel dominated the intellectual scene at Berlin; and Karl Marx soon became an ardent young Hegelian of the left. He had connections with Edward Gans and Bruno Bauer, the latter an atheist professor on the theological faculty. When Bauer was removed from his post, Marx decided to submit his doctoral dissertation, on differences between the materialist philosophy of Democritus and that of Epicurus, to the University of Jena. He received his Ph.D. in philosophy, *in absentia* from Jena, in 1841. Marx could not teach philosophy, however, because of his radicalism.

A friend, Moses Hess, was at that time arranging the publication of a liberal businessmen's newspaper in Cologne; he got Dr. Marx to submit articles. After only a few months, Marx became editor-in-chief, and, by making his *Rheinische Zeitung* into the principal radical organ in Germany, he became famous in his twenty-fourth year. When the Prussian censor suppressed the paper, Karl married and went into exile in Paris. Of this, his earliest newspaper career, Carr says, "It is one of Marx's minor titles to fame that he was the first noteworthy German journalist." [4]

Marx subsequently lived for a short time in Brussels, but from his thirty-first year, in 1849, until his death in 1883, Marx lived in London. There he reared his family, wrote articles for the *New York Herald Tribune,* made speeches to worker organizations, and toiled at the British Museum on his chief work, *Das Kapital.* During the earlier years in London, Marx and his family suffered extreme want, despite frequent receipts of notes from his close friend and collaborator, Friedrich Engels. Engels provided not only money, but also his considerable knowledge of military, foreign, and commercial affairs, and his literary talents. Eventually, when Engels retired from the Ermen and Engels cotton-spinning firm in Manchester, he moved to London and bought proper houses for both himself and for the Marx family and undertook to pay Marx 350 pounds a year.[5] Marx suffered various disabilities in his later years,

[4] Edward Hallett Carr, *Karl Marx, A Study in Fanaticism.* London: J. M. Dent and Sons, Ltd., 1934 and 1938, pp. vi and vii.

[5] F. A. Hayek refers to Engels as "a wealthy patron who enabled him [Marx] to devote his life to the elaboration and propagation of doctrines which the majority of his contemporaries heartily detested." *The Constitution of Liberty.* Chicago: The University of Chicago Press, 1960, p. 128.

but he was able to travel to English and European spas, and even to Algiers.

### BRIEF COMMENT

Marx's early supporters in Berlin and Cologne looked upon him as the enemy of "medieval religion and politics," not of capitalism. Marx became an opponent of capitalism in consequence of philosophical, economic, and social speculation, and following on observation and study of the horrible conditions under which industrial workers lived on the Continent, but especially in England. The fundamentals of the position for which he is famous were first worked out between 1843 and 1845 in Paris. He then "arrived at a clear position personally and politically." [6]

Carr remarks, in light of the impression that young Dr. Marx made even earlier on Hess (who himself is "credited" with having converted both Marx and Engels to communism), that "The dominant personality of Marx, capable of inspiring the strongest attachment as well as the strongest repulsion, reached its full stature at a remarkably early stage of his career." [7] In any case, there is much evidence that Marx had a happy childhood, that he became a radical, not from weakness and frustration, but out of strength and conviction. Berlin says, that Baron von

> Westphalen had humanized and strengthened that belief in himself and his own powers which was at all periods Marx's single most outstanding characteristic. He is one of the rare revolutionaries who were neither thwarted nor persecuted in their early life. Consequently, in spite of his abnormal sensitiveness, his *amour-propre,* his vanity, his aggressiveness and his arrogance, it is a singularly unbroken, positive and self-confident figure that faces us during forty years of illness, poverty and unceasing warfare.[8]

Since 1883, no doubt to the chagrin of the Bolsheviks, Marx' body has lain buried in Highgate Cemetery in London. All his observations of, and harsh judgments on, capitalism and its social consequences were made a hundred years ago. *The Communist Manifesto* was written by Marx and Engels in the winter of 1847–1848; *Capital* (Vol. I) was published in 1867. Marx devoted his life to the study of capitalism as a then existing fact, and to communism as

[6] Berlin, *op. cit.,* p. 80.
[7] Carr, *op. cit.,* p. 18.
[8] Berlin, *op. cit.,* p. 33. Reprinted by permission.

something not then anywhere existent.[9] The capitalism and industrialism observed by Marx were of early English and Continental variety, dating from before and during the American War between the States.

Who, however, can lay Marx' ghost? The image of capitalism and the image of us held by Marxists the world over, however anachronistic, exist; and in their essential traits they are taken from the works of Karl Marx. Of course, the differences between capitalism as described by Marx and capitalism as it exists today are not the only points of misunderstanding and confusion. Mr. S. C. Allyn, Chairman of the Board of the National Cash Register Company, said, after his trip to Russia:

> When we added up our findings on our way home, we decided that there is more misinformation about the United States in Russia, and more misinformation about Russia in the United States than ever existed before between two leading powers of the world.[10]

Mr. Allyn adds that Russia must take the essential blame for this. However, we have to face the facts of the case, and one important fact in the total situation is that Marx's thought and works are a kind of fundamentalists' bible to the Communists. We have to deal with Russian and Chinese peoples whose images of us are permeated through and through with Marxist paints. These images are drawn from many sources. *Das Kapital* is not widely read by Russians and Chinese, but it is of course read by many intellectuals, and through them affects the mentality of all. The *Communist Manifesto* is widely read, and we shall look briefly at capitalism as Marx and Engels there described it.

## THE COMMUNIST MANIFESTO

In October, 1847, a revolt began in Sicily. It turned out to be the beginning of a whole series of revolutions. Marx and Engels were drafted by the Communist League to write a manifesto in order to present the League's world outlook and to propagandize for a major proletarian revolution.

Marx and Engels aimed to understand the present as the embodiment of the past and the womb of the future. They conceived the flow of events in terms of conflict among classes, and the classes in terms of industrial and economic roles and groupings. The questions

[9] The Paris Commune was in existence for two months in 1871.
[10] From NCR Factory News, 1956. Reprinted by permission.

Marx asks concern the effects of basic industrial changes on our larger loyalties and interests. It was Marx' conviction that the proletariat could only accede to power and form a classless society, after war to the death with the other classes. The Marxist morality in non-Marxist countries descends directly from this belief. Any action is right, if it leads to confusion and dissolution of existent institutions.

Marx was not at all disposed to belittle the accomplishments of capitalism. He and Engels lay stress on two great accomplishments of capitalism: the vast increase in physical production and the organization of vast networks of social relations, especially for production. They look on the colossally increased production as a step toward the revolution. They praise it fulsomely, as if history meant it for the nourishment of the communists. But capitalism is also praised for having beaten down guild restrictions and monopolies, for the political defeat of the aristocracy, for opening up the world market, and for providing railways and other communication systems. Capitalism "has been the first to show what man's activity can bring about." Its wonders surpass Egyptian pyramids and Roman aqueducts. During a rule of scarce one hundred years, the bourgeoisie

> has created more massive and more colossal productive forces than have all preceding generations together. Subjection of Nature's forces to man, machinery, application of chemistry to industry and agriculture, steam-navigation, railways, electric telegraphs, clearing of whole continents for cultivation, canalization of rivers, whole populations conjured out of the ground—what earlier century had even a presentiment that such productive forces slumbered in the lap of social labor?

So there is full admission of the seven wonders of capitalism, including its power over social relations in the interests of getting work done. But this power itself is conceived as uncontrolled.[11] Capitalism, Marx says, is like the sorcerer who cannot control the powers that he has called up. From Marx' perspective, then, capitalism can't be more than transitional. It will have to land somewhere, and the only place it can land is on revolutionary ground.

The only significant classes under capitalism, according to the *Manifesto,* are the bourgeoisie—the capitalists, the owners and employers—and the proletariat—the wage-laborers "reduced to selling

[11] The pride of capitalism has been, in respect to its ethical character, that an entirely objective and impersonal institution, namely the free market, distributes wealth with justice. Marx denies the validity of the market as arbiter and looks on the creative power of capitalism as a whole as something wildly veering from crisis to crisis. We shall raise questions about Marx' historicism and his rejection of objectivity in principle and *in toto* a little later on.

their labor-power in order to live." [12] Marx pretended not to pass moral judgments on particular capitalist employers; blameworthiness on the part of the individual capitalist was of little account. The bourgeoisie as a class was held to have outlived its usefulness; indeed the very activities of the bourgeoisie advanced the doom of capitalism and capitalist. Expanding his commercial and industrial activities, even spending time and money to fight off agitation and revolution, the capitalist was only performing his historical role, advancing the ingress of post-capitalist society, sealing the fate of his own class.

## A SHOCKING PARADOX

Capitalism, like science, is adventurous, willing to incur hazards, ready to embark on journeys of uncertain destination. "Let us go where the enterprise—or the events, or the facts—leads us." Though it may be a shocking paradox, a main component of the animus of the world's greatest revolutionary is his feeling that capitalism is too revolutionary. Marx finds capitalism too restless, moving too fast in the dark, too rapidly metamorphosing the social relations involved in production and exchange.

> The bourgeoisie cannot exist without constantly revolutionizing the instruments of production, and thereby the relations of production, and with them the whole relations of society.

All earlier industrial classes had fought to conserve old modes of production in unaltered forms; but

> constant revolutionizing of production, uninterrupted disturbance of all social conditions, everlasting uncertainty and agitation distinguish the bourgeois epoch. . . .

Having an orderly, synthesizing mind, Marx found revolutionary capitalism unbearable. Change ought to be rational and comprehensible, but the transformations from 1840 to 1870 were mad with speed, unpredictable, incomprehensible. Did Marx hate change as only aristocrats can hate change? Or was Marx impressed by the hardships change imposed on workers and their families?

Even the cheap prices for which capitalism was notable were viewed in the light of their disrupting effect.

> The cheap prices of its commodities are the heavy artillery with which it batters down all Chinese walls. . . .

[12] The deliberate neglect to mention the European aristocracy was remarkable in 1848. Although Marx knew the aristocracy "was there," he considered it powerless, essentially dead.

## THE WORKER REDUCED TO A CHEAP COMMODITY

Marx saw the worker with his power to do work as if reduced to a commodity, forced to sell himself piecemeal, "exposed to all the vicissitudes of competition, to all the fluctuations of the market." The laborer had become a mere appendage of the machine; capitalism organized workers "like soldiers" into industrial battalions.

> We see the workers in the noisy mob of business people only when they troop off to the factories in the gray light of the early morning or hurry home again in the dusk when the factories eject them in droves after the day's work.[13]

The worker is alienated from the system. He has no title to it either in letter or spirit. Moreover, he has no security in it. He is used when needed; and when he is not, he is tossed off like an obsolete piece of machinery. His insecurity is specially guaranteed by "the epidemic of overproduction." The laboring man is alienated, excluded, made insecure, reduced to proletarian status. Besides all that, according to Marx, he is robbed.

Although the *Manifesto* credits capitalism with great accomplishments, it accuses the system of having realized such feats at the expense of labor. The workman sinks deeper and deeper. Pauperism "develops more rapidly than population and wealth." The theory of the systematic robbery of workers is developed in *Das Kapital,* Marx' major work. Labor is seen as the primary constituent of exchange value, but wages are determined on a competitive market which keeps laborers at the subsistence level. The factory owners require their employees to work far beyond the time necessary to maintenance of that subsistence, however, and pocket the difference. In brief, workers get enough to keep them in existence; but they work long hours to keep the owners rich. Marx' primary account of the origin and increase of capital is that it came out of this surplus, a surplus actually expropriated from labor.

One can see at once that the combination of this labor theory of the origin and increase of value and this theory of profit originating in expropriation is well fitted for propaganda against capitalism. "Capitalism has been called the profit system, and Marx made it synonymous with exploitation." [14]

[13] The preceding quotations are from the *Manifesto.* This one is from Marx' "official" biography: Franz Mehring, *Karl Marx,* translated by Edward Fitzgerald. London: George Allen & Unwin Ltd., 1936, p. 377. Reprinted by permission.

[14] L. M. Hacker, "The Anticapitalist Bias of American Historians," *Capitalism and the Historians* (Ed. F. A. Hayek). Chicago: The University of Chicago Press, 1954, p. 91.

As for the low wages and the terrible conditions of employment under early capitalism, there is no denying them. But there is much evidence that conditions on the farms of England and Ireland were much worse still. Two reasons why we have so much historical documentation of the bad conditions in factories are (1) the opposition of Tories to the ascending capitalists, and (2) the reports of bureaucratic factory inspectors.

> People entered, or imagined that they entered, a mill and saw the little factory hands engaged in monotonous routine; and they thought 'how much more delightful would have been the gambol of the free limbs on the hillside; the sight of the green mead with its spangles of buttercups and daisies; the song of the bird and the humming of the bee . . . (but) we have seen children perishing from sheer hunger in the mud hovel, or in the ditch by the wayside.' Compared to the factory workers, the agricultural laborers lived in abject poverty, and the work to which country children were put was far more exhausting than factory labor.[15]

Engels, already in 1844, published his *The Condition of the Working Classes in England*. One of the most dramatic passages in all Marx' own writing is the section of *Capital,* Vol. I, "Illustrations," in Chapter 23, "The Universal Law of Capitalist Accumulation." Marx used statistics to show that the richer England became, the poorer became her workmen, representing a capitalist "law of increasing misery." Through lengthy quotations from official Public Health reports, Marx showed that there were in industrial areas as many as 16 persons sleeping (sometimes in stages) in one room; in another case, 26 in two rooms; that there was "mass starvation in London," and that generally the diet of workers and their families was inadequate.

This picture of the wickedness of early capitalism is still very much with us. Thus, Bertrand Russell said:

> The industrial revolution caused unspeakable misery both in England and in America. I do not think any student of economic history can doubt that the average happiness in England in the early nineteenth century was lower than it had been a hundred years earlier; and this was due almost entirely to scientific technique.[16]

[15] W. H. Hutt, "The Factory System of the Early Nineteenth Century," *Capitallsm and the Historians, loc. cit.,* p. 180. The quotation contained in the above is from William Cooke Taylor, *The Factory System.* (London, 1844), pp. 23–24.

[16] B. Russell, *The Impact of Science on Society.* New York: Columbia University Press, 1951, pp. 19–20. Reprinted by permission. One wonders anyway how a subjectivist or emotivist like Russell can compare so objectively the average happiness in England in the early eighteenth and early nineteenth centuries. It's nonsense.

As Professor Hayek comments on Russell's bland assertion, "The intelligent layman can hardly be blamed if he believes that such a categorical statement from a writer of this rank must be true." [17] But it is only the theory of the paperbacks. Economists and economic historians have long since given up believing that the workmen of the nineteenth century were worse off than their grandfathers and great-grandfathers. The condition of the laboring class was poor; but it was better than that of the poor in the country,[18] and better than that of earlier generations of laborers.

* * *

The only way that the workers can prevent themselves from being systematically robbed, according to Marx, is to become an organized proletarian class and rid themselves of the capitalist system. The *Manifesto* explicitly proclaims that the fruits of victory for the laboring class lie *not* in immediate results (*e.g.*, lowered hours and higher pay), but in ever-expanding union to be turned against the capitalist class and the capitalist system.

The proletariat may be confident, meanwhile, says Marx, that it must inevitably win. For the advance of capitalism brings on its own inevitable ruin by reducing all workmen to the same miserable status, by ruining unsuccessful bourgeois themselves, and at the same time by bringing larger and larger numbers of workers together, associating them, combining them into an overwhelmingly powerful enemy of the capitalist class. "What the bourgeoisie therefore produces, above all, are its own grave-diggers."

Precisely in performing their normal function successfully, the capitalists, as a class, carry capitalism through a series of stages to a narrow monopoly of wealth and capital and a correspondingly enormous, angry, organized proletariat, and thus to revolution. The way capitalism is, Marx said, it can't last, can't help destroying itself, destroying its own highest class—the capitalists themselves spearheading the destruction of their system. The inevitability of the process, of the movement through capitalism to revolution and communism, inheres in the very nature of capitalism.

## CLASS WARFARE AND OBJECTIVITY

Marx was influenced in his thinking by Hegel and by Feuerbach. He agreed with Hegel in the criticism of abstract moral principles and in

[17] F. A. Hayek, *Capitalism and the Historians,* p. 13.

[18] The condition of many of our own agricultural people in America today is ignorance and poverty. My wife teaches in a rural consolidated school. A seven-year-old girl was added to her class the other day. The girl had missed school for three months, because she had no shoes.

the rejection of abstract principles of explanation. Hegel had begun by asking himself, among other questions, why the French Revolution had failed, why it had only culminated in Napoleonism and then reaction. Hegel's answer was that the French Revolution had put too much stock in abstract rationality. He tried, himself, to incorporate the empirical and the historical with the rational, and said that "the rational is the real, and the real is the rational." He insisted that any lasting change of institutional structure must be related to roots that are even older than those torn up. Any permanent or significant progress must be nourished from roots deep beneath the surface of history and politics.

The essential weakness of the French Revolution that predetermined it to failure was that it stood on abstract principle. It was born, but it could not grow. It could tear down; but it could not build, for it had no foundation on which to raise a substantial superstructure.

> The advance of the doctrine that all men were brothers, that national, racial and social differences were the artificial products of defective education, was arrested by the Hegelian counter-thesis according to which such differences, for all their apparent irrationality, expressing as they do the peculiar genius of a given race or nation, are grounded in some historical necessity. . . . Reform must spring from traditional soil. . . .[19]

Hegel found that the entire cultural panorama was a manifestation of the spirit of the age. Spirit is always in movement and has a fundamental direction. Every process is one of tension between opposing forces, the thesis and the antithesis, and these are transcended by new synthesis. The transcending is sometimes by a sudden leap, *e.g.*, by a political revolution, and the synthesizing outcome incorporates both earlier forces. For Hegel, this process is dialectical; and, at least retrospectively, it is rational and understandable.

Marx found meaning in Hegel's attempt to understand historical events as following dynamic laws that do not show on the surface. But he accepted Feuerbach's criticisms of the notion of "spirit" and "spirit of the age." He soon came to agree with Feuerbach that the substance underlying historical and social phenomena was not spiritual but material. For one thing, from Feuerbach's perspective, the spirit of the times was only the totality of the phenomena composing it; to say that it determined the phenomena was only to substitute a foolish redundancy.[20] Feuerbach found a more adequate explanatory principle in the sum of the material conditions of the

[19] Isaiah Berlin, *Karl Marx: His Life and Environment.* London: Oxford University Press, 1948, pp. 56–57. Reprinted by permission.

[20] *Ibid.*, pp. 75–76.

time. Men live as they must, given their needs, the material environment, and the techniques known to them for coping with physical stuff in the interest of filling their needs.

Both Feuerbach and Marx are "Social Freudians": They "discovered" that men in their material distress seek to escape into a spiritual life and construct fantasy realms of art, religion, and ethics. In particular, Marx criticized the established political economy, contending violently that its theories expressed a bourgeois or class doctrine, that it was really based on class interests and class prejudice.[21] The classical economists opposed legal restriction of hours (opposed a statutory ten-hour day), and Marx very likely got from them the idea that "the struggle for a standard of working time was the most important part of the struggle" of the capitalist and laboring classes.[22] Marx' theory of surplus value and expropriation can thus be understood as a generalization of conditions that prevailed in the mid-nineteenth century. Marx first labeled political economy as,

> a rationalization of the interests of the ruling class, and then generalized this contention into a statement that ideas, conceptions, art, literature, law, religion are a superstructure built on the basis of productive forces. . . . Marx first applied to public and scientific consciousness what Freud later applied to individual consciousness. . . . Marx contended, not that the bourgeois economist is a hypocrite or a humbug, but that the real sources of his ideology, as a rule not realized even by himself, lie deeper down, in unconscious beliefs and myths related to the interests of his class. Marx's 'Social Freudism' therefore existed before Freud, just as Malthus' Darwinism existed before Darwin.[23]

This "Social Freudianism," of course, implies the relativity of human knowledge. In Marx, it implies particularly the relativity of knowledge to unconscious economic interest. It was especially this set of ideas that impressed Lenin, whose preoccupation was to grasp the future; and the one great clue that he found was the Marxist dialectic, which he described as,

[21] Ferdinand Zweig, *Economic Ideas: A Study of Historical Perspectives.* New York: Prentice-Hall, Inc., 1950, pp. 11–12. Nassau Senior was then the most influential economist in England and in the forefront of the battle against new social legislation. The relevant tract by Marx is *Zur Kritik der politischen Oekonomie* (1859).

[22] *Ibid.,* p. 12.

[23] *Ibid.,* pp. 12–13. "Ideology is a process accomplished by the so-called thinker consciously, indeed, but with a false consciousness. The real motives impelling him remain unknown to him, otherwise it would not be an ideological process at all. Hence he imagines false or apparent motives." Engels' letter to Mehring, 14th July, 1893, Marx-Engels Correspondence. London: Martin Lawrence, Ltd., 1934, p. 511. *Ibid.,* p. 13.

> the doctrine of development in its fullest and deepest form, free from one-sidedness. The doctrine of the relativity of human knowledge which provides us with a reflection of eternally developing matter.[24]

Summarizing, and following Hunt, we can say that:

> It was from Feuerbach that Marx got the idea that all the products of the human mind were the reflection of material conditions. Only while Feuerbach taught that material conditions determine being, Marx taught that they determine *social* being, that is, the life of the community.[25]

Lenin accepted from Marx the dialectic, with its materialist interpretation, the doctrine of class struggle, and, in general, the application to capitalism. He found capitalism and its dialectical antithesis, socialism, to have historical meaning for Russia, even if Tsarism slowed down the development, and even if the land was mostly given to agriculture. He accepted "the Mission of Capitalism," *i.e.,* its historical role in the economic development of Russia, and he anticipated the same transformations, antagonisms, and contradictions: "centralization, concentration, proletarianization, monopolization, expropriation and pauperization." [26]

Our own primary concern in all this will be the relativity of knowledge—the rejection of objectivity—and the doctrine of inevitable class warfare.

## THE EMPHASIS ON THE PRACTICAL

*. . . philosophy stands in the same relation to the study of the real world as onanism to sexual love.—Karl Marx.*

Marx' primary criticism of other philosophers was that they concerned themselves with knowing rather than with doing. Thus he wrote:

> The chief defect of all previous materialism—including Feuerbach's—is that the object, reality, sensibility, is conceived only in the form of the object or as conception, but not as human sensory activity, practice [Praxis], not subjectively. . . . (Feuerbach) does not conceive human activity itself as an objective activity. Consequently in the *Essence of Christianity,* he regards only the theo-

[24] From *On Dialectics,* 1915. *Ibid.,* pp. 58–59. Lenin read Feuerbach while in Siberia, and studied Marx all through his adult life.

[25] R. N. Carew Hunt, *The Theory and Practice of Communism, An Introduction.* New York: The Macmillan Company, 1951, p. 10. Reprinted by permission.

[26] Isaiah Berlin, *Karl Marx,* p. 79.

retical attitude as the truly human one, while practice is conceived and fixed only in its dirty-Jewish form. Hence he does not grasp the significance of 'revolutionary,' or practical, critical, activity.[27]

As Professor Hook has emphasized, the true middle term for Marx between nature and history lies in the concrete needs of men. "The interaction between physical conditions and social organization is history. Philosophies themselves are critical historical activities which arise to fill some social need. . . ." [28] "According to Marx, the whole of theoretical culture, including science, arises either directly or indirectly as an answer to some social want or lack." [29]

> In Marx's eyes, the whole theoretical tradition of western-European philosophy with its apotheosis of Reason, its conception that thought has an underived and independent history, its identification of theoretical activity with divine activity, and when divinity was no longer fashionable, with the "highest" type of human activity—all this represented a religious pattern of behavior. He found this tradition moulding the outlook even of those who imagined themselves extremely radical.[30]

Marx thought of *Praxis* as fundamental. It was not something to be contrasted with science, because science itself had its practices and its connections: "Marx rarely discusses science without underscoring the influence of modern commerce and industry upon its development." [31] Marx' second thesis on Feuerbach is:

> The question whether human thought can achieve objective truth is not a question of theory but a practical question. In practice man must prove the truth, *i.e.,* the reality, power and this-sidedness of his thought. The dispute concerning the reality or unreality of thought—which is isolated from practice—is a purely *scholastic* question.[32]

The eighth thesis is, in Professor Hook's terms, "a heuristic principle of the first importance":

> Social life is essentially practical. All mysteries which mislead theory into mysticism find their rational solution in human practice and in the understanding of this practice.

[27] Quoted from Sidney Hook, *From Hegel to Marx: Studies in the Intellectual Development of Karl Marx.* New York: The Humanities Press, 1950, pp. 273–274. Reprinted by permission.

[28] *Ibid.,* p. 278.

[29] *Ibid.,* pp. 277–278.

[30] *Ibid.,* pp. 279–280. Reprinted by permission.

[31] *Ibid.,* p. 281.

[32] *Ibid.,* p. 281. Reprinted by permission.

The tenth thesis is most often quoted:

> Philosophers have only interpreted the world differently: The point is, however, to *change* it.

Professor Hook, who found here a major contribution to philosophy and the conception of truth, comments that:

> Practice, on every conception of philosophy except Marx's own, is a foreign element in philosophy. It involves decision, conflict, an element of partisanship in behalf of one among a number of possible alternatives. The kind of philosophy Marx called for and which his own activity illustrated, involved not merely risking an idea but risking one's whole person in carrying it out. Without an attempt at carrying out ideas, philosophy becomes a mere playing with possibilities unrelated both to the quest for truth and the furtherance of the good life—its professed objectives.
>
> Philosophical activity may be conceived as action in behalf of values and interests which have been criticised by knowledge and reason. The very fact that philosophy is an activity in a world of space, time and incompatible interests, makes it clear that its goals cannot be absolute truth or absolute justice. But the fact that action is thoughtful makes it possible to achieve beliefs which are truer; the fact that thought leads to action makes it possible to achieve a world which is more just.[33]

## SUMMARY, COMMENT, AND CRITICISM

I agree with Professor Wayne Leys that Marx raises some questions which have significance in social ethics:

> What are the fundamental changes in the mode of economic production? What economic classes are created by these changes?
>
> What forms of organization and government, what ideas and customs are being undermined by these changes and conflicts?
>
> How are various issues related to class conflict? How do class interests determine ideology?
>
> Is there a long-term, perhaps inevitable, change that will be required to overcome the disequilibrium? [34]

Marx is one of the first philosophers to have studied the industrial revolution. He rejected Hegel's interpretation of history, believing that it depended too much on nationalism to explain historical conflict. Marx saw that "the disturbing causes were economic, and the

[33] Hook, *loc. cit.*, pp. 305–306, 306–307. Reprinted by permission.

[34] Wayne A. R. Leys, *Ethics for Policy Decisions*. New York: Prentice-Hall, Inc., 1952, pp. 142–143 and pp. 190–191. Reprinted by permission.

conflict was between classes." [35] Marx accordingly elicits the further questions:

> How are the opinions of all individuals and groups determined by their class bias, and which partisans are to be opposed because they do not represent our class, regardless of the "reasonableness" of their opinions?
>
> How can every action in every circumstance of life, including even science, the fine arts, and humor, be directed so as to accelerate the crisis and bring it to a head? [36]

Anyone who today did not put these questions to himself in relevant ethical deliberations would be unrealistic. There are, however, some equally important questions that should be fired back.

Is there no valid loyalty higher than loyalty to one of the conflicting groups?

Is there no thinking better than class-motivated thinking? If not, is Marx only representing the proletariat, a class to which he did not belong?

What about the main line of Western thought and its insistence that the truth about man and the world is the proper goal of scientific observation and thought? If Marx rejects this goal, does he then confess to standing on a position of sand? Is his "truth" only class truth?

What firm basis can the revolutionary proletariat find for believing that the society to follow will be classless? That the proletariat will not remain just that, the proletariat? How distinguish legitimate reform or revolution—on Marx' terms—from mere restlessness and foolish adventuring? Does Marx not promise "down with those who are up," but fail to give any real promise of concrete betterment for those who are now down?

Marx hit the point hard that class differences may be irreconcilable, and that class warfare may be the only sensible action. But how are Marx and Marxists to put the pieces back together again? Do they not arouse apocalyptic expectations, *e.g.*, among any gullible Negroes inside the U.S.A., rather than probable and really credible ones? And what does Marx have to offer the underdeveloped nations? Hate, followed by foundering?

If minority classes and underdeveloped nations want concrete progress, they will have to face up to the facts of political and economic life—of human life in all respects. They may then well consider the possibility that Communist propaganda is nothing more than an ideological bunny-hop.

[35] *Ibid.*, p. 141.
[36] *Ibid.*, p. 143. Reprinted by permission.

In the long run, the failure to attach significance to objectivity, truth, and science will be more than the Communists themselves can endure. To look on science as fundamentally conditioned by class struggle and class ideology is to betray science. It is interesting that, although Mao Tse-Tung quotes Lenin, "Practice is more important than (theoretical) knowledge because it not only has the virtue of universality but also the virtue of direct reality," he himself hurries to include a role for "scientific experiments." For he says:

> According to the Marxist, man's social practice alone is the criterion of truth in his cognition of the external world, for in actuality human cognition is verified only when man arrives at the results predicted, through the process of social practice, namely, through the processes of material production, of class struggle, and of scientific experiments.[37]

The cost to the Soviets of such an attiude toward basic research and science as is characteristic, not only of Marx and Lenin, but generally of Mao, too, will be dreadful in the end. For basic science, be it physical or social, is not a product of economic classes engaged in a class struggle, but of men intent on knowing the truth. Of course, *intent on knowing truth* implies that one is willing to risk his person and welfare, to commit himself: But for truth, not for some other thing. We may grant also, with Lasswell and others among our own social scientists, that a difficult self-reappraisal and revaluation may be required. But we are not inclined to confuse Marx' Bandwagon Argument and Mao's propaganda with science. Playing on Marx' understanding of philosophy as "changing the world," Mao sets forth the struggle of the proletariat as "to reconstruct the external world; to reconstruct their own subjective world, that is, to remold their faculty of knowing."

> What is meant by the external world which is to be changed includes the persons who are opposed to that change. To be remolded they will have to go through a stage of compulsion before they enter in a stage of remolding of their own accord.

We call it force and brain-washing. It is not science.

## NIKOLAI LENIN (VLADIMIR ILYICH ULYANOV) (1870–1924)

The first man to institute and rule a great Communist state was Lenin. His father was a distinguished school administrator; when Lenin was three, his father was made a member of the Russian petty nobility.

After his father had died, but when Lenin was not yet seventeen,

[37] Mao Tse-Tung, *On Practice* (1937). Italics added.

his beloved older brother went to St. Petersburg to the university. He studied chemistry, and he provided the explosives for a naïve and feckless plot on the life of Tsar Alexander the Third. He was hanged.

In her memoirs, Lenin's wife wrote:

> When we had become closely acquainted, Vladimir Ilyich once told me about the attitude of the Liberals towards the arrest of his elder brother. All acquaintances shunned the Ulyanov family . . . There was no railway at Simbirsk at that time, and Vladimir Ilyich's mother had to go by coach to Syzran in order to go on to St. Petersburg, where her eldest son was imprisoned. Vladimir Ilyich was sent to seek a companion for the journey. But no one wanted to travel with the mother of an arrested man. Vladimir Ilyich told me that this widespread cowardice made a very profound impression upon him. This youthful experience undoubtedly did leave its imprint on Lenin's attitude towards the Liberals.[38]

Lenin spent the rest of his life thinking, writing, organizing, studying the works of Marx and Engels and other socialists and revolutionaries, developing his own (Leninist) doctrine of revolution in and for Russia. The last six years of his life he dominated the ruling party of the U.S.S.R.

Lenin modified Marxism in various ways.

First of all, Marx had for the most part anticipated that Communism would arise first in highly industrialized countries, say, in Germany. The Communist society was to be an inevitable consequence of advances of capitalism. Lenin's problem was to develop a program for an immense country that was predominantly agricultural. Instead of revolution in a country controlled by a tight capitalist oligarchy, with a large, trained proletariat, Lenin planned for a revolution by a small minority of industrial workers and intellectuals. Revolution and the dictatorship of the proletariat are more important by far in Leninism than they are in Marxism. Lenin planned to use intense force swiftly and cultivated revolutionist cells in Russia. When the Great War ruined Russia, and the Kerensky government could not maintain order, Lenin's Bolsheviks and their cells were the strongest native force in Russia.

Second, Lenin was less "internationalist" than Marx and Engels. His first concern was to make the Revolution stick in Russia. Stalin carried Lenin's policy even farther.

[38] Quoted by permission from Bertram D. Wolfe, *Three Who Made a Revolution.* Boston: Beacon Press (by arrangement with Dial Press), 1955, p. 64. Perhaps there is here a lesson for liberals: Might the course of history have been a little modified, if at least one liberal had befriended Lenin's mother in that time of stress?

Third, Lenin looked on the capitalists as exploiters of the proletariat, but he also looked on the workmen of the industrialized countries as themselves exploiters of the people in underdeveloped countries. The colonial natives were the real proletariat. This doctrine of imperalism has been a major propaganda force in the Far East, where the noncommunist labor movements in America, Britain, and Europe are themselves sometimes suspected of imperialist policy.

Like every other politician and statesman, Lenin has often been charged with opportunism.[39] He was an opportunist, but that is a significant charge against him from the perspective of one or another Marxist orthodoxy, not from our own point of view. More important for us is that the Leninist Revolution succeeded in Russia; that the defense under Stalin held in World War II; and that today we face Communism as a great existing fact in Russia and in most of eastern Europe and China.

[39] "A veteran Communist once told me that, in an argument with Lenin, he quoted a passage from one of the latter's books which contradicted current Soviet policy. Lenin asked him for the number of the page, which he smugly produced. 'When you get home, tear that page out,' he was told." Mervyn Jones, "The Time Is Short." *Conviction*. London: MacGibbon & Kee, 1958, p. 188.

# 11

# CAPITALISM

## TRANSITION

Marx was not the first person to disapprove the bourgeoisie. Madame la Marquise de Sévigné, a sensitive aristocrat of seventeenth-century France, expressed in one of her celebrated letters a complete absence of feeling for sixty bourgeois who were to be hanged on the morrow and for a sixty-first who had already been cut in quarters and exposed in the four corners of Rennes.

Two centuries later, while Marx was toiling on *Das Kapital,* John Stuart Mill composed this glowing tribute to the bourgeois, this recognition of his accomplishment, his ideology:

> For, what is the peculiar character of the modern world—the difference which chiefly distinguishes modern institutions, modern social ideas, modern life itself, from those of times long past? It is, that human beings are no longer born to their place in life, and chained down by an inexorable bond to the place they are born to, but are free to employ their faculties, and such favourable chances as offer, to achieve the lot which may appear to them most desirable. Human society of old was constituted on a very different principle. All were born to a fixed social position, and were mostly kept in it by law, or interdicted from any means by which they could emerge from

it. As some men are born white and others black, so some were born slaves and others freemen and citizens; some were born patricians, others plebeians; some were born feudal nobles, others commoners and roturiers. . . . Among the industrious classes, only those who were born members of a guild, or were admitted into it by its members, could lawfully practise their calling within its local limits; and nobody could practise any calling deemed important, in any but the legal manner—by processes authoritatively prescribed. Manufacturers have stood in the pillory for presuming to carry on their business by new and improved methods. In modern Europe, and most in those parts of it which have participated most largely in all other modern improvements, diametrically opposite doctrines now prevail. Law and government do not undertake to prescribe by whom any social or industrial operation shall or shall not be conducted, or what modes of conducting them shall be lawful. These things are left to the unfettered choice of individuals. . . . The modern conviction, the fruit of a thousand years of experience, is, that things in which the individual is the person directly interested, never go right but as they are left to his own discretion; and that any regulation of them by authority, except to protect the rights of others, is sure to be mischievous. . . . It is not that all processes are supposed to be equally good, or all persons to be equally qualified for everything; but that freedom of individual choice is now known to be the only thing which procures the adoption of the best processes, and throws each operation into the hands of those who are best qualified for it. Nobody thinks it necessary to make a law that only a strong-armed man shall be a blacksmith. Freedom and competition suffice. . . . In consonance with the doctrine, it is felt to be an overstepping of the proper bounds of authority to fix beforehand, on some general presumption, that certain persons are not fit to do certain things.[1]

Business and bourgeoisie continue to represent vulgarity to some people. An American professor wrote a few years ago:

> Now business is in power again; and with it will inevitably come the vulgarization which has been the almost invariable consequence of business supremacy.[2]

Another professor, however, exceeds even Marx and Engels in praising capitalism for its accomplishments. Nor does he confine himself to technical and industrial achievements but credits capitalism and the bourgeoisie with the great ethical and cultural achievements of Western man.

[1] John Stuart Mill, *The Subjection of Women,* Second Edition. London: Longmans, Green, Reader, and Dyer, 1869, pp. 29–30.

[2] Arthur Schlesinger, Jr., "The Highbrow in American Politics." *Partisan Review,* vol. 20, 1953, p. 162.

> The much abused "shopkeepers" have abolished slavery and serfdom, made woman the companion of man with equal rights, proclaimed equality before the law and the freedom of thought and opinion, declared war on war, abolished torture, and mitigated the cruelty of punishment. . . . Bourgeois civilization has created and spread a well-being, compared with which all the court life of the past seems meagre.[3]

The quiet broad favor that our system elicits suggests that it is something more than just the interest of capital that is at issue. Reasonably consistent support of our system by labor unions suggests that its advantages do not all accrue to stockholders, bond owners, and banks.[4]

Capitalism cannot be correctly appraised apart from its relationship to libertarian tradition and principles. As an existent fact, capitalism is much older than Marxian Communism. It has more on its conscience, and more to its credit. Its inherent growth pattern lies more revealed, more self-revealed. It is more experienced and sophisticated, but also more contorted by age and by the historical situations that it has had to face. Capitalism is a tough system, and its muscles deserve appreciation. Capitalism deserves to be observed in its own traits and tendencies but also in its various relationships.

The Communist picture of the life of American business and labor is discolored and distorted. The Communists are not quite certain whether to paint the American workman as beat, stumbling off to unsafe factories before sunrise with only a Ry-Krisp or two in his lunch pail, or to paint him instead as the younger brother of the capitalist ogre, holding hands with him under the table, and drinking coffee grown for both by Brazilian peons, the slaves of capitalistic imperialism.

In our own image, businessmen do not hold all the aces and do not pull all the strings. To make a profit these days requires successful collective bargaining with labor unions and successful negotiation with state and federal commissions, and often even with legislatures, over prices, costs, taxes, and markets. It has always required selling products or services to customers who—as a rule—can go

[3] Ludwig von Mises, *Socialism*. New Haven: Yale University Press, 1951, pp. 440–441. Reprinted by permission. Nor are Von Mises and Von Hayek the only students of capitalism and socialism who prefer the former.—It is interesting that Fidel Castro and others are contrasting the accomplishments of Communism with those of Christianity. Castro is reported to have said, "Why pray for daily bread—Communism provides it." But to date, the record of capitalism is best in providing bread; but it may have provided Cuba with too much imperialism and too little bread.

[4] Nor do we say with Sumner H. Slichter, "We do not live, as we used to think, in a capitalistic society but in a laboristic one."

elsewhere, and obtaining supplies and credit and work from suppliers and bankers [5] and workers who also—as a rule—"can go elsewhere." The brewing and distilling industries have had the experience of seeing their business "liquidated in the public interest"—or, to be exact, turned over to smugglers and bootleggers.[6]

Pure capitalism has never yet been national policy anywhere, certainly not in the U.S.A. In the twenties, America had the graduated income tax, the Eighteenth Amendment, high tariffs. Today, one might better say that pure capitalism has been ruled *out* as national policy. The Employment Act of 1946 has these declared purposes: (1) provision of employment opportunities for those able, willing and seeking to work; (2) promotion of maximum employment, production and purchasing power; and (3) deference to other needs and obligations and other considerations of national policy.[7] Our government is significantly, officially, powerfully, in the act. And little objection is heard today against the *principle* of government participation in the economic and financial picture, so far as the Employment Act of 1946 is concerned, or the Federal Reserve System and Board, the FCC, the FTC, the NLRB, the FSC, the other FSC, *etc., etc.* Control, regulation, and incitement are admitted. Still, actual entry by government into business is not; it remains highly exceptional.

## CAPITALISM

In capitalist countries, most factories, machines and machine tools, stores and warehouses are owned by private persons or by associations of private persons. The accepted incentive to undertake production and trade is the chance to make a profit. Characteristic of capitalism are private ownership of the means of production and the investment in, and employment of, such means to make a profit. Saving and investment are primarily functions of individuals and free associations, not of the state.

All definitions, in the end, contain an element of arbitrariness; and definitions of capitalism are no exception. Capitalism is not belied by the government of the United States if it stockpiles food and

[5] The founder of the First National Bank in Chicago is said to have turned out his largest account, since he morally disapproved of one of its practices.

[6] These industries are still specially sensitive about their public relations. Brewers, distillers, and sometimes even automobile manufacturers propagandize against drunken driving.

[7] Quoted here from Wayne A. R. Leys and Charner Marquis Perry, *Philosophy and the Public Interest.* Copyright, March 1, 1959, by the Committee to Advance Original Work in Philosophy. P. 61.

ammunition for governmental purposes; nor is the U.S.S.R. capitalist because some of its nationals buy government bonds from personal thrift. As we shall here have to limit ourselves primarily to theoretical and general considerations, exceptions could be found to many of our assertions.

We depend on private companies to see that there is milk at the door in the morning, that we shall have a shirt to cover our back, that our house and garage will get built. Private, profit-seeking companies provide most transportation, sell vehicles, build roads, and deliver most electricity and gas.[8] We correctly look on our country as capitalist, despite the ownership by federal and state government of roads, highways, canals, and rivers, lakes, and postal service, and despite full federal control over the armed services [9] and federal, state, or local control of the police, firemen, *etc.* Atomic energy is produced by agencies of the federal government. Utilities, transportation systems, and broadcasting companies operate under license and report to federal and state commissions; the railroads are perhaps in some ways over-controlled. Moreover, income tax is paid not only on wages and salaries, but also on profits. The system is not operated wholly by capitalists for capitalists.

Many other nations that are usually classified as capitalist countries and that are generally thought of as allied with us in their economic habits have state owned monopolies in areas where we do not, especially in utilities and railroad transportation, but sometimes also in various heavy industries, tobacco, and entertainment.

For all that, there is a contrast, sometimes a sharp one, between capitalism and Communism. In U.S.S.R., there is almost no private industrial capital whatever. Even fruit-water stands and hot-dog stands are generally owned and operated by government and served by government servants. *All* major economic functions are performed by the state. Decision concerning investment is made by officers of the state. Prices are set by officers of the state.[10] Higher education is controlled by the state.

We in America are ultimately dependent on our private economy and also on our private institutions of learning, publishing houses, hospitals, clinics, and so on. There is a real difference of both ide-

[8] Water is provided by private companies in some American communities, *e.g.*, in Peoria, Illinois.

[9] The East India Company used to maintain a navy and a 40,000-man army in India. Some companies may have their own police force, but we do not expect private companies to have armies.

[10] There are free markets for vegetables and other produce here and there, but the amount of land which can be diverted to private production for sale in these markets is strictly limited.

ology and organization that is not adequately symbolized by *free enterprise*. Free enterprise rather narrowly denotes undertakings to make profit.

For many years, half our college students have attended private institutions, none of which make a money profit. The solvency of these institutions depends on philanthropy. Their support comes from individual rich men, corporations, foundations, alumni organizations, churches, and unions, none of whom can be forced at law to give. Many other universities and colleges receive support from states and municipalities, but none are directly financed by the federal government except West Point, Annapolis, and the Air Force and Coast Guard Academies.

Although working for profit is characteristic of many private corporations, of others it is not. By definition, nonprofit institutions do not seek a profit. But we also do not ordinarily think of seeking higher wages and salaries as "seeking a profit" (which is not to say that labor negotiators have their eyes closed to corporation profits). Much earned profit is in fact paid to employee stockholders: Sears, Roebuck Company is "controlled by itself." Much profit is paid into foundations, and passed on by the foundations to institutions of higher learning, hospitals, and other nonprofit concerns. Much more is paid to insurance companies, and by them in turn to annuitants and beneficiaries.

A related point ought also to be made as a psychological point. Many executives, even major ones, rarely think in terms of profit. They do their jobs as do other employees. For instance, if you are the head of public relations for a company, your job is to see to the company's public relations, not to make a profit on your budget.

Perhaps these points would hardly warrant mention, except to straighten out the comparison with Communism. In the U.S.S.R., approximately one-third of the national product is syphoned off by the state for purposes of state. The comparable figure for the United States is only twenty per cent. Most of the difference, about eleven per cent of the gross national product of the United States, is invested by private companies in new plants and other facilities. (In 1960, sixty billion dollars were spent by U.S. companies in capital investment.)

In both the United States and the U.S.S.R., nationals consume about two-thirds of the gross national product. In the U.S.S.R., the rest is invested or otherwise spent by governmental or Party fiat for purposes of state. But in the United States, government spends only one-fifth, and the rest—ten to twelve per cent of the gross national product—is invested by private interests.

Our conviction is that persons, alone or freely joined together, can do most things better than the state, better than the masses, can. We let these persons and corporations reap part of the profit and bear most of the losses. Under ordinary circumstances we should say, "It's their property," and we should assume that they will do with it as they will. From the same conviction, we also depend on private parties to support and orient nonprofit corporations—not only colleges and hospitals, but also trade, professional, and research organizations and labor unions. We do depend, not just on business and government, but also on this third great class of organizations, the nonprofit category. The private ownership and administration of production facilities is but one consequence of our overarching philosophy and of its acceptance from motives that are not just economic, but also political, religious, and aesthetic. Perhaps today no one is more wary of government intervention than organized labor, which has recently, ironically and paradoxically, been under more and more pressure from free enterprise to accept it.

### EGOISM AND ALTRUISM

Egoism is a policy of self-seeking. It is too narrow and restrictive a policy for anyone in his right mind. The man who concerns himself always with his own good grows too self-conscious, with the result that he finds less and less enjoyment. This psychological fact is known in ethics as the Hedonic Paradox: If you always seek your own pleasure, you'll grow bored with yourself, pained by your pleasures. Egoism is thus self-defeating. Self-concern, moreover, can blind us to the environment and thus inhibit our knowledge and strength, and cut us off from allies. Institutions that are self-centered suffer similar disabilities; the strength of institutions always in some sense or other consists in the services that they render. The corporation that has no further aim than to hold on to what it has got is decadent.[11]

A great ethicist and psychologist, Bishop Joseph Butler, pointed out that self-love is restrictive as an explanatory principle in a double sense. Not only does it falsely explain our highest actions, which are outgoing and have as their target the welfare of someone else, but it misinterprets the nature of human passions. To act directly from some passion or other is not to act from self-interest or egoism, is not to act in the interest of the self, but is to act as impelled by the pas-

[11] In this connection, one may think of the expansionism of Sears after World War II *versus* the caution and long-on-cash position of Wards.

sion. Unless hypnotized, I act from my own impulses and motives; but my impulses and motives do not always have my self as object.

Altruism (a word coined by Auguste Comte) is a policy of seeking the good of others. It is vague and not clearly limited in denotation; it encourages do-gooding in individuals and paternalism in the state and other institutions. It has not been very widely adopted as a term of praise; most persons would arch an eyebrow at hearing a man called "altruistic," quite as they would were he called "egoistic." It is likely to symbolize catering or even condescending attitudes. But why should so much suspicion greet a policy or attitude of seeking the good of others? There are several reasons. (1) If the policy is announced, it may conceal an iron fist; we tend to doubt the integrity of someone who claims to be giving something valuable away. (2) Our self-respect is damaged, if we look on ourselves as the beneficiaries of altruism. A policy of altruism is likely to help us less than it belittles us. (3) Altruism tends to make its beneficiaries dependent and, if pressed far enough, to enslave them.

This distinction between egoism and altruism has lost its standing in psychology and economics, and in ethics it is certainly at least suspect. We should like to know, not whether capitalism rests on egoistic human impulses, as often charged—and sometimes even *claimed*—but what it does to people who participate in it in various capacities, and how it relates to other institutions and habits. We should like to know of Communism, not whether it is altruistic, but what it accomplishes, and what *it* does to people.

We might well ask, incidentally, *who* is supposed to be altruistic under Communism? If the leaders, then to that extent Communism is reduced to paternalism, and its subjects are reduced to the condition of dependent children (whatever is given them, moreover, must be produced by their own labor). If the citizens generally are supposed to be altruistic, then we might well fear such a flood of benevolence that even the strongest individuality will be washed away.

As a matter of fact, the Bolshevik government *is* afraid of too much internal peace and advertises persistently on billboards all over the U.S.S.R.: "Criticize. Criticize constructively and you help to do a good job."—Our own government, fortunately, does not have to go begging for criticism!

## INDIVIDUALISM

"Individualism" is for many an honest contemporary thinker a pejorative term. This is owing to its peculiar historical association with "free enterprise," with governmental inactivity in The Depression, and with the egoist and the quaint Yankee. It has been said that today in American big business—of all places—the most widely accepted meaning of "individualist" is "socially unadaptable."

Individualism can still be meant, however, to stand for the notion that the individual is the chief locus of value in society. It then means, negatively, that the social whole "has no value or significance not derived from its constituent individuals." (Webster's.) It implies that all social practice is subject to final judgment in terms of consequences to individual men.

Besides this meaning of individualism as end, it has another as means. It means fostering the education and initiative of the individual in the social interest. It means placing our blue chips on the ingenuity and fertility of individuals in order to attain social results. As social policy, individualism implies maintaining the political and economic independence of the individual, fostering his initiative, his education, his personal interests and objectives. As Mill stressed, society needs the energy of strong, matured individualities. The improvement of society is difficult of achievement, and only the strongest minds and wills can bring it about. Individualism means that the laggard gets stirred into action. It means a point of origin for new ideas, new perspectives, new movements, new pressures.

Individualism means, instead of thwarting the idiosyncratic interest of the specialist, eliciting it, drawing it out, giving it rein to find its gratification. A policy of individualism, consequently, is likely to maximize the benefits accorded by the division of labor. It delights the specialist and encourages him in the acquisition of intricate skills and technologies, and thus it contributes to the achievement of more and of more diverse, social values.

Social value,

> is definitely not confined to those things which are useful or gratifying to all of us alike. . . . What is useful to or gratifies any member of a society and brings no harm or distress to any other, has by that fact some measure of impersonal and social value.[12]

The serious student and the intellectual, with their highly individual interests, should be among the first to recognize this truth.

A remarkable feature of capitalism, with its individualistic orientation, has been its success in delivering goods—and careers—to men and women of the greatest diversity of need and interest. Social

[12] C. I. Lewis, *The Ground and Nature of the Right.* New York: Columbia University Press, 1955, p. 71. Reprinted by permission. Tendency to the misconceived contrary view is "one root fallacy of totalitarianism and the regimented society."

values that do not sooner or later come home to roost in individual lives are frauds. The personal values [13] that ought to be final and consummatory have real opportunity of realization under our system. Fraudulent values are generally found out and buried by free consumers and critics.

## COLLECTIVISM

Collectivism contrasts with individualism. Collectivism does not entail totalitarianism, but totalitarianism and collectivism have been closely associated historically. Collectivism means collective control by society as a whole, especially by the state and its corporations, over the production and distribution of economic goods and services, and hence also over industrial employment. It implies a single administrative bureaucracy in charge of everything, including any efforts made in the direction of decentralization and pluralism. But how any real bastions of independent thought and criticism, of taste and discrimination, of economic production for minorities, can be constructed or kept in existence is not at all obvious. The manager reports to the central administration, the union executive reports to the central administration,[14] and the political commissar and his deputies all report to the central administration. If you please, the central administration reports to the people; but then the people's courts and the people's armies, meanwhile, report to the central administration.

The collectivist may emphasize service to others and the collective good; but there are really no *independent others,* there is no systematic way of cognizing what things make up the collective good (like free markets and elected parliaments). Altruism is just one more name for the relation between the state and its subjects. A monolithic collective power, it seems, will always in the end be more worked up about its own security than about any other value that might conceivably be presented for estimation. In Russia this has been equally true of the Tsarist and the post-Revolutionary bureaucracies.

Besides the obsession with security, there is a mistake in economic principle. Since decisions about production and payroll, as well as decisions about offerings and prices of merchandise, are all made by one central administration, how well can the economy be expected

[13] "Personal values—value to me, value to you, value to John Doe." *Ibid.,* p. 70.

[14] As early as 1933, William H. Davis was pointing out that we were "centuries ahead" of Russia in industrial relations: Our great vertical unions do represent the interest of masses of laborers at the bargaining table; in the U.S.S.R. there is no such really independent, fighting representation.

to aim at the gratification of individuals, or at optimum satisfaction of the aggregrate of individuals? Economy takes the form of efficiency, and efficiency of simplicity: Any growing tendency toward variety and complexity will be put down, unless it happens to associate itself immediately with the urge toward collective security. Simplicity and standardization will be imposed on all wares, on employees, on buyers, on everything and everybody. The collective altruism provides potatoes, turnips, and army-style canned meat; but those who want rice, fish, coconut, poi-poi, steak, champagne, or gin (instead of vodka) must proceed through political channels. Abstinence [15] is built into the system. The "inevitable" blandness is worse, even worse than all the TV programming, commercialism, vulgarization of government, and opera bouffe of bourgeois society.

The system accused of reducing all values to money can be reformed in the interest of human beings. The system that would "give to each according to his needs" is the one that passes over the individual and neglects his wants. In the collectivist society there will be, sooner or later, only one audience, one market, and one arbiter.

### THE ACTUAL SITUATION

To describe the actual situation requires recurring effort, for the actual situation changes. Fortunately, we are not here required to concern ourselves with events that change from day to day.

The American public is, in any case, understandably concerned about our relative power and progress, and it is wise to recognize at full value the great accomplishments of the Communists in Russia, as Marx recognized at least some of the accomplishments of capitalism. The Communists have established their capacity to carry through great collective projects. They have tossed satellites into orbit and speared the moon.

We should not necessarily attempt to stay in the forefront in every single technique and tactic. A country that won *all* the gold medals in the Olympics would be overemphasizing sports.

We should, however, look to our fences. Our system at its best is more than adequate to all the stresses put upon it by Communism. Our duty is to maintain it in good faith and with great energy. We shall be strong, if our people do not elect loutish legislators to harass the scientists and engineers on whose spontaneity and genius we de-

[15] Ambrose Bierce defined an abstainer as a weak person who yields to the temptation of denying himself a pleasure. Collectivists yield on behalf of all of us.

pend. We shall be strong, if fair procedures are maintained in industrial relations, and the full vigor of industry and labor is steadily elicited. We shall be strong, if we undertake without fear or quibbling, great governmental projects, appropriate to the times and circumstances.[16] We shall be strong, if we maintain well-considered national and international goals, if we intelligently, sternly, universally, learn and educate.[17] The great means of conservation and progress is to do our best in our own way.

### THE NECESSITY OF CHOICE

We must, however, really do our best in our own way. To be defensive, to applaud prolixity from the right bench, is not enough. Instead of capitalism, the rightists often support feudalism.

Facts must be faced, problems must be faced up to, choices made, and decisions energetically carried through. Insistence on some narrow statement of our ideology only makes it more difficult to see and solve problems. Capitalism is not cut and dried. Such terms as "laissez-faire," "the Industrial Revolution," "the spirit of capitalism," and "capitalism" itself have, for the most part, been manufactured and propagated by enemies of capitalism.[18] Our great economists, emphatically including the conservative ones, have looked on capitalism as an evolving economic order. The very success of capitalism results in change of form. Debtor countries, like the United States before 1914, become creditor countries—and must adopt policies to fit their new status. Highly competitive industries turn into monopolies because of the success of certain firms in the market. Monopoly industries can be made over into competitive ones.

[16] How many and how great projects the state and federal governments shall undertake is best decided according to need and experience. A priori decision that projects are "socialistic" or taxes too high, based on dollar amounts without consideration of the need for the projects, violates empirical principle.

[17] "Honesty requires the reporter in Russia to note again and again that the Communist educational system does not waste talent. It recognizes it, and it sees to it that it is given opportunity. Our critics may protest, but there is a very real reason to say there is more opportunity for the talented in Russia than at home. This talent is used, of course, for objectives different from our own, many of which we properly reject. But we would be foolish to avoid knowing that in Russia the boy or girl who shows ability is recognized and given every educational chance, whereas, too many of ours do not have a chance because of geography or the economic status of their parents."—Ralph McGill, *Dayton Daily News*. Moscow dateline, August 1, 1959.

[18] T. S. Ashton, "The Treatment of Capitalism by Historians." In *Capitalism and the Historians*. Ed., F. A. Hayek. Chicago: The University of Chicago Press, 1954, esp. pp. 54–62.

The ideology of privilege should not be allowed to pass for conservative capitalist thought.

> Although a communistic revolution is often feared as the most likely cause of widespread redistribution of wealth, several stock market panics in the past fifty years have shifted property rapidly enough to delight the heart of Karl Marx.[19]

Historically, capitalism has not favored the privileged. For instance, predatory undercost selling has been opposed, both in ethics and law, because it does favor the longest purse. The fittest are those best fitted to do the world's work, not those who, perhaps by luck, have the longest purse.[20]

One cannot say, of course, that the privileged never get favored. But capitalism as a system of fair competition almost certainly separates people from their undeserved privileges more quickly than does any other system. Long before Marx, capitalists of note not only detested privilege but also anticipated "Social Freudianism." Thus, James Mill wrote, ". . . people who are privileged invariably rule in their own interests, even when they think they are serving the community, for they deceive themselves as to their true motives." [21]

Communist theory opposes privilege, especially privileges accruing to capital. In practice, there are classes of persons who have limousines and chauffeurs and fresh vegetables. These people are said to manage successfully in finding good places for their sons and daughters in the hierarchy.

Most people, no doubt, put up with the political economic order that they are born into until they find some adequate reason to aim at another one. Were those Minnesota farmers who, in the Depression, had rope around the neck of a judge who was carrying through a foreclosure action even aiming at fundamental change? Prosperity is the best preventive of revolution and rebellion.

Managers and executives tend to take things as they come in practice, knowing that they are safer than others in a change of economic order. Experience under Labor governments in Britain has confirmed that the men who know how to manage operations are the best insulated. Paradoxically, the reasons for labor support

[19] Harold M. Finley, *Everybody's Guide to the Stock Market.* Chicago: Henry Regnery Company, 1956, p. 125.

[20] Frank Chapman Sharp and Philip G. Fox, *Business Ethics: Studies in Fair Competition.* New York: Appleton-Century-Crofts, Inc., 1937, p. 169.

[21] Mill's *Commonplace Book.* Quoted in W. H. Burston, "James Mill on the Aims of Education." *Cambridge Journal,* VI, 2 (November 1952), pp. 79–101.

of capitalism are stronger. Big government does weaken the labor movement, while big business offers the precise challenge that elicits the most powerful vertical unionization. Under Communism there is no autonomous representation of labor. Government encompasses everything. In our own system there is real dependence on organized labor to keep up the market by an exertion of effective economic and political power. Perhaps it is too much to ask that all businessmen should appreciate this fact, but those who sell to ultimate consumers appreciate it.

Some organizations and professions are unduly concerned with the danger of government intervention and social legislation. The American Medical Association has been painfully concerned about state interference with medical practice and research. Meanwhile, much important medical research is directly supported by the federal government anyway, *e.g.*, at Harvard Medical School and for that matter at the Graduate School of Business Administration (Fatigue Laboratories). Physicians cannot easily be interfered with in their profession by government or by anyone. One could easily gain the impression, listening to A.M.A. commercial squibs, that what it is trying to protect is not the practice of medicine, but privilege. However professional, generous, and busy one's own physician may be, one might gain the impression from A.M.A. propaganda that doctors spend more time reading investment than medical journals.

Over-defense can boomerang. The same day that Gagarin made the first space flight around our planet, thousands of Harvard alumni received a mail request for a contribution from Veritas Foundation, an organization of alumni that alleges that the Harvard Department of Economics teaches too much Marxism and Keynesism. The objection against Marxism is anachronistic. Almost all economics professors in the United States would agree with Kenneth Boulding that Marxism represents a fossil image, a fossil image and orthodoxy maintained by the coercive power of the state. But they would also agree that the Keynesian system "is easily seen as the generalization of the classical system." In its own way, the Foundation comes near saying the same thing:

> Marxism uses the regularly recognized economic terms in propounding its theory while Keynesism has invented an entire new nomenclature to replace the accepted terminology used in our classical economics. Thus, in one fell swoop, the Keynesians have attempted to side track, by-pass and confuse all minds previously educated in economic thinking, relegating them, so to speak, to the scrap heap. The new terms which are more abstract and vague than

> the time tested old ones, make it possible to indoctrinate an entire generation of college students exclusively with Keynesian dogma; while leaving it totally ignorant of the workings and benefits of our classical economic society.[22]

One is tempted to quip that the Foundation should put its time and money in adult education. It is not to quip, however, to point out that the avowed general purpose of the Foundation, namely, to educate the staffs, students and alumni of American colleges and universities on Communism is not identical with an intent to teach the most true and useful economic theory. The Keynesian economics—though it is not all really Keynesian—has won acceptance because it allows of superior understanding and operation of capitalism. Incidentally, it is no fault on the part of Lord Keynes, if his views interested National Socialists and Communists. It is rather our fault, if we ignore his views.

No responsible federal government could restrict itself to the "classical economics" any more than it could prevent the Air Force from operating beyond the "classical mechanics." What is the line between conservatism and reactionism? Disrespect for new conceptions has frequently been associated with reactionism. Surely conservatives do not want to let their struggle deteriorate into a phase of the classical "class struggle" between youth and age. Brilliant young minds will go their own way—and must do so. In the case of economic theory, it may well be that the new terms are more abstract. The great merit of the new theory, with its related program of gathering and presenting information, is that it allows us, *e.g.*, as a nation, to know where we stand all the time and to do something about it. Those who never want to make a move in response to new intelligence are fighting, not against ideology, but against reality.

### MEN AND CAPITALISM

Emerson said, "The true test of civilization is not the census, nor the size of cities, nor the crops—no, but the kind of man the country turns out." We all give some lip service to this self-realizationism and should be interested in the penetrating recent criticism of capitalism from the standpoint of what it does to people.

The older criticism, to the effect that capitalism impoverished the worker, can hardly be maintained in the more advanced coun-

[22] Letter from the Veritas Foundation to Harvard alumni.

tries. Nowhere are the masses so well provided for, materially speaking, and workers in particular. Our material standard of living is the highest.

The newer criticism takes a different tack. It grants that the grandchildren of our grandfathers have access to the horn of plenty, that we have largely achieved our material aims. "But what," we are now asked, "is the eventual psychological good of all this material success? Has it made us happy? Has it made men of us? Or are we not all become bloated capitalists and nothing much more than that? Are our lives devoted to a ritualistic worship of Baal?"

One of the brightest and most knowing of these newer critics is the psychoanalyst Erich Fromm. However, we do not accept his criticisms. We shall see that much of his criticism—and with it most of the newer criticism—is attitudinal. It rests on a certain bias of feeling that could be changed—without affecting capitalism—from disfavor into favor. For instance, "Capital, the dead past, employs labor—the living vitality and power of the present." [23] Why should we equate capital with the dead past? Capital either as represented by investment in physical instruments of production or as represented by free money seeking to exploit new opportunities can look very fresh. Capital augments the "living vitality" of labor as baby food augments the living vitality of babies. Capital immensely augments "the power of the present." There is nothing more "dead" inherent in massing one's capital than in massing one's strength for a pole vault. Of course, if one insists on contrasting the wealthy old dowager, sitting late at night in Las Vegas, her thin, bluish fingers limp over a mass of chips, with the healthy young male jauntily swinging his lunch pail on the way to work in the early morning, he will get a contrast hard on capital. Why not compare this dowager with other old women? Why not compare the jaunty young worker with a banker just out of Harvard or Yale?

Then there is the correlative "conflict between two principles of value: *that between the world of things, and their amassment, and the world of life and its productivity.*" [24] To state the conflict in this way suggests that capitalists are not creative, while laborers are: Which is not only to beg the question, but also to camouflage the facts by evocation of all the medieval usury images.

As for the alienation concept, the alienation in modern society of the individual from his tools and from any clear conception of how his work contributes to the community is no greater under

[23] Erich Fromm, *The Sane Society*. New York: Rinehart & Company, Inc., 1955, pp. 94–95.

[24] *Ibid.*, p. 95.

capitalism than under socialism or Communism. That more and more persons are manipulators of symbols and people and less and less of things has to be granted. But it has to be granted the world over. Besides, to deplore the acquisition of new instruments of power is but to kick at the pricks. What we are entitled to deplore is inhumanity in their use.

Dr. Fromm speaks of alienation of the consumer. Under capitalism, and especially among Americans, much consumption is of symbols.

> With a bottle of Coca-Cola we drink the picture of the pretty boy and girl who drink it in the advertisement, we drink the slogan of 'the pause that refreshes,' we drink the great American habit; least of all do we drink with our palate.[25]

Are we then to remove the symbolic from consumption? Eat our dinner on the run, so long as our palate is de-psychologized?

> We do not know how bread is made, how cloth is woven, how a table is manufactured, how glass is made. We consume, as we produce, without any concrete relatedness to the objects with which we deal; we live in a world of things, and our only connection with them is that we know how to manipulate or to consume them.[26]

But the answer to this is knowledge. And are we so bad off on this score in any fair comparison? Did the peons and villeins of yore know why the wheat grew or did not grow? They worked and often starved in the fields, in the heat of the sun, in coruscating ignorance.

## THE HIGH PRICE OF RICHES

Is it a secret that the possession of riches leads to new problems? Riches have always been subject to abuse. In morals, riches have always carried responsibility in their wake. Riches have always meant special and incisive psychological problems for their possessors: They invite foolish pride, smugness, narrowness, a false feeling of superiority. In today's world, there is some danger of their leading to opposite vices: false humility, lack of self-confidence, lack of concentration. But anyway, one can easily provide a counter list of sins and failings associated with poverty: bitterness, slave mentality, greed, and the eccentric smugness and narrowness of penury. A third list could be provided for that staunch class between the rich and the poor. We all have our problems: The mistake was in ever

[25] *Ibid.*, p. 133.
[26] *Ibid.*, p. 134. Reprinted by permission.

thinking that capitalism, if it led to wealth, would lead to a world in which all problems were solved. No "ism," no social, economic, or philosophic programme leads to that world. But the basest problems are those of poverty. Capitalism has made it possible to attack some new problems, at a higher level of human interest. We have not sacrificed more than we have gained, and it is hard to believe that anyone seriously thinks so.

Many complaints that we are sick minds, that we are moving *en masse* toward self-destruction, and so on, are spokes in a cycle of fads in judgments about American or capitalist morality.[27] Erich Fromm deserves more respect. He stands outside the cycle. As a psychoanalyst, Fromm is disturbed to see some of the attitudes that are presumably held partly in response to the popularization of psychoanalytic theories. The efforts of the Freudian school to understand and free the self may have contributed to a widely accepted "principle of nonfrustration." This principle may *thin* the self which we would understand and free, sometimes almost liquidate it. Acceptance of this principle is placed to the account of capitalism, because "the marketing orientation" implies titillation of wants immediately followed by their gratification; it implies not facing up to deeper wants that cannot be immediately filled. This situation and this personality are clearly a long ways removed from the "Protestant Ethic" of William Whyte, Jr., Tawney, and Weber.

Fromm protests the absence of responsibility coupled with conformity to "anonymous authority," the slavish following of the mob. Individuals will not so much as try to judge for themselves what things are good and right. Fromm's sharpest indictment is that we are unrealistic. How can we claim to be realistic when we are "playing with weapons which may lead to the destruction of all modern civilization . . . ?" "To speak of our realism is almost like a paranoid distortion." [28] Modern man "has covered up the whole reality of human existence and replaced it with his artificial, prettified picture of a pseudo-reality, not too different from the savages who lost their land and freedom for glittering glass beads." [29] Are these flights from sense, is this euphoria, owing to the marketing orientation? To the use and abuse of human beings as customers, to be sold? Is all our attention given to baubles and nonsense? Instead of assuming that this degradation is inherent in capitalism, can we look to capital-

[27] See Meg Greenfield, "The Great American Morality Play." *The Reporter,* June 8, 1961, pp. 13–18.

[28] Fromm, *loc. cit.,* p. 170.

[29] Fromm, *ibid.,* p. 171.

ism and to capitalists for initiative in the direction of improvement of the public mentality and feeling? If capitalism provides centers of power that can provide initiative, where are they? One answer to this question is that, whenever a capitalist takes a position that is unpopular, he at once comes in for name-calling; and the one name he does not get called is "capitalist." Thus, Cyrus Eaton, one of the most powerful capitalists in the United States has stood firmly for co-existence and peace. As a result, he is assailed from the floor of the Senate as "a materialistic, meddlesome, evil old man." He is a "Communist," a "well-known apologist for world communism." But *in reality,* he is a tycoon, a banker, an industrialist, a multimillionaire, a capitalist. In an earlier time, Henry Ford tried to arrange a peace, too; but Americans thought the Kaiser had buck teeth to eat babies with; then they scorned Keynes' prognostications, and did not foresee the Third Reich.

## THE HIGH PRICE OF KNOWLEDGE

One complaint against capitalism must be taken seriously. Capitalists are disposed to use whatever resources fall into their hands. Among the newer resources is the knowledge provided by psychology and related fields. These resources are an even greater menace in the hands of government and of political factions, but everyone ought to use them with restraint.

To begin with, the ethics of psychologists tend in any case to be conservative. Psychologism and sophistry are destructive of ethical standards, but even psychologists have to take a stand somewhere. Individual psychologists may become radical, and others may turn to a serious consideration of the problems of criteria of conduct (Fromm would be a case in point). But the general tendency is to fall back on conservatism.

Perhaps you, too, have heard personnel counselors assert that "tact is 50 per cent of social living." But what about the other half of living?—The other day, I heard a trust officer of one of the largest banks in the country say, "It certainly is not like the old days. Today you are just another cog in the trust machine, and nobody really stands for anything."

Both Mr. Fromm and Mr. Whyte (in his *The Organization Man*) have declared against the abuse of psychology, "counseling," "consulting," "testing," *etc.,* in industrial relations, executive recruitment, assignment, and reward. Both find that the use of these instruments is often prejudiced, not so much in the interest of the corporation, as of the biases of individual administrators and executives. They condemn not only the use of profiles and tests of taste that disfavor free intelligence and modern and realistic sensibility, but also techniques that are used for the evasion of worker and executive frustration. The refusal to face up to frustrations is surrender of personality. *All* these devices can be, and sometimes are, turned into tools for the manipulation of men. Mr. Whyte would like us to see that the natural upshot of capitalism in the way of human product is not skinless franks bearing a corporate seal.

Sharp and Fox [30] tell of a manufacturer of desiccated cocoanut who was one day surprised by an offer of cash for a large supply of refuse shell. When he found out that the shell was to be ground up and mixed with pepper, and the mixture marketed as pure pepper, he refused to make the sale. Now, if a little manufacturer of desiccated cocoanut can, from conscience, refuse to sell shell, cannot a large corporation refuse to buy dishonest or dubious psychological practices? "Responsibility is not like pie." It cannot be cut into independent pieces. Corporations are responsible for their personnel offices.

### CAPITALISM AND THE INTELLECTUALS

The intellectuals of the earliest days of capitalism were associated with the rising bourgeois; together they made up the avant-garde and fought the value systems of mercantilism and feudalism. Bertrand de Juvenel considers the alliance typical of the seventeenth and eighteenth centuries, but it continued in existence in the nineteenth century. Professor Hayek has seen even the relation between Marx and Engels as a relation between intellectual and capitalist patron—which, of course, it was. Today we find it hardly credible that anyone could manage to be so much a capitalist as Engels was and yet be a significant intellectual; but Engels easily did it.

De Juvenel reflects on the sudden switch that intellectuals made in the nineteenth century away from logic and intensive logical training toward—less empiricism than—romanticism. Romanticism without logic allowed the following proceedings.

> The intellectual is really of two minds about the general economic process. On the one side, he takes pride in the achievement of technique and rejoices that men get more of the things they want. On the other hand, he feels that the conquering army of industry destroys values and that the discipline reigning there is a harsh one.

[30] Sharp and Fox, *op. cit.*, p. 56.

These two views are conveniently reconciled by attributing to the "force" of "progress" everything one likes about the process and to the "force" of "capitalism" everything one dislikes.[31]

De Juvenel likens that proceeding to Manichaeism. The division made between intention and actual consequence sets the "metaphysical tone" of most criticism of capitalism:

> One hears Western students stating that the welfare of the workers must be the aim of economic leaders; that, although this aim is achieved in the United States and not achieved in the U.S.S.R., it does inspire the Soviet leaders and not the Western leaders (or so the students say); and that therefore the former are to be admired and the latter condemned. Here one finds one's self very clearly in a case of jurisdiction *in temporalia, ratione peccati.* The secular intellectual in this instance does not judge social devices as devices (and the device which achieves the workers' good out of the leaders' indifference *ex hypothesi* is surely an excellent device as compared to that which produces no workers' good out of the leaders' solicitude!), but he steps into the shoes of a spiritual guide, with perhaps insufficient preparation.[32]

Today science leads the world, and it certainly makes a magnificent contribution to business, to politics, and to the military. Yet neither scientist nor humanist has the primacy that the intelligentsia once owned as a part of the First Estate. The intellectual does not wield the greatest power nor possess the greatest wealth. He does not understand why it is so.

De Juvenel speculates that, in economic jargon, "the market value of the intellectual's output is far below factor input." [33] The intellectual is, therefore, inclined to be dubious about the value of whatever yields a margin of profit. To give the public what it wants makes a poor writer or thinker and a poor missionary of the Truth.

> The trader who fails to turn to the more salable product is adjudged a fool, but the missionary who would so turn would be adjudged a knave.
>
> . . . the businessman's normal conduct appears blameworthy if judged by the criteria valid for the intellectual's conduct.[34]

The intellectual is not mistaken, of course, in using his kind of tackle to try to improve the situation of the workers and of the popu-

[31] Bertrand de Juvenel, "The Treatment of Capitalism by Continental Intellectuals," *Capitalism and the Historians,* Ed. F. A. Hayek. Chicago: The University of Chicago Press, 1954, p. 115. Reprinted by permission.

[32] *Ibid.,* p. 116.

[33] *Ibid.,* p. 119.

[34] *Ibid.,* pp. 118, 120–121. Reprinted by permission.

lation at large. But he can easily commit "the scholar's fallacy" of looking on the whole wide world as a community of scholars and scientists. In that case, he may look on persuasion as the only good form of authority.

> He sniffs at the mild form of authority given by the massing of capital in the hands of "business czars" and recoils from the rough sort of authority given by the massing of police powers in the hands of totalitarian rulers. . . . The intellectual's effort to whittle down the use of alternatives to persuasion is obviously a factor of progress, while it may also, carried too far, lead society into the alternatives of anarchy and tyranny. Indeed, the intellectual has been known to call upon tyranny for the propping-up of his schemes.[35]

American intellectuals find this last charge incredible. But any emigré professor from Nazi Germany can give you a list that will warrant reflection.

In any case, intellectuals should be able to find a better alternative for the ethics of business than—

> *Fiat justitia, pereat mundus;* which means: Fie on what's called justice in this wicked world, sir! [36]

Like Lundestad, the businessman has *tried* to compromise with the newer ideas: That is how, in America, he became the Organization Man.

> *Lundestad.* I've read in old story-books about people who could summon up spirits, but could not lay them again.
>
> *The Chamberlain.* Why, my dear Lundestad, how can a man of your enlightenment—?
>
> *Lundestad.* I know it's mere popish superstition, Chamberlain. But new ideas are like those spirits: it's not so easy to lay them; the best plan is to compromise with them as best you can.[37]

In no case will the most superior intellectuals assume full responsibility for routine operation of the practical world. They should therefore not be too harsh in their judgments of the business community, until the community of political leaders, or some other alternative community of leaders, has proved its greater merit. This is all the more so, if De Juvenel is correct in saying:

> . . . that the intellectual community has waxed harsher in its judgments of the business community precisely while the business

[35] *Ibid.*, p. 118. Reprinted by permission.

[36] Henrik Ibsen, *The League of Youth.* New York: The Modern Library, p. 217. Reprinted by permission.

[37] *Ibid.*, pp. 233–234. Reprinted by permission.

> community was strikingly bettering the conditions of the masses, improving its own working ethics, and growing in civic consciousness. Judged by its social fruits, by its mores, by its spirit, capitalism of today is immeasurably more praiseworthy than in previous days when it was far less bitterly denounced.[38]

Of course our primary concern is not that businessmen should be given more praise—or profit, either—but that the situation of the workers and of the population at large should be improved and, emphatically, *not* worsened.

[38] De Juvenel, *loc. cit.*, p. 122. Reprinted by permission.

# 12

# TOTALITARIANISM, LIBERTARIANISM

## I TOTALITARIANISM

The first thinkers to foresee the advent of totalitarianism were John Stuart Mill [1] and Alexis de Tocqueville. It was in America, England, and France that they observed increasing pressures making for mass uniformity and for conformity to the masses.[2] They saw totalitarianism in the withering away of institutions and institutional devices that could stand against mass opinion or against the more prejudiced, fanatical formers of mass opinion. They found it in the thought and disposition of Auguste Comte and other zealous reformers and intellectuals. They anticipated that democracy could move, in the most advanced countries, in only one or the other of two directions, namely, totalitarianism or libertarianism.

Totalitarianism is not just an order in which there is highly centralized government under the control of one political party or dictator. Nor is it instituted merely by concentrating in the government power over economic programs and operations. The much more

[1] This prophetic nightmare is today paramount among Mill's valid claims to fame.

[2] Mill thought of Germany as fatherland of the von Humboldts, as the seat of liberalism.

ominous significance lies in a complete grip by the whole people, or what passes for the whole people, on the entire thought and feeling of every individual person. Mass coercion and the police power of the state support a single unquestioned ideology and a single authority over the interpretation of that ideology. Instead of each ruling himself in his own way, all together rule every individual in their mass way. Totalitarianism is "total" in a two-fold way: First, it affects everyone; but second and more important, it penetrates and permeates the whole personality, dominating all outer and inner aspects, of every man's life.

Perhaps central political and economic control encourage totalitarianism. They do not define or constitute it. Democracy itself is already rule by the popular will, or in accord with it; and there is in principle nothing undemocratic about economic democracy. To see why the U.S.S.R., China, and the United States all call themselves "democracies" is not difficult. They are essentially correct in doing so, even if they have unlike ways of manufacturing the popular will. But we count on the fertility of the individual mind and personality, count on a real spontaneity and individual liberty; *they* do not.

We shall have to use our imagination, if we are going to understand totalitarianism. Not only is it foreign to our experience and temperament, but we have not been so much informed as we have propagandized about it. Italian-Americans who visited Fascist Italy were often amazed at how little Americans understood Mussolini's program, at how little we knew of what actually went on over there.

### THE NAZIS

The vast majority of Germans who were National-Socialists did not run from meeting to meeting, from the Grünewald Stadium to the Sportspalast, to give vent to their organized mass hatreds. True, they hated the Poles and the Jews, and especially "the Polish Jews," and most of all "the Jewish High International Finance." [3] But the National Socialist German Workers Party set out in practice to fill the lives of all good Germans with—shall we say?—value, aspiration, and pride. To the women of the Nazi welfare organization, Dr. Goebbels was not a wicked propagandist, but rather a brilliant

[3] The principal international bankers who influenced the situation in Germany and Austria from 1925 to 1933 were, in fact, gentile Americans. When Hitler became Chancellor (January 1933), Germans owed the Chase National Bank alone seventy-seven million dollars in short-term credits. Payment was deferred under a series of "stand-still agreements."

manager of relief and recruitment, a loving, *gemütlicher* husband and father. He was devoted to the Leader, the Party, the People. The women knew the names and ages of his children. They knew where Hitler and Goering were, and what they were doing (more or less). They followed the Nazi versions, in the *Angriff* and other party newspapers, of the continual streetfighting among their own Horst Wessels and the Communist Youth. To them, Hitler meant German unity, national recovery and purpose, and the recovery of national pride. To us, Hitler was associated with shouting, but to them, with their immediate welfare.

### THE NAZI YOUTH

The Nazi Youth Movement was not a newly fabricated pattern. Before 1933 there had been a number of separately organized youth movements: Catholic, Evangelical, Jewish, those which were motivated by political aims and beliefs, such as the Weimar Socialists, the Communists, and the various rightist, nationalistic, and pseudo-militaristic youth organizations. There was also a number of spontaneously organized youth groups, of which the Wandervogel, initiated by a group of university students to encourage informal outdoor life and camping, and in protest against the academic, family, and community conventionality and authoritarianism of the period, was one of the most active. The motivations behind these movements and groups included those of group recreation, romantic escapism, co-operative work, and (on the part of the adult) leading youth toward particular religious or political aims and beliefs.

There was much in these earlier movements which met the genuine needs of adolescents: the need of belonging; the need of being thought important; the need of feeling oneself independent of the older generation; the need of participating in social service or community affairs; the need of identifying oneself with ideals and with admired leaders. The activities of these groups also met the interests of adolescents: group organization, informal outdoor life, athletics, singing, dancing, practical service jobs in groups, and campfire discussions.

The leaders of the Nazi Youth Movement were extremely clever in the way they appealed to the young generation. They took advantage of the unfortunate situation in Germany after the first world war, which came about through the inflation and later led into a long lasting depression. They impressed upon youth that all the misery they were suffering, the insecurities and deprivations they had to endure were the result of wrong political and educational ideas and of ineffective,weak and unclear leadership. They blamed the democratic efforts of the young Republic for the failure to achieve economic stability, more political power and prestige, better opportunities, and a more hopeful future for youth.

They hammered into the minds of each and every young German, that democracy was identical with weakness, that it inevitably resulted in decay and misery. Weakness became one of, if not the most despicable and despised attributes in Germany. In its place the ideal of and demand for force, hardness, and bravery were vigorously implanted. Incorporated into these aims and ideals were the above mentioned group activities and through these many of the genuine inner needs of youth were met. Much fanfare of public recognition, uniforms, insignia, parades were added, all of which had strong appeal to masses of youth who had come to feel that they had no real place in society.

Because they had lost all confidence in themselves and in their ability for self-direction, they easily and voluntarily submitted to firm leadership. The years of unemployment, of economic deprivation, of lack of purpose and incentive in life, and bound up with this a sense of not being needed and wanted, had made young Germans extremely vulnerable. Thus, they accepted blindly an organization which promised fulfillment of many of these very needs and wants. They responded eagerly to Hitler's call for total self-commitment and total self-surrender. They believed what they were told: that the hope for a free, powerful force, coming out of the combined efforts and achievements of all German youth and based upon their undivided loyalty and unquestioning obedience, a strong, mighty, and proud German nation could be developed. Whatever ideas, measures and activities were introduced and forced upon the various Nazi Youth groups were always given and explained as justified and imperative for achieving this supreme goal.

A large number of these young boys and girls accepted the restrictions imposed upon them without inner conflicts and reservations, because they had earlier been brought up in the tradition of acceptance of authority and obedience in their daily lives. It was difficult for those few who had been active members of the young Socialist Youth Movement and who had through living and participating in the efforts toward a realization of democratic ideals grown to identify themselves with these ideals and goals. Many of these were extremely unhappy when they saw their own movement abolished and destroyed and when they were forced into the Hitler Youth. There were some who never gave up their inner resistance and held on to their former loyalties. For others the discrepancy between the ideals of brotherliness, equality and sense of membership —as taught and practised in the Socialist Youth groups and the barrenness and acute miseries and needs in their every-day lives, had weakened or shaken their belief in these ideals. After more or less severe conflicts they became converted by National Socialist indoctrination.

In an attempt to understand this process of total surrender of youth and the absence of any large-scale, strong, organized resistance, one has to bear in mind that hand in hand with their appealing slogans and offerings, the Nazi Youth organizations did not hesitate to use all overwhelming power at their command to impress upon and threaten the young. There is no doubt that the element of fear, though unconscious to most—the fear of the isolated and insecure, and resulting therefrom the unconscious need for mass protection and identification with something powerful and strong—played a large part in this initial phase of development.

It also has to be seen and understood, that from the very outset of their taking over—simultaneously with the incorporation of all former youth organizations into the Hitler Youth—a matchless and holeproof scheme was set in motion through which all German children, almost from their very first day of life, were subjected to Nazi-dominated ideologies and practices. Everything they saw, heard and learned, the air they breathed, was permeated by Nazi dogma so that their adherence and uncritical loyalty and desire to follow was built up as a matter of course.[4]

## NAZIS AND COMMUNISTS

One could say that National Socialism was a movement which began essentially in the elementary schools and found its first significant support among frustrated school teachers. It moved on into the secondary schools, and finally swept up even such prominent professors as Werner Sombart and—for a moment—Martin Heidegger. It allied itself with such anti-Communist business leaders as Fritz Thyssen—and then rejected them, when it had taxing power and no longer needed their voluntary contributions.

Thyssen was exiled, Sombart made an idiot of himself, Dr. Goebbels killed his wife, his children, and himself. But, we should not forget that the Nazis did achieve albeit a forced and hysterical national unity and a war machine of immense power, mobility, and progressiveness—a comparatively *democratic* war machine. Neither Russia nor we ourselves could afford to make concessions to the Nazis. Stalin, to his shame and sorrow, made a pact with them; and then he did not build up his armed might fast enough.[5]

[4] *Education and Child Care Institute in Germany, 1949.* Ed. Katherine Taylor. Unitarian Service Committee, Inc., in co-operation with Arbeiter-Wohlfahrt (Boston and Hanover [20a], respectively), p. 23–26. Reprinted by permission.

[5] This is "the lesson of history and experience"—for it is much less a matter of philosophy—that makes Khrushchev so intent on possessing military power. The Russians lost at least 15—but probably 20—million people in the Second World War, in contrast to our own 400,000. I know a Russian woman who lost all four brothers and both brothers-in-law.

Neither will we make, nor can we afford to make, unbargained concessions to totalitarian Communism. One of our major tasks is to make that clearly understood in terms of intent and power.

## IDEOLOGIES

An ideology is a manner of thinking and feeling, and a scheme of ideas about life and the world. An ideology may belong to an individual, a class, or a nation. It differs from a philosophy, but is perhaps equivalent to "a philosophy of life." It differs from a philosophy not only in being less reflective and critical, but also in being more intimately and unconsciously related to day-to-day patterns of living. Logical simplicity and ability to withstand penetrating criticism are criteria of philosophies, but ideologies are judged by other standards. An ideology may display its power in effective evasion of criticism, in appearing so natural that its critic is laughed out of court—or lynched. Social acceptance is the normal test of an ideology.

Some famous ideologies are bourgeois ideology, liberal ideology, Bolshevik ideology. Marx seized the initiative in the description of ideologies and, from his Hegelian sort of eyrie, accused the bourgeoisie of imposing its ideology on all the world. No doubt, the widespread conviction, especially the *unconscious* conviction, that certain attitudes should be held by everyone, leads to attempts at enforcement. This is all the more likely, where conviction relates directly to work, distribution of goods, and patterns of consumption. Marx aimed at liberating the proletarian from bourgeois ideology, saying, "Law, morality, religion, are to him so many bourgeois prejudices, behind which lurk in ambush just as many bourgeois interests." He spoke of capitalism making everything over into its own image. He called the executive of the modern capitalist state, "a committee for managing the common affairs of the whole bourgeoisie."

Why not frankly admire this peculiar Marxian interpretation of the bourgeois position as one of the shrewdest subversive devices ever invented? It makes every capitalist investment and every capitalist's exhortation look like something nefarious, so that the proletarian imagination will not be satisfied until it has "found" how, in every situation, the capitalist really manages to lap up all the cream. There is hypocrisy here. But how much of it lies with capitalism? Marx was flatly wrong, if he meant to say that there is *no* objectivity under capitalism. And this masterful deceit is now used, all too effectively, to conceal the fact that Bolshevism offers next to nothing. It is used to conceal the fact that Communism thrives abroad on hunger, penury, and agitation, while capitalism makes real inroads in coping with real problems.

For instance, nothing is more needed by the underdeveloped nations than capital goods. As Lord Home said at Harvard:

> The total sum which is exported in investment and aid from the Western countries today to the underdeveloped world has reached a total this year of *over six billion dollars.* Ladies and gentlemen, the Communists contribute twenty times less than that. Sometimes you would think from the propaganda that goes on that it is the other way around. And we ought to tell the world the story; that whereas the Communists contribute 300 million dollars in investment and aid, the West's investment is six billion dollars a year.[6]

This is the problem that Pope John calls the number one social problem facing the contemporary world: the bringing out of the underdeveloped nations. To its solution, the Communists have contributed words and confusion. Accordingly, we are all faced not only with the bitter economic problems of the underdeveloped nations, but with the further problem of "telling the world the story" despite a much propagandized Communist ideology that blackens the storyteller, that demands a look into the mouth of every gift horse.

There are real reasons why, in respect to ourselves, we should ignore and purposefully overlook the Marxian interpretation of our ideology altogether and in principle. We are not perfect, and there is much work and reform to be done. We must, therefore, be self-critical and receptive, too, to any legitimate criticism from abroad. We have enough tendency on our own part to be cynical and anxious, without receiving the Communist myth of a Gila monster under every capitalist stone. That myth does not make for objectivity. It does not even pretend to do so.

There is ample legitimate criticism. It was not Khrushchev, but Paul Getty, "the richest man on earth," a man who hobnobs with sheiks and pashas, who compared most American business executives to the "educated barbarians of ancient Rome." Like the barbarians of Rome, they have mastered commercial, engineering, and military techniques, Getty said (UPI).

We have our own course of reform and progress to follow, and we cannot afford to stop pursuing it because of the carping cynicism of the extreme left and right.

## II LIBERTARIANISM

But, *is* our own tradition nothing more than liberal ideology, bourgeois ideology, or something of the sort?

[6] *Harvard Alumni Bulletin,* July, 1961. Reprinted by permission.

Against the background discussion of Liberty in our Part II, we can confidently answer no. By no means is libertarianism just another concoction of intellectuals, commerçants, and propagandists, just one more alternative in a cafeteria serving up ideologies. It is rather the carefully wrought system which alone offers a real likelihood of more and more correction, insight, and advance. It is the one order that can systematically discover and adopt new truths and new perspectives across the whole range of human interest and concern. It can envisage and adopt any possible Marxian truth and perspective, while the Bolsheviks succeed only in copying from us industrial technique and science in the narrow and technical sense. Despite Khrushchev, we are not really the Communists' teachers, for *they* are not full-fledged learners. Copying is not learning.

The fundamental principle of libertarianism is: Face up to the facts, including the facts about value. This principle has the negative implications: Do not get stuck with an ideology, for it may be blinding and restrictive. And do not get stuck with interests that are merely class interests, for we are human beings before we belong to any class.

### POLITICAL DEMOCRACY

According to E. F. M. Durbin, the totalitarian countries have paid our plain old-fashioned political democracies a great compliment by holding so-called elections.

A few years ago many "liberal" socialists who did not mean to align themselves with totalitarianism made such statements as J. A. Hobson's, "Effective political democracy is unattainable without economic equality." Durbin objected that this identifies "democracy" with the conception of social justice itself and dissociates it from the political practice of any present society. "A community is a 'true' democracy only if all cause for sighing and weeping have passed away." [7] None of the great democracies—America, Britain, France, Sweden—can meet that standard.[8]

The criteria of political democracy, according to Durbin, are three. First, the power of a people to choose a government. In practice, this turns out to have its significance in the ability of a people to dismiss a government from office.

The second criterion is that there be a real choice before the people. Otherwise there is only Hobson's choice. Freedom to oppose

[7] E. F. Durbin, *The Politics of Democratic Socialism.* London: Routledge and Kegan Paul Ltd., 1940, p. 235. Durbin was a Labor M. P.

[8] The U.S.S.R. can't satisfy the criterion either.

the Government, to prepare an opposition party able to take over the power after an electoral decision, is an institution essential to political democracy. This is where the modern dictatorships pay democracy "the sincerest form of flattery—that of imitation."

> They copy the device of the "General Election." But it is an empty and silly imitation—like that of an ape reading a newspaper or a baboon playing on a violin. It deceives no one, except those who wish to be deceived. Of course, no amount of electoral machinery, nor platform eloquence, nor secret balloting, nor "equal voting," has the slightest real significance if there is finally nothing to vote about, no choice before the voters.[9]

The "great tribute votes" turned in for the Nazis and the Communists, running to 98 or 99 per cent of the votes polled, are a dead give-away. The toleration of opposition is the *acid* test, and all that we can "admire" in Hitler's Herr Goebbels is the extremeness of his fanaticism:

> All we National-Socialists are convinced that we are right, and we cannot bear with anyone who maintains that he is right. For either, if he is right, he must be a National-Socialist, or, if he is not National-Socialist, then he is not right.[10]

The third characteristic is less obvious; Durbin calls it *the cause* of democracy. He argues that "democracy is the epiphenomenon of a certain emotional balance in the individuals composing a nation . . ." The result of this can be seen in "the existence of *an implicit undertaking between the Parties contending for power in the State not to persecute each other.*" [11]

### CORRIGIBILITY

The implicit understanding not to persecute is supported by more than fear of civil war. It is a resultant of respect for the ideas, interests, and rights of other persons and parties. It amounts to a recognition that no man or party holds a monopoly of truth or of insight into value.

All we men are fallible and corrigible, but we are not all big enough to admit it. The frank recognition of one's human fallibility is in practice a great source of strength.

Don Blasingame of the Cincinnati Reds, in his seventh big league season, went to his field manager and said:

[9] *Ibid.*, p. 239. Reprinted by permission.
[10] As quoted by Durbin, *ibid.*, p. 241. Reprinted by permission.
[11] *Ibid.*

Hutch, I might as well tell you; I haven't been making the double play as well as I did when I played for you in St. Louis. I wish you'd check me.

What Blasingame told him, Hutchinson already knew. He also knew "Blazer" was not a particularly good double-play man when he had him before. The trade made for him was almost a desperation deal.

It was considered a miracle that a team could continue to win as the Reds did through May and early June of 1961 with a weakness like this down the classic middle.

All this time, Blasingame, the little veteran, was getting special instructions, particularly on the double-play pivot. Sometimes Hutchinson worked with him; often it was Reggio Otero.

They discovered the basic weakness was that in coming across the bag as the middle man, he was throwing off balance; he wasn't getting the proper leverage. Blasingame worked as hard as a kid in a rookie camp to correct the fault.

Blasingame got on to it, and the Reds began to make consistently the logical double plays. The line down the middle was strengthened because a veteran major leaguer was willing to admit he needed help on a fundamental facet of his position.[12]

If one is not satisfied with an illustration from baseball, let him consider the implications of an advertisement of United States Trust Company of New York addressed to a class of very wealthy Americans.

The investor who says, "I am locked in—my profits are so large I can't afford to sell and pay the taxes," will do well to take a fresh look. He may be following his emotions rather than logic.
. . . The question of profit-taking is part of a larger picture: it involves investment objectives, family, and estate considerations.[13]

What a fine thing that even the investor who is thus "locked in" can be appealed to by the thought that he may be following his emotions rather than logic. It is this capacity for criticism and this reach of experience which enlist the majority of America's extremely wealthy families on the side of libertarianism, at least when the chips are down.

The basic system of real election and independent political party in the Western countries is, in one aspect, an institutionalization of this capacity for criticism and of this "emotional balance." We have

[12] Adopted from Si Burick, *Dayton Daily News* Sports Editor.

[13] *Harvard Alumni Bulletin,* July, 1961. Reprinted by permission of United States Trust Co. of New York.

the moral strength to go to the hustings and then to accept the result.

FURTHER ON CORRIGIBILITY

Philosophers are notorious for reminding us of occasions on which what looked like gold was not, what seemed a man turned out to be a puppet. From these disappointments some of them pretend to demonstrate the impossibility of knowledge.[14]

Disillusion is often turned to the good uses of men and nations. Disillusion *with false disillusionment* can be of emphatic service. For instance, we might recognize that Religion with a capital "R" has been a fairly bad set of historical phenomena and yet have the courage not to deny the invaluable good in religion. It is "religion without ethics" that is blind. The knowledge of our own ignorance, the truth about our intimate and ultimate fallibility, is one of the greatest blessings of civilization. But "what is truth?" It is not a cynical dogma and doubtfully an academic or any ultimate sort of scepticism. Philosophers can also remind us of many occasions on which what did not look like gold was, and what seemed to be a puppet turned out to be a man. What passes for disillusionment is sometimes no more than a failure of imagination, energy, or constructiveness.

John Wisdom continues:

> Poets, dramatists, and novelists continually present the shocking continuities between love and hate, devotion and infatuation. . . . shall we, like Dostoevsky, Freud, and many other explorers of the spiritual world, have the courage to refuse to deny the evil and also the further courage not then to deny the good.[15]

We concern ourselves with a delicate balance.

> Metaphysical paradoxes such as "Ethical discussion is propaganda," "Reflective thought is thought about words," are dangerous and need to be balanced by the re-assertion of the old truths in their opposites. Psychological paradoxes are dangerous, too, and call for a dialectical process in which they are balanced. For example, the psychological paradox "We are all mad" needs to be balanced by its opposite "We are all sane" and by the re-assertion of "Some of us are mad, but some of us are not"—only now the old truth will not blind us to the continuities the paradoxes have revealed. . . .

[14] John Wisdom, *Philosophy and Psycho-Analysis.* Oxford: Basil Blackwell, 1953, p. 261. From "Philosophy, Metaphysics, and Psycho-Analysis."

[15] *Ibid.* Reprinted by permission. And, *admittedly,* "The worst of it is that Dostoevsky is extremely confusing."

> To gain a new apprehension of any part of reality we have to shake off old habits of apprehension crystallized probably in a well-known mode of presentation. . . . Oscar Wilde says [*The Decay of Lying*] "There may have been fogs for centuries in London. I dare say there were. But no one saw them, and so we do not know anything about them. They did not exist till Art had invented them." [16]

The philosopher, the scientist, the mathematician make their points in different ways, and the way of the philosopher is the most difficult. Like the psychoanalyst, the philosopher has come off fairly well if only he has *rather* proved his point. The investor and the politician are in the same boat. What we ordinarily think of as induction and deduction do not fully cover the prophecy, the insight, or the intuition of experience that are involved in those decisive acts, which control our individual and social futures. No philosopher that I can name chose philosophy for his field by unassisted deduction from premises or by induction from data.[17]

Careful naming—insightfully and purposefully related to the data—is an ingredient of good philosophizing, doctoring, psychoanalyzing.

> Psychoanalysts, in order to reveal to us things about ourselves, modify and sophisticate our conceptions of love, hate, jealousy, envy, sympathy, sense of responsibility. They use familiar words not with a disregard of established usage, but not in bondage to it.[18]

It does not follow that the psychoanalyst or the ethical philosopher cannot *prove* his statements. But it suggests that we have here to do with areas in which *demonstrative* proof eludes us. To the extent that statements insightfully expressing new truth are not expressed "in strict accord with convention," they "will never be proved in strict accord with convention." [19]

## A LITTLE FURTHER STILL ON CORRIGIBILITY

Professor Wisdom continues, protesting what he refers to as "bogus acceptance." We all admit we make mistakes. We all admit limits to our imagination, our insight, our reasoning power. People accept Freud, but then add: "No doubt he is using sexual in a special sense of his own." That's a bogus acceptance.

[16] *Ibid.*, p. 263. Reprinted by permission.

[17] C. S. Peirce says, one should choose Truth as one chooses his beloved. I suppose he means, as one *should* choose his beloved.

[18] John Wisdom, *loc. cit.*, p. 271. Reprinted by permission.

[19] *Ibid.*

We do not have to stay inside the context of Professor Wisdom's discussion. A bogus acceptance is any acceptance that is not heartfelt, not brought home, not energetic. To thine own self be true! But when is one really true to himself? Only when he has the energy, the courage and knowledge, and the opportunity, really to know himself. Experience shows that "self-criticism" can be extremely false to self and to any man. In fact, "criticism" and "self-criticism" are fetishes of Communism and well-known devices of brainwashing.

Major William Mayer, an Army neuro-psychiatrist, who has made himself expert on the brainwashing of Americans held prisoner of war by the North Koreans and Red Chinese, presents the following article from a camp newspaper, written by a soldier with less than eighth grade education:

> I wish to express my profound and heartfelt gratitude to the members of the Chinese Peoples Volunteer Army for teaching me to read and write English, because in the capitalist imperialist community of Pittsburgh, Pa., from which I come only the sons of wealthy capitalists are ever permitted to read and write English.

The boy was repatriated and interrogated about that statement, which is perhaps even more amazing to teachers of English than it is to Pittsburghers.

> He freely admitted he'd written the article and that he couldn't see that there was any point in not doing it because—and this is something we began to hear over and over and over—everybody else was doing it, which made it all right.

Habits of bogus acceptance and rejection and habits of name-calling, informing, and other bogus criticism are dangerous to us all. There is profound reason for that basic American precept: no tattling! Yet our extreme left and right wings have been doing their utmost to annul it. The notion that everyone's life and sentiment must be brought out into the public view is totalitarian.

As for bogus rejection, our fear and offhand rejection of Communist literature leave it its full shock value. Mao's tactics have proved themselves on the battlefield, but his writings, when subjected to open and honest criticism, turn out to be not only wrongheaded and vague, but boring. It is in part the absence of any serious—or witty—criticism that gives them their political force in China. Our rejection of Mao's "practical" Communism should not be a bogus one. It should be an informed and sincere rejection.

A meritorious corrigibility depends, in brief, on intelligence and insight, but also on nerve. The libertarian is not aiming at security and protection of his lowly self, but at knowledge and value. He is too sophisticated to seek certainty, but he wants a probability as well-warranted as is practically attainable. His ego and id, even if he is a veteran big leaguer or a millionaire, he will not allow—God willing—to intrude or to obstruct his quest for truth and life. He certainly is interested in his own welfare, but he wants no counterfeit, no lead nickel preferred by mad society or by any unhealthy machination of his own ego.

And for his own society and the world community he wants nothing less. He wishes them the greatest health and welfare, *real* health and welfare. Without ever being cynical, his social experience, his tradition of scepticism, will not allow him to think a cause is pure just because it aims at what *its* spokesmen call "People's Democracy." Nor will he be deceived by the routine cry of "Anti-Communist" either: Wolves will wear any kind of make-up to conceal their teeth.

The free spirit will never clutch at mere words. It wants the reality that should be behind them.

### ECONOMIC DEMOCRACY

Perhaps you have seen the motto, posted in some dark corner, "If You're So Smart, Why Ain't You Rich?" One can easily imagine a motto of contrary sentiment, to be posted in Las Vegas casinos or Wall Street brokerage offices, "If You're So Rich, Why Ain't You Smart?" These two questions would then nicely express, respectively, the smugness of the rich and the smugness of the poor.

The Bolsheviks have made all they could of the motto, "economic democracy." We have noticed also that so significant a thinker as J. A. Hobson said, a few years ago, "Effective political democracy is unattainable without economic equality." Durbin called Hobson's assertion a confusion of democracy with the conception of social justice itself.

But does our highest conception of social justice imply an absolute economic equality? If so, why is such extreme economic equality even more rare than moral excellence and Christian martyrdom? Why have the Communists, who proclaim it, so totally failed of achieving anything even remotely resembling it?

Only a few years ago, E. A. Burtt wrote:

> In its ultimate ideal communism is, however, essentially right; to reorganize our social life on the basis of the Marxian principle

> "from each according to his ability, to each according to his need," would but express in economic relations the valid ideal of subordinating selfish gain to the love and service of others.[20]

This view has manifest deep roots. Jesus beheld a young man and loved him and He said to him:

> One thing thou lackest: go thy way, sell whatsoever thou hast, and give to the poor, and thou shalt have treasure in heaven: and come, take up the cross, and follow me.[21]

But Jesus spoke also in parables about investment of talents and about proliferation from mustard seed; and He spoke of the prosperity of the righteous and Himself accepted the gift of Mary of Bethany. Exegesis and history indicate that Christianity and Judaism take generally a position of sympathy *and* of superiority toward both rich and poor, and toward the *issue* of rich and poor. The life of the spirit is above riches and above poverty, above the smugness of power and the smugness of weakness and infirmity.

In contrast, the materialist ethic of Marxian Communism expresses a fanatical obsession with the question of wealth and poverty, an obsession, incidentally, that is not so much proletarian as it is lower middle-class. "Share the wealth" and "Every man a king" were slogans of Huey Long.

Contemporary social science has given considerable attention to social and economic stratification and to questions of class ideology. One finding, or upshot, is that men compare themselves as a rule with those in their immediate environment. The teamster does not envy the airline pilot and certainly not John D. Rockefeller or the latest receiver of a baseball bonus; no, he envies some other teamster who gets five cents more per hour. But it's only a psychological foible. We need not pay everyone the same amount. And to pay according to need is properly a matter of compassion (and sometimes of good sense), *not* of an ideal of justice or economic equality.

Plato gave some attention to communism. He proposed that the rulers of his ideal state live together on the same terms, without conventional mates and without individual or family property. His intention was to confine the loyalty of his rulers to the rule of the state and to the subjects. This proposal may have been fantastic, but it does not give warrant for speaking of Plato as having supported communism or economic democracy. We strive from identical motives to keep our judges and justices above any economic bias:

[20] Edwin A. Burtt, *Types of Religious Philosophy,* Rev. Ed. New York: Harper & Brothers, 1951, p. 353. Reprinted by permission.

[21] Mark 10:21.

It is their function to interpret and apply the law impartially, but also insightfully and excellently. The notion that "the people" or peoples' courts can perform these functions better than intelligent, skilled, and objective justices is ridiculous. The people generally, and those people in particular who want to impeach the justices, are much more commonly biased than are the judges and justices.

We know reasonably well how to pay people for accomplishments. To pay them according to recognized need is a matter of mercy; but to pay them according to need, if "need" is interpreted to involve psychological desire, would require unlimited resources.

The first aim of every economy is production; the common ideal of economic democracy is lopsided in considering only characteristics of the distributive system, as well as in unduly emphasizing bodily concerns.

### "JUST PLAIN EQUALITY"

The plain equality of men emphasized by Thomas Hobbes (1588–1679) deserves careful estimation and appreciation. Hobbes pointed out that one man is not much stronger or weaker than another. Weapons reduce natural difference in size and strength to nothing.

If you go to the great old church in Wasserburg, in south Bavaria, you can see there the bones of nobles carefully preserved under glass. Some of them are still lying after six or seven hundred years in their robes, their skulls crowned in jewels. We are all born and all die, and we all have the same calcareous, vertebrate structure.

But this equality is only a physical equality, an equality of physical structure and strength in an unregulated state of nature, perhaps modified by the presence of firearms. From a description of this equality, nothing follows, unless perhaps a revelation of the lack of realism in arrogance.

### EQUALITY OF OPPORTUNITY

The principle of equality of opportunity appeals not only to our brute sense of justice or of equality, but also to our desire for individual and social value. Opportunity means *inter alia* opportunity to invent, develop, and enjoy *new* values and new knowledge, technology, and application.

As John W. Gardner [22] has said, "You *can* keep a good man down." You can do it by the institution of hereditary privilege, the underside of which is underprivilege. Our society and our culture

[22] John W. Gardner, *Excellence: Can We Be Equal And Excellent Too?* New York: Harper & Brothers, 1961, p. 3.

are noted for rejecting arbitrary restrictions on individuals and classes.

They are noted for offering opportunity to ability and for rewarding those who produce results. But the free opportunity does not lead to equality in ability nor to economic equality. "Many a feudal lord would have given his drawbridge to enjoy the power and glory of the industrial barons who pushed him into the history books." [23] A major purpose of Mr. Gardner's book is to show that when societies give up hereditary stratification, they can either take the path of equalitarianism or simply "let the best man win." But in their moderate forms, both equalitarianism and competitive performance are ingredients of a healthful society; or, as the author notes, "each point of view can be carried to harmful extremes."

We are always the victims of our own ideals, and Americans have been somewhat victimized by the paradoxical, somewhat incompatible, set: equalitarianism *and* competitive performance.

> As a result, any bright [American] schoolboy can write an essay on the disadvantages of hereditary stratification. Hardly any could write an essay on the disadvantages of extreme equalitarianism or of extreme emphasis upon individual performance. But such essays must be written. [24]

## EQUALITY AND EXCELLENCE

The only inexhaustible resources are the resources of creative men. But creative men are not born, they must themselves be painstakingly created and cultivated. There is always something or other there to develop, if it is only elicited and not stifled. Children who are understood and loved "do a tremendous amount of work themselves developing their own characters and discipline," says Dr. Spock. But there are good reasons for believing that even "old rascals" can be reformed and have something good in them that will transform their whole lives, if the right catalytic agent is once applied. Nazis can be de-Nazified, and Communists can be de-Communized.[25] And we should remember, a reformed criminal is not a criminal.

What we want is not the reduction of all people to one unhappy—

[23] *Ibid.,* p. 5.

[24] *Ibid.,* p. 6. Mr. Gardner does not mean to imply that there is no nepotism or local aristocracy among us. He draws special attention to our aristocracies of profession.

[25] This is a subject that should be pursued farther by psychologists, neuro-psychiatrists, *etc.,* far beyond what it has been to date. For the long pull, the art of bringing people to their senses is far more significant than brainwashing or propagandizing.

and inevitably somewhat neurotic—level of life and consciousness. Our aim is rather the establishment of equitable and humane conditions under which anyone can rise.

There are certain pitfalls for us in our egalitarian *and* competitive performance society. One is that selection should be too often and too exclusively from above. For in the long run that would mean selection by elders; and while our elders deserve that love and respect commanded by the Old Testament, they will not and cannot bear the responsibility of the future. Moreover, the older generation is always likely to suffer from a misplaced daring. It constitutes the field managers and the home guard, but never the front line. Even more important, its sense of excellence is confined inside well-worn grooves. The older generation appreciates and recognizes the excellence of old painting, architecture, music, literature, politics, ways of doing business, *etc., etc.* But is it able to appreciate new forms of excellence? Equality of opportunity should mean equality of opportunity to choose forms, and new kinds of ways, as well as established grooves. In youth and growth we trust.

Another pitfall relates to competitive performance. The mad desire for education, or at least for the degrees and other trappings, results, perhaps necessarily, in great emphasis on testing and test results. But a man's talent and a man's career must at last come to a better test than any invented by professors, namely the test of life itself.

# PART V

# The Individual in Liberal Democratic Society

# 13

## RESPONSIBILITY I

In liberal democratic society, the individual leads a difficult life. He is directly responsible for the consequences of his own actions, and he shares responsibility for social policy and its execution. Hence nostalgia for older orders or longing for simpler ones is not infrequent; for surely everyone from time to time, consciously or unconsciously, wants to shirk his responsibility.

Under libertarian and capitalist régimes, the scientific, industrial, and social contexts of human life have become more and more complex. All individuals find that the situation in which they live and the field of their decision-making grows always more difficult to understand. Through the very action of competition in free markets, economic power has become more and more concentrated in a few great institutions. Through a plurality of free choices of men, social existence has become more and more intricately organized. The individual person finds the exertion of control more difficult and oftener frustrating today than yesterday. But the more that is required of him, the more the individual requires the free, full development and use of his powers. The more complex the problems of human beings become, the more liberty is a condition of successful adaptation and function.

The suggestion was made, already in Chapter 2, that liberty is compatible with intelligent social decision. Liberty was said to be compatible with the execution of policies that have been democratically formulated and legislated. But now we shall have to go beyond those suggestions to consider whether liberty is not even *a necessary condition* of intelligent and democratic decision and action.

The key to a solution of the problem of the relation between liberty and intelligent society lies in the concept of responsibility. But if responsibility is this key, it must be a key that is exquisitely, but also sturdily, manufactured. Any impression that "responsibility" is just another of those words that are easily grasped, but which, once in hand, melt quickly and disappear like snowflakes, must be illusory. Responsibility certainly has always been a major burden on society, but it has never been so heavy and so widely distributed as in the social dynamics of the present. Any illusion that it is nebulous or evanescent is owing to poor vision—that ought to be corrected.

Let us look first, in this chapter, at some of its more mundane meanings and functions, and then see if we can possibly, in the next chapter, ascribe substantial meaning to the higher, the less clear and settled, responsibilities.

## "THE FOURTH R"

Because of the acknowledged importance of teaching it in the schools, responsibility has been called "the fourth R." [1] Responsibility in this traditional usage means accountability by each for the consequences of his actions.

> A responsible person holds himself accountable for his conduct and behavior. He takes the initiative in solving his own problems, using the lessons learned through experience. He informs himself in areas in which he must make important decisions. In accepting consequences for what he says and does, he accepts also the consequences of failure to act when the occasion demands.[2]

Responsibility implies voluntary obedience. It implies either acceptance of the rules established by law and custom, or, in seeking their modification, respect for merit and adherence to democratic procedures. It implies action on the basis of a pattern of values and beliefs, development of one's talents, and concern for others in an ever-widening circle. On crucial issues it may at times mean holding to one's own beliefs at considerable personal cost.

[1] "Responsibility: the fourth R," title of the Superintendent's Annual Report, Cincinnati Public Schools, 1956–1957.

[2] *Ibid.*, p. 10. Reprinted by permission.

Responsibility of one sort or another is widely taught inside our schools and families. Even as taught in the nursery and primary grades, in a liberal democracy, responsibility is a most complicated subject matter. A pedagogy, an art that is adequate to elicit and mature it, is not easy to come by.

### "HIGHER" AND "LOWER"

However much the meaning of responsibility may resemble a snowflake, we all have at least some vague sense of responsibility in handling other peoples' money and goods; we all recognize responsibility to our fraternity or firm or family. At home we know responsibility for jobs assumed in an informal division of labor, but also "the family responsibility for smoothing things over." We recognize a parental responsibility to instruct respect for women and property, and for tradition generally, but we may also recognize a responsibility to encourage sensitivity to newer ideas, and adaptation to the attitudes and notions of our childrens' peers. We know that an administrator is responsible first of all for his department or bureau and its work; but ought he not "to be man enough" on occasion to act from a broader loyalty? We uniformly acknowledge that a congressman is responsible to his constituents; but then many of us think he should also be held responsible to his country as a whole, or even to humanity. Should a congressman have the courage of his own moral convictions and know when to try to change the majority opinion among his constituents?

We first learn responsibility as children by having specific duties assigned and carrying them out, but the profile of adult courage is more likely to be of a person whose crucial decision turns on finding, insightfully, what his responsibility in life really is, and then, if necessary, bravely rejecting his formal but shallow "duty in the eyes of the world." If we try to spell out the higher responsibilities, we may risk finding ourselves deep in briars and tangles. Every specific responsibility might seem to hold only for a certain level of discourse. We could, instead of rising to a higher level, sink into a slick hypocrisy. But if we then rejected all the higher and subtler responsibilities from fear of hypocrisy, or from any kind of fear, we would be plain cowards. We should be no more reluctant to face and study our responsibilities than to carry them out. But for good psychological reasons, we usually are.

### USAGE AND LOGIC

Our usage will vary with the strength of our mind and character. If we are even a little subject to envy, we may easily confuse responsibility, in our perception of the lives of others, with extraordinary power and freedom. Thus an executive may be envied—de Juvenel suggested the case—because he is "free" to fly to Japan in March and to Argentina in April. But the man himself may enjoy his flights very little. To him they may only mean having to take leave again and again from his family, or more routine work, more risk and nervous strain. Do we not all agree, in any case, in granting at least *some* degree of subjectivity in judgment as to where rights end and responsibilities begin? Subjectively, the line is not sharp. Many a young man, well started on a brilliant career or rapturous love affair, has waked up to find himself chained to serious responsibilities from which he could no longer extricate himself.

Responsibility names a triadic relation. We can always logically ask of a responsibility,

For *what* is it?

For *whom* is it?

To *whom* does it belong?

It may consist in an action or inaction or a readiness; somebody owns it; and it advantages someone. Since our conception of advantage is relative to our knowledge of the good, or is a constituent of our theory of value, responsibility will always raise problems of a philosophical order. And the theory of decision as to *who* is responsible, and to *whom,* is central to ethics. The more concrete, practical answers to these questions come no easier, unfortunately, than do the philosophical ones. Thus: To what extent is your local school board responsible to the pupils, and to what extent to the taxpayers? If the home is typically responsible for the child, what if it fails? Is the school then responsible? or the church? or some political unit or other? an aunt or uncle, perhaps?—We are not all in agreement in our answers to these questions. We shall find corresponding disagreement in a philosophical analysis that tries to relate legal, political, and domestic responsibility.

Linguistic usage is confusing, sometimes even deceiving. We for instance very frequently use forms of "responsible" to name a character trait. Without any clear-cut reference to whom or for what they are responsible, we speak of certain individuals as "responsible persons." But in sharp contrast to that usage, we often speak of responsibility—in court, for instance—as an entirely objective relationship, and one to which characterological responsibility and felt sense of responsibility are totally irrelevant. A department store is responsible in law for the condition of its escalators, elevators, and fire escapes, but this has nothing to do with how the store owners or managers happen to feel about it or whether they are decent men or not.

Yet there may be sound reason to move in *both* these directions that usage indicates. Surely it does matter that the municipal inspector of escalators should always perform his work with responsibility, for the department store manager may be given to bribing, and his customers to claiming exorbitant damages. Someone needs to be responsible in his own person. We have to go beyond the objectively clear cases of full triadic meaning. The linguistic drift towards the characterological and the subjective is almost inevitable.

Supposing you appoint an administrator, will you know just what his responsibilities are? He must be given administrative discretion, and you are forced to count on his responsibility-in-general. If you are unlucky, you may even have to weigh his reputation for responsibility against his reputation for professional skill. Your eventual success or failure in appointing him will depend on his acts in objective situations and on how those acts affect numerous people. Responsibility is not all that counts, but it *does* count, and eventually in its full triadic nature.

Responsibility does not, then, belong to action just as (brute) action: It may be either relevant or irrelevant to pulling a switch or turning the lights on. And action conceived of as responsible or irresponsible is thought of as having consequences that affect other people and that could be intended to.[3] Objectively, responsibility is the ability and habit of performing up to standard in the light of claims of persons or institutions. Subjectively, the *sense* of responsibility is respect for interests, felt constraint. —However, to say that we want responsible persons is not equivalent to saying that we want worriers, people who habitually and temperamentally "feel constraint." The heaviest responsibilities have to be placed on people who are "strong," who by temperament and habit do not unduly "feel constraint" and can, therefore, go home and sleep it off. And so it is obvious that health and energy, self-discipline, a habit of excellence, and—somehow—conscientious feelings, all are elements of the character that can carry responsibility of high degree.

## RESPONSIBILITY AS MANIFEST ACCOUNTABILITY

The origin of the word "responsibility" suggests that it means accountability, for it derives from a Latin form of "respond to," or

[3] Responsibility exists at the ontological level that Peirce called "thirdness." Thirdness applies where one thing stands for another in respect to some third thing or third party.

"answer to." To be responsible is to be answerable for something to someone.

Debt is usually a manifest obligation for which I can be held answerable. I am responsible for a debt, because I have freely incurred it and received something of value in return from somebody else.

Agency of any kind implies manifest accountability to a principal. If I perform a function of trust or representation, I am accountable to those whom I represent or whose trust is placed in me.

In the most primitive social unit, the family, part of the responsibility is manifest. Husbands are accountable to and for their wives, and fathers to and for their children. Marriage means the free assumption of responsibility for one's spouse, and having children implies the voluntary assumption of responsibility for their support and training. Generally speaking, no one else could be expected to accept identical responsibilities with equal interest and understanding.

In our way of looking at things, accountability in all these kinds of cases implies the *free* assumption of obligation to perform in certain ways or kinds of way. Liberty and responsibility are inseparable. Beyond the acknowledged specific debt, in our political-economic order, stands the whole system of free contract among individuals or freely associated parties. We not only agree to this or that exchange. We have also at least tacitly agreed upon an entire system of exchange in which economic values are freely traded.

Agency, again, is acknowledged only where there is a presumption of its having been voluntarily assumed. And our legal tradition has aimed to restrict and carefully demarcate parental responsibility. Parents are not accountable for children who have attained their majority, but the courts have been most reluctant—perhaps unduly reluctant—to hold them responsible even for minors. On the other hand, if one has children he is accountable *to* them, and it is generally agreed that one has a negative responsibility *not* to have children for whom one cannot care. There is, however, no legal punishment for having too many children, and both the state and many corporations make allowances.

### LEGAL AND MORAL RESPONSIBILITY

Responsibilities can be enforced by law, to the extent that they are manifest. The law crystallizes responsibilities that are already acknowledged and that are testable. "Responsibility has become primarily a legal concept, because the law requires clear tests to decide when a person's actions create an obligation or make him liable to punishment." [4]

The law works with coarse tools, and it is desirable anyway to keep legal machinery as far out of sight as possible. Where loyalties run deep and integrity is all but universal, performance is generally good without intrusion of the law. Law takes up the slack: It is no general substitute for voluntary performance.

A good lawyer aims to clarify responsibilities, to make a just estimate of future problems and probabilities, to assure in advance the satisfaction of all parties, and so to obviate the necessity of litigation. Not enforcement, but the exact depiction of responsibilities, where social relationships are complicated or rapidly evolving, is the primary work of the law.[5] Law is needed to insure parties to business transactions that they know to what they are committing themselves, to foresee the implications of contracts. It is needed in the establishing and proliferating administrative agencies. Statistics would indicate that lawyers are at a premium in legislative and major executive positions. In brief, the work of the law is to make responsibility as manifest as possible.

Of course, this work simplifies the detection of irresponsibility and thus makes it easier to identify, corral, and bring in the stragglers. When a disproportionate amount of legal attention is required to cope with enforcement problems and to solve issues of criminal responsibility, it is a sure sign of near-hysterical fear and suspicion or of breakdown of public morality. "The looser sexual morality, the more shot-gun weddings."

Nothing is more important to a high standard of public morality than clear sanctions. Unfortunately, in a rapidly evolving society—and today society is rapidly evolving the world over—sanctions are not clear.

> If we are surprised about the lack of moral scruples which in some Asian countries are connected with petty thefts, we should remember that men used to be hanged for stealing a sheep in eighteenth-century England.[6]

[4] "But it is, of course, no less a moral concept, a conception which underlies our view of a person's moral duties. In fact, its scope extends considerably beyond what we commonly consider as moral." F. A. Hayek, *The Constitution of Liberty*. Chicago: The University of Chicago Press, 1960, pp. 75–76.

[5] The more advanced colleges of law are preoccupied with the development of new international law, administrative law, aviation and space law. Legal research, like all research, is typically forward-looking.

[6] K. J. Newman, "Punishment and the Breakdown of the Legal Order: The Experience in East Pakistan." *Nomos III: Responsibility,* Ed. Carl J. Friedrich. New York: The Liberal Arts Press, 1960, p. 137. Reprinted by permission.

But who today would approve of hanging a man for stealing a sheep? Who blames Jean Valjean for stealing a loaf of bread? Who blames a slave, the legal property of Simon Legree, for running away?

> Even in Europe, law enforcement became almost impossible when, as in the case of duelling, the moral code did not uphold the legal one.[7]

If duelling is ruled in by the moral code, it cannot be successfully ruled out by the legal code. Of course, in a very moderate degree, the law may forecast morality to come, but such "prophetic" law is never well enforced.

In general, where moral codes and views are rapidly changing, where punishment is becoming more humane and retribution considered obsolete and unjustifiable, neither responsibilities nor sanctions will be entirely manifest. In such cases, the libertarian tradition ever since John Locke has supported the sharp enforcement of minimal law. Public order always demands good enforcement, but only that minimal law which is almost universally supported by public morality can be well enforced. It is illiberality, intolerance, and suspicion that insist "there ought to be a law. . . ," and moreover support a policy of retribution towards violators. But illiberality, intolerance, suspicion, and retribution are today properly frowned on as themselves immoral. Of retribution, Winston Churchill said, in essence:

> The mood and temper of the public toward crime and criminals is one unfailing test of the civilization of any country. A desire to rehabilitate those who have committed crime, tireless efforts toward the discovery of curative and regenerative processes, and an unfaltering belief that there is worth, if you can but find it, in the heart of every man—these are the symbols that mark and measure the stored-up strength of the nation.[8]

But to overplay legal responsibility and to desire always to enlarge the law's net constitute psychological dispositions closely affiliated with the demand for retribution.

## IN FAVOR OF PARCELED RESPONSIBILITY

Embezzlement is a national scandal. Norman Jaspan has estimated that it accounts for the loss of a billion dollars a year—twice the

[7] *Ibid.* Reprinted by permission. When I studied in Germany, members of the conservative fraternities, or *Burschenschaften,* still salted and proudly wore their duelling scars.

[8] As stated by Henry Weihofen in "Retribution Is Obsolete," *ibid.,* p. 127. Reprinted by permission.

loot of all burglars, armed robbers, and auto thieves. Embezzlement is not the crime of teen-agers but, generally, of an older generation with a too widespread, sadly distorted sense of values according to which one's integrity has less worth than money.[9] We should not be overimpressed by this and similar national scandals. Our hope lies with youth, teachers, and the public at large. The integrity of the public is a fact, if we are talking about individual conduct and not spoken, generalized opinion. Finance companies report only minuscule losses on personal loans.

A man who had some years before inherited a small town bank committed suicide. The discovery was then made that he had lost more than a quarter million dollars gambling at the horse races. The money he had lost belonged to depositors at his bank, and most of it was fully insured. Why did he embezzle? Why did he committ suicide?

Is not a sense of responsibility fulfilled part of the normal individual's psychology? Perhaps of all human frustrations, the most intense and painful is the one a man imposes on himself when he rejects and seeks to bury a responsibility that he himself immediately acknowledges. But to some careless people, to "borrow" insured bank deposits is easier than to pass by a beggar on the street, easier for a time.

In America, to instance one Western country, responsibility has been very widely scattered and parceled out. It has never been so in Russia or China. Some foreign observers have protested vigorously that the locus of accountability, like that of sovereignty, is extremely hard to discover. There certainly is no inevitability about the sort of extreme division of responsibility that has generally held among us. Among many peoples, for instance, parental responsibility does not cease when offspring reach maturity. Neither does political responsibility require to be assumed by all the people; as was mentioned earlier, most Russians hardly know how to begin a discourse about political issues.

Whatever may be the origin of our intensive division of responsibility, it is supported by reasons that parallel those that argue for individual liberty. Specific responsibilities freely assumed have the greatest likelihood of being carried through with consistent high quality performance. Moreover, if responsibility is undertaken by individual initiative and intention, the *burden* is minimized or is at least balanced by contemplated rewards.

Sometimes, to be sure, we don't know "where the grocery got the canned goods." But then we count on a *chain* of responsibilities

[9] Violation of antitrust legislation is again no crime of teen-agers, but it rests on a confusion that can more easily be cleared up by the government.

in which each link is freely assumed: The grocer is responsible to the consumer, but the jobber is responsible to the grocer, and the canner to the jobber. Each responsibility is incorporated in a contract, and the obligations thus freely shouldered all have the force of law behind them. Government can oversee the entire chain or inspect any link, but we hardly expect government to take as much interest in economical production and distribution as do most individual contractors. The general run of men, with their lack of scope and imagination, and with few courses in philosophy to their credit, respond more consistently where accountability is addressed to specified individuals. And then their energy is elicited, not only by sense of responsibility, but also by interest, by both short-term and long-term interest.

Inside government and inside business concerns, serious attempts are, and of course must be, made to *assign* responsibilities. Even so, responsibilities assigned quickly become organic, get integrated with work, and take on a character that can be studied by anthropologists. The primitive undertaking is almost always owing to the initiative of individuals or free associations, be they business establishments or political parties. Men do *decide* to run for President. Nor would we allow the highest responsibilities to be assigned by birth or party or self-perpetuating trusteeship.

Our seemingly high, wide, and handsome division of responsibility does not lead to irresponsibility. Rather, it assures the interest and care for detail that are requisite to success. Hence, for instance, our farmers have produced more and more and have greatly increased productivity in recent decades, while Russian collectivized agriculture has limped. There is some evidence that the most efficient farming in the U.S.S.R. is done on plots assigned to individual peasants. But beyond that, the stress on one grand responsibility—"hedgehog responsibility"—to the state, or to the Russian—or German—people or nation or soil turns, by the pressure of events and the magic of propaganda, into fanaticism. If men do not have adequate immediate interest and sense of responsibility, then they must be prodded, whipped up, forced. Responsibility gels quietly and even more firmly when mixed with opportunity. We do not trust fanaticism, and we don't like psychological and physical force.

We have divided responsibility even at the highest level of government. We look on the division as necessary to the maintenance of adequate checks and balances. We have here on the grand scale the same organization that holds in a clothing loft: Some design clothing, some make it, and others inspect it. The customer, not the tailor, passes final judgment on the garment. A major negative strength of our order is that it curbs every tendency towards the assumption of total or permanent responsibility.

### THREE KINDS OF RESPONSIBILITY

The most fascinating conflict in the Western world is the clash between responsibility for maintenance of the status quo and responsibility for progress. Maintenance of the status quo includes the preservation of moral values; progress includes moral progress and betterment of the social order. Both kinds of responsibility are institutionalized. The continuing recognition and resolution of this conflict is itself the core of ultimate political and ethical responsibility today.

A third kind of responsibility, namely the responsibility to keep things going, is too obvious to belabor. It is rubbed into us from boyhood, so to speak, when we learn to swim and keep swimming and not to leave trunks and towel on the living room couch. This responsibility for operations ought, in any case, to be respected. Supplies must be kept coming. Analytically, and these distinctions are for the most part only analytical, this kind of responsibility should be sharply differentiated from responsibility for the status quo, which has to do with structure, conditions, and procedures.

We propose to discuss all three kinds of responsibility. First, the mundane but not always so pedestrian responsibility for keeping things going. We elect in this connection chiefly to discuss responsibility in business. Then something will be said about maintenance of the status quo. The next chapter has to do with responsibility for progress and then with the highest responsibilities.

### RESPONSIBILITY FOR OPERATIONS

That power inheres in operating positions rather than in reform movements is inevitable. That it does so is one great peril that every society faces in times of world change. The burden of state and of defense, the burden of big business and of big labor, are burdens of responsibility universally acknowledged. It is the acceptance of major responsibilities of this kind that is most highly paid for throughout the world. Major-generals in the U.S.S.R. earn 156 times the base pay of conscript privates. Intelligence, education, experience, and a habit of deciding and commanding are well-known requirements of fitting a man for the assumption of responsibilities such as those of a general officer.

Leaving Russian generals to their caviar and vodka, there can in any case be no serious question that some kinds of operations must be maintained. Mouths must be fed. Clothing and shelter must be available and adequate, work done and payrolls distributed. Established ends and given ends can be attained, only if the necessary means are made available.

In *Point of No Return,* his father is forever promising Charles gifts; but Charles never gets them, because the money does not turn up. Marquand says:

> Yet there was one thing that Charles could not understand then or later. Why should anyone promise something unless the means were there for making that promise good? That was the weakness behind it all, the insidious, deceptive plank which destroyed all the rest of the structure.[10]

Presents, like punishments, should be promised only when seriously intended. The disillusionment in not receiving the one or the other, when promised, may be bitter.

Every society depends substantially on persons and institutions who look to the means. In our country, the Collector of Internal Revenue is counting on comptrollers having records clear and funds ready for payment on April 15th. (In some other countries, the rich don't know—and don't want to learn—how to keep their books. It was Henry James who said that double-entry bookkeeping is a mark of high culture.) Responsibility for means, including liability for funds to be appropriated by legislatures, in our country rests largely on business. Social scientists have usually taken more interest in other kinds of responsibility, doubtless with good reason: Questions of political responsibility and administrative discretion are ultimate questions. Nevertheless, business operations provide our wealth and affect us all in many ways. We should be prouder than we are that our economy is a good provider and that we have been able to serve as the arsenal of democracy and to support devastated and underdeveloped countries.

Day to day responsibility for means is carried, then, by business firms and their executives. In order to meet it, they must maintain careful audits and a solvent position—they must "stay in the black" —and to do that, they must keep orders coming in, customers satisfied, and collections made.

## PSYCHOLOGICAL CONSEQUENCES OF FOOTING THE BILL

One may expect to find a conservative frame of mind, or "psychology," generated by the carrying of this kind of responsibility. We know, however, that Marx did not think of the bourgeoisie as con-

[10] John P. Marquand, *Point of No Return.* Boston: Little, Brown, and Company, 1949, p. 188. Reprinted by permission.

servative, but as forever revolutionizing production and industrial and social relations.

Whoever must regularly pay the piper is likely to put a high rating on ability to meet bills. The contrast of outlook normally associated with this role and that of the scholar, the scientist, the artist, or that of the politician or soldier, is sharp. But it is not precisely the contrast that outsiders and critics think they perceive. It is responsibility that makes for business conservatism. It is not that executive and ownership classes have wealth so much as that they must pay. The ethics indigenous to business is an ethics that puts first stress on the capacity to fulfill promises. To speak of that reponsibility as a responsibility for maintenance of the status quo is clearly to over-abbreviate. It is really no more than an accommodation to popular opinion.

Businessmen tend to be wary of politicians, because politicians must succeed in making a broad appeal that sometimes fails to count the cost. Big business adapts to high taxes and supports foreign aid. "It all depends." I have heard millionaires say, "The more surtax I pay, the richer I am."

Despite the common image of the businessman as a pillar of the local church, as hymn-singing protector of fundamentalism and "community stability," the more natural tendency of the businessman is toward hard-headed realism. The great theorists of capitalism, *e.g.*, James Mill and David Ricardo, were secularists. If a senator wants to criticize Harvard for secularism, he might do better picking on the great overseers, trustees, and benefactors than on faculty and undergraduates. (It is true that Harvard does not have fraternities: There is hardly time for Harvard rituals *and* fraternity rituals.)

Business is not dully conservative and monolithic in its attitudes toward education. In the South today, pre-eminent business leaders carry the ball for integration of the schools. The pro-liberal arts movement in higher education since the Second World War has been vigorously supported by corporate administrators.[11]

Above all, businessmen cannot afford to be too conservative in business. The contradiction between responsibility and reactionism is blatant. Reaction is expensive. Executives are always making changes, and it is of course industrial processes, social relations, attitudes toward work, toward products, that they are changing.

Max Weber has pointed to the flood of moral indignation that

[11] Every year around April Fool's Day, business recruiters visit American colleges to fool and confuse the graduating seniors. Nothing could be more deceptive than the picture of business painted by some of these representatives of the personnel office.

accompanied the rise of capitalism.[12] It has torn down old codes and ancient rituals. Perhaps in practice capitalism still poses a sterner challenge to the traditional morals of village cultures than that posed by Communism.

According to Weber, moreover, "the process of rationalization associated with the movement from traditionalism to capitalism was accompanied by the catastrophic degradation of taste in the style of articles of everyday use." [13]—That is, of course, a value judgment. One could be equally impressed by the democratic spread of aesthetic education associated with capitalism. One could be impressed by the support capitalists have given to the advance of architecture, by support given to Louis Sullivan, Root and Holabird, Frank Lloyd Wright, and Saarinen.[14]

### "BUSINESS IS BUSINESS?"

A farm management executive was relating the other day how he reduced the number of families working a Georgia plantation from twenty-six to three in the first year of his contract. The twenty-six families had had a median annual cash income of $200 per family. The three families who remain now earn nearly $400 the month each. The other families have moved to town, where they have good incomes and live in new government-subsidized houses with indoor plumbing. Their children begin to receive a modicum of education. —This same executive had to order all wrenches removed from the new $6,000 combine on that farm to keep the hands from "making adjustments" and damaging the combine. He succeeded in gaining respect for the new Deere plows (always green) by painting them bright red. His "crackers" have turned into farmers, and someday they will be good mechanics, too.

This kind of "revolution," sometimes on a gigantic scale, is almost routine in the business world. Capitalists have not just introduced steam, gas, electricity, and petrol and gravity feed, mass production, the assembly line, and automation; they have also moved the country into the city, transformed the hill-billy into the suburbanite and the city-dweller, and, in Marx' phrase, "conjured up whole populations out of the earth." By contrast, the Communists have been, for the most part, mere copy-cats. The paramount responsibility for the

[12] Max Weber, *The Protestant Ethic and the Spirit of Capitalism.* New York: Charles Scribner's Sons, 1958, p. 69.

[13] *Ibid.,* p. 200, note 26.

[14] The Chicago Art Institute made a fine show of the architecture of Chicago capitalists in the '80s and '90s. That architecture includes early skyscrapers and the first air-conditioning.

really Faustian leap into the dark by modern man rests squarely on enterprise and capital.

A bankrupt artist or politician or school teacher is not necessarily a failure, but a bankrupt businessman is a failure. Business directors have always assumed responsibility for profits and losses. But now what about responsibility for guaranteed annual employment? What about responsibility for the provision of enough jobs for all the nations' employables? What about responsibility for re-training those displaced by automation and other technological shifts? Is there such a thing as business statesmanship? *Is* business run in the interest of the whole polity? —The business community has had to take more and more responsibility for consequences beyond mere profit and loss, especially since Myron C. Taylor decided to proceed with collective bargaining. "Business is business," or the kind of narrow professionalism once espoused by Andrew Carnegie, has become little more than a dodge. Whitehead said, "A great society is a society in which its men of business think greatly of their functions."

Since most working citizens are employed by big business, it makes a great difference, what kind of organizational structure holds sway within our larger corporations. Some American corporations have more employees than Rousseau would grant citizens to a sovereign state. James Worthy has made a double point in favor of conscious and persistent delegation of responsibility and authority in big business. Delegation is needed, since senior executives do not have time to make decisions that junior executives can make. But second, distribution of responsibility is needed in order to keep high the number of autonomous and responsible citizens on the total American scene. So many people are employed in big business, that if it were narrowly hierarchical in its structure of power and responsibility, the sources of leadership would shrink dangerously. His own company, Sears, Roebuck, "is widely known in management circles for the unusual extent to which authority and responsibility are delegated down the line." [15] Nor should one downgrade either the realities or the possibilities of business as a supporter of community enterprises (and political undertakings), or as a school for the cultivation of men of action and vision.

## BUSINESS AND POLITICS

The record of so-called "business government" is mixed. Administrations dominated by businessmen often prove uninspired.

[15] James C. Worthy, *Big Business and Free Men.* New York: Harper & Brothers, 1959, p. 94.

Businessmen naturally have some disposition to look on economic values as fundamental; and indeed they are, but not "more fundamental" than certain other classes of value. Long experience with commercial problems and values cannot easily be adapted to the hustings. Businessmen and soldiers are sometimes impatient of the "inefficiency" that inheres in democratic political and legal processes and rituals. Politics is "inefficient" in that it comes round to a matter of votes; but also it *is* sometimes concerned with ultimate values. The exceptional businessmen who have performed greatly in politics and government are men, say like Senator Couzens, who gave up business and energetically entered on a second career, and who adopted new perspectives and habits. A sort of proof of the pudding is Mr. Worthy, who, after having urged part-time participation by businessmen in politics, resigned from Sears, Roebuck to work full-time in politics.

### BUSINESS VERSUS GOVERNMENT

The interest and responsibility of government are not the same as the interest and responsibility of commerce or industry. Municipal, state, and federal government represent all the people in all their capacities and interests. The federal government has power to declare war and to make peace; it commands troops and can send them into battle. It is true that very large corporations like General Motors prosper or languish with the national economy—and *vice versa.* National refusal to trade with mainland China has restricted the foreign market, *e.g.,* of our earth-moving and tractor companies. The Marshall Plan has undergirded the foreign market. Wars and involvements such as that in Korea obviously affect industry.[16]

To force or pretend identity or harmonization of interest is not always sound. Certainly the government has to establish its own course with no more consideration for any corporation than is warranted by its being a useful and efficient producer and employer. Too great an involvement of government personnel with corporation officials, *e.g.,* of military officers with suppliers, is a menace against which the Congress and the Executive are properly on guard. From a business perspective, in the long run, the danger is just as great. A corporation has its own interests and should be, under our laws, carefully protected against expropriation by government.

[16] Transport aircraft were called into military use in 1950, greatly reducing American trans-oceanic service. Electric manufacturing companies had to cancel "ECA" contracts with Greece and Turkey and let the business go to Siemens and other German concerns.

It is not an exaggeration to say that, to the extent that government and the business community have one identical interest, totalitarianism has infected the economy.

### FISCAL POLICIES

Modern fiscal procedures make intervention and interference in business simpler and more feasible than they used to be. Public opinion polls reveal that the public at large does not realize how much strain is put on business by taxes and is not even aware of the surtax rates on either individuals or corporations in the higher brackets.

Our most profitable—and presumably most efficient—companies often pay more in federal taxes than is left over for dividends, reserves, and expansion of facilities. The S. D. Warren Company is a small, high-quality company in paper manufacture and commercial printing. It long ago celebrated its centenary and has often proved its ability to withstand industry-wide and even general depression while maintaining its labor force. In 1960, S. D. Warren Company made a net income before federal income taxes of $11,039,623, up 7 per cent from 1959. Its net income after taxes was $5,258,429, up 6 per cent. The President of the Company commented in the annual report for 1960:

> Do you ever realize that, with a 52% Federal tax on corporation profits, the U.S. Government has a greater interest in our success than do our own stockholders? Yet the Government has put up none of the money, while our stockholders have put up all of it! On the face of it, this is an unsound situation.
>
> And this is further confirmed in my visits to the various mills of our foreign licensees. I am forever amazed at how some of our foreign friends who may be one-fifth our size in plant, capacity, sales volume, and the like, can undertake building and equipment projects that would give us pause—even though we're five times their size. Sure, their wage and construction costs are less than ours, but it's more than that. Their governments *encourage* them to spend on plant. They have *incentives* to modernize and expand. The tax situation is *favorable* to a growing company.
>
> But not so in this country. In fact, it is quite the reverse. And so—with no other way out of the dilemma—the small fellow is forced to merge with the big—thus making the bigs bigger.
>
> This trend is not good for the long-range American economy. The old-time entrepreneur, the guy who is willing to work his heart out to build a business, should have a chance in this country and

should not be hamstrung and hobbled by punitive Federal taxation and by outmoded depreciation policies.[17]

Either taxation or appropriation can result in undue advantage to some firms, less than their due to others. Corporations having large military contracts may be favored with cost-plus contracts, with contracts not competitively bid, or with special arrangements for paying the costs of scientific and technological research.

The government has the right, if not the obligation, to spur the production of what it needs. But the responsibility attaching to fiscal decisions is immense. Some corporations having major defense contracts or subcontracts spend immense amounts of money on advertising, public relations, and sales and entertainment expense. To the extent that such money is classified as expense, it is not taxed. Yet it is used to control the public mind, and to secure new contracts.

Surely public utilities have the right to present their perspective to the public and to develop public relations programs. Yet these programs can be used to soft sell the public on high utility rates and to propagandize justly or unjustly against those who want low utility rates. Perhaps the extreme manifestation of confusion is simultaneous support by fiscal practice of the "free enterprise" propaganda of privately-owned companies and of the public relations of REA and TVA.

It is not justly the responsibility of some business firms, through the vagaries of taxation and appropriation, to support the extravagances of other business firms. While direct responsibility to see that this does not happen rests on government, in the nature of the case the business community must assume indirect responsibility and initiative to prevent it.

## RESPONSIBILITY FOR MAINTENANCE OF THE STATUS QUO

Responsibility for the status quo is responsibility for maintenance of the political and moral economy as an order, for fundamental principles and institutions as they have evolved. It implies the maintenance of conformity; but how much conformity, and conformity in respect to what, are questions that require the most serious consideration. Narrowly conceived, it is the responsibility for enforcement of law and custom, the prevention of sabotage, the radical elimination of subversion. Broadly conceived, it is also the responsibility for the avoidance of such kinks, bottlenecks, and failures as

[17] George Olmsted, Jr., President, 89 Broad Street, Boston, Massachusetts.

make for disillusionment, desperation, and destructiveness. It includes the protection of property by night-watchmen; but it also includes protection of the *system* of private property by legislation to prevent abuse and protection of the *system* of individual right by just administration.

Where there is general agreement in respect to values, ethics, and the essential nature of the legal order, there is ordinarily no special difficulty in maintaining the status quo. The police power of the state can then be brought to bear without equivocation in its support. Most of us would like to look on that as the normal and desirable situation. Most of us would agree that actual and potential offenders ought to have conveyed to them a clear expression of public disapproval in the form of known legal punishment.

Agreement in respect to values, ethics, and the legal order does not, unfortunately, always exist. For example, the action against the Nazi war criminals was an unprecedented action, one that is still much disputed. Whether it was a legitimate legal action by international authority or a morally and legally inexcusable maneuver by the victorious Allied nations, depends on the point of view one adopts. If our point of view is right, it is not so because of vindictive feelings, but because, in present world circumstances, actions like those of the Nazis we intend to look on as criminal in the interest of humanity.

This brings us to the question of the nature of the status quo. And we have to admit that, since the values and ethical principles of a society evolve and new laws gain moral and legal sanction and old ones lose it, the status quo varies from time to time and from place to place. Individuals do not interpret it in the same way.

> The world is living through a period of swift and far-reaching upheavals. Standards and institutions which have remained unchanged for centuries are breaking down. Millions who have hitherto passively endured their place in life are clamoring for a new and more worthy existence.[18]

We in the United States are not insulated against these changes. Because of our power and prominence we are sharply, if not always accurately, judged according to our shifting attitudes towards these upheavals. Inside the United States, continuous consideration of the nature of the status quo warrants the application of the highest intelligence and judgment combined with the best will. Lack of agreement and confusion about our position are leading not only

[18] From the first page of the "Rockefeller Report" on the problems of U.S. Defense. Copyright 1958 by Rockefeller Brothers Fund, Inc.

to much more expensive, but also to contradictory enforcement and use of police power.

To choose at random a field or two where our effective morality and law are obscure, one may consider our positions on trust-busting and internal security, though our sexual mores would be equally interesting in this connection.

Does the denial of trust and cartel maintain the status quo and protect standards of free competition, or is it an anachronism that inhibits the normal development of capitalist enterprise? We have the Sherman and Clayton anti-trust legislation and the prosecution against the electrical manufacturing companies; we disapprove of the use of wealth to beat down competitors. Do we also fear bigness as such? Have we sometimes taxed chain stores from hatred and envy? Working in the other direction have been the National Recovery Administration with its price codes and the disposition of the Department of Defense to favor large contractors with their promise of large results. Bank mergers are being approved, and big banks often mean a kind of interlocking control over industry, and hence over competition.

We have become more and more concerned by questions of internal security, especially in response to the threat of Communism. Our institutions warrant the full protection of the law against internal and external enemies and against concealed ("black" and "gray") propaganda. However, some of the prominence (and perhaps some of the success) of Communism has always been owing to the disproportionate fear of it and to its use as a political football and in name-calling. Is the status quo protected by our one thousand rightist organizations, or is it changed and degraded? Are the nations' citizens more patriotic because of the activities of the House Un-American Activities Committee, or less respectful of the "Bill of Rights" and the Fourteenth Amendment? Have so many intensive security checks been worth their cost in money and preoccupation and in obstruction of recruitment of scientific, technological, and military personnel? Against what lying subversive do test oaths—with their entirely unmeasured cost of administration—protect us? Is segregation the status quo, or is "equal rights"? What are the criteria of loyalty to America and the American tradition?

Perhaps we can find some solace in knowing that we are not alone in the possession of contradictory conceptions of status quo. In order to maintain their orthodoxy of Communist internationalism, the Chinese have had in practice to fall back on a policy of isolationism! And Khrushchev is still trying to live down that pact which Stalin made with Hitler to protect the status quo.

# 14

# RESPONSIBILITY II

The more advanced and sophisticated the moral economy becomes, the more dependent we are on the excellent fulfillment of individually assumed, freely assumed, responsibilities. To force a man *not* to do something is, comparatively speaking, very simple. To make him positively do something, and do it with a high degree of perfection, is not easy.

## EDUCATION FOR A NEW WORLD

Our system crucially depends on the work of teachers. The deeply interested and responsible work required of them certainly cannot be requisitioned by statute or by policeman's night club. Minimal standards can, of course, be maintained by law and administration: college courses can be required, an outward show of patriotism and loyalty to the local community, regular appearance at 8 o'clock Monday mornings, sobriety and conservative attire. But the kinds of teachers who save or even improve the system find their deepest responsibilities inside themselves, in their pupils, in the subjects and arts to be taught. To a certain extent, these deeper responsibilities can be inspired and encouraged by devices of selection and recognition. However difficult judgment about teachers may be, still wealthy and intelligent school systems and colleges do manage to hire with discrimination—which is not to say they never make mistakes.

The responsibility of teachers is not exclusively a responsibility for progress, nor is the responsibility for progress in education exclusively on the shoulders of teachers. Nevertheless, given our cultural arrangements, a heavy burden in this respect is borne by teachers and professors. The duty to educate young people so that they can live successfully in both the present and the future, so that they will be well adapted to their own times, and thus flourish in their years of maturity and, so to speak, be *in command of* their own times, is a duty all but impossible of performance. The mere act of informing young people about what is already known, without a critique, is difficult enough; but serious parents are not satisfied with that. As has often enough been pointed out, who only understands accepted meanings really fails even to understand them. The burden of the past needs always to be transmuted into something relevant and useful to the future. The pupil who does not learn how to generalize, and thus to project into the future, but who rather literally learns only how things are done now, gets neither a humane nor a useful education.

Whitehead stressed the importance of the present, and his point of view is compatible with our own. Whatever actually happens, happens in some present. Events, including the event of learning, can only occur in the present tense. The student has to learn to live in *his* present, and to use *his* time. Young people want to learn to master themselves and *their* environment.

The knife-edged *NOW* is not, however, all the time there is. The present is full of the future, and the future will be. "What shall be the properties of that future?" is our most important human question, from a practical point of view. (The preceding statement is a tautology, but it is a tautology of supreme importance for the conduct of life.) Education is a leading forth, and it should be not only a leading out into the light but also into a future of maximalized satisfactoriness.

A crucial question for any philosophy of education is, what is "maximalized satisfactoriness"? But philosophers, poets, and religionists have not succeeded in reaching any consensus as to what is the meaning of "maximalized satisfactoriness." As we well know, Kant said it is an ideal of the imagination. The libertarian strives to take this unsatisfactoriness of "satisfactoriness" seriously into account, on the ground that an open question deserves frank recognition as such.[1] But while he may regret that so much of life's meaning and value reside in an ideal of the imagination, he will not on that account allow himself to be either fanatical and desperate *or* cynical. Imagination can be controlled, and the issue, in this point of view, is really whether we are going to control it in our own interest as individuals or have it controlled from outside or "above."

The main-line Western philosophers have stubbornly tried to face up to the problem. They have eschewed apocalyptic expectations. Whether the social result of this stubborn effort—representative, of course, of unspoken attitudes of men-at-large—has been greater *happiness* for the main-line Western masses than for the Nazi, Fascist, Falangist, and Communist minorities would be extremely difficult to establish. But, at least, it has meant greater sanity. "Sanity" means reasoned choice of happiness as one's target, and the choice of experientially tested means of attaining it.

[1] In sharp contrast to Lenin, who was combatting an inability to act which characterized pre-Revolutionary Russian intellectuals (including physicians), but which is—we may hope—uncharacteristic of Americans, including American intellectuals. Professor Sabine writes concerning Lenin:

"There is a revealing remark in one of his [Lenin's] notebooks to the effect that clericalism is indeed a sterile flower, yet one growing on the living tree of a prolific, true, powerful, omnipotent, objective, and absolute human knowledge. This sentence shows pretty clearly what Lenin thought science ought to be, and also what he thought Marxism is. It is as authoritarian as clericalism itself. Marxism, he said, is like a solid block of steel; you cannot omit even one of its assumptions 'without falling into the arms of bourgeois—reactionary falsehood.' 'Freedom of criticism' contains an inherent falsehood. 'Those who are really convinced that they have advanced science would not demand freedom for the old views to continue beside the new views.' It is not surprising that Lenin's party, as a rule, has found it easier to co-operate with political reactionaries than with political liberals.

Lenin's Marxism was actionism and intellectualism within the tight band of a dogma that in essence was a religious revelation, and this copied quite faithfully an attitude native to the Russian stereotype. . . . It is the glittering vision of a far-off future in which, like Tolstoy and Dostoevski, Lenin believed that the world and man are to be made perfect. Such a philosophy needs its sacred writings, and just as Tolstoy in his later years turned to exegesis of Scripture to learn what Christianity really means, so all the twists and turns of Lenin's devious politics had to be defended with texts from the gospel according to Marx. Within such a philosophy a difference of belief is a moral issue; a dissenter is not wrong but bad, indifferently bad because he is wrong or wrong because he is bad."—George H. Sabine, "The Ethics of Bolshevism." *The Philosophical Review*, July, 1961, pp. 316–317. Reprinted by permission. This position has been called by Silone, "the primacy of morals over intelligence"; and as Professor Sabine remarks, the line between the primacy of morals over intelligence and plain cynicism is very thin. Lenin metamorphosed the Russian intellectual into an activist, but only reinforced his disposition to dream apocalyptic dreams. The value absoluteness of these apocalyptic dreams reduces the value of every reality and every alternative ideal to near zero. Everything else is either means or obstacle. Totalitarianism requires nothing further for its existence but the socialization of this dream (its widespread, say national, acceptance) and bureaucratic control over "the steps toward its actualization," *i.e.*, statism, party control, dictatorship, national madness.

A good education is, accordingly, an education that results in holding ideals that are worth holding, that relate to the needs of the individual and his fellows, and that are appropriate to the times. A good education results in a steady, firm grip on reality.[2]

### JOHN DEWEY

There is a consensus among American philosophers that the central concept in Dewey is responsibility. Dewey was concerned that men should accept responsibility for the consequences of their actions; and he conceived that to accept such responsibility was to be ethical. Moreover, according to Dewey himself, his educational philosophy is central to his whole philosophy.

Of course, Dewey did not think that educational responsibility was exclusively responsibility for progress. Educating is at once teaching our social heritage—teaching what we know about, and teaching what we know how to do—*and* teaching critique, eliciting criticism in the interest of progress. Since critique is accomplished by the exercise of intelligence, *e.g.*, in recognizing, formulating, and solving problems, the concept of intelligence is also of paramount importance. Since situations change, contemporaneous understanding of heritage implies alertness. If meanings stand idle, their denotations move away from them. Hence, as for Mill, responsibility for maintaining tradition and responsibility for maintaining progress may sometimes prove to be identical. To be fully clear what we stand for is to be clear what we intend in the present situation.

E. A. Burtt[3] says that by about 1890 Dewey was thinking that,

> all human action, including thinking as an important part of action, has consequences; and that the vital difference which men in general and philosophers especially are concerned about is whether responsibility for those consequences is accepted or not.

Again quoting Mr. Burtt's statement of Dewey's views:

> Education is the social function through which every older generation communicates its heritage of wisdom to the younger generation and guides it toward the realization of its new possibilities. It will fail of its role if it falls into either of two extremes—indoctrinating the young in what their elders take to be established truth, tolerating no room for freedom and growth, or permissively allowing children to fumble their own way toward adulthood without

[2] This position represents a consensus of all parties, realists, idealists, progressives, and both Freudians and Jungians.

[3] Edwin A. Burtt, "The Core of Dewey's Way of Thinking." *The Journal of Philosophy,* Vol. LVII, No. 13 (June 23, 1960), p. 406. Reprinted by permission.

> wise guidance from the lessons and resources of their heritage. . . . Education, rightly conceived, is the intelligent reconstruction of human experience as a whole, in its temporal passage from one generation to the next; experience itself is essentially a process of education which will be engaged in either well or ill.[4]

Dewey may have taken his model for responsible action too exclusively from the educative process. One could charge that he had not left his Idealist forebears far enough behind. To be sure, learning and the kinds and ways of acceptance characteristic of learners are components of comparatively passive forms of deciding and acting. In the realm of education, conflicts are decided on their merits; *social* conflicts in educational areas are often decided from above or from outside. The teacher will not serve as a model universally, for the simple and obvious reason that he is not engaged in the thick of practical life. The only method of compromise that the teacher accepts in principle is compromise on the basis of merit, but in fact he wields power over the future, and not over the present, and so situations develop where he may bend under pressure of actual events.

No great teachers have wanted to present themselves to youth as their exclusive models and paradigms.[5] Great teachers want to cooperate in the growth of their students, but the pattern of growth is to emerge out of the nature and experience of the student. The optimum consequence of great teaching is great people, *not* disciples. Thus so conservative a thinker, writer, and teacher as James Weber Linn could be a teacher of importance in the career of James T. Farrell. Of course, teachers often *do* get chosen as exclusive models —but that is not their fault.

For all that, responsibility, education, and liberty, too, are somehow inextricably bound together in the popular imagination: And not without reason. Education aims to bring people to the point of responsibility, to a point of no return beyond which they can and will assume responsibility for the consequences of their actions. Individual strength is that without which no community can maintain itself in progress. It is persons of developed strength who can and do assume responsibility. And the cultivation of individual strength in the young (certainly including strength in group situations) is the special department of educators.

Not the disciples of great teachers, but the eventually strong individualities who have indeed been influenced by them are the great bearers and upholders of responsibility, inclined to, and capable of,

[4] *Ibid.*, p. 413. Reprinted by permission.
[5] Except Jesus and Socrates?

upholding their own rights and the rights of others. *They* can see, and they can do what the weak and irresponsible cannot see and do.

The revolution wrought by Dewey in the field of education was a revolution aimed at responsibility and realism. What the chief figures in the counter-revolution (Hutchins, Admiral Rickover, Bestor) seem to be congenitally incompetent of understanding—as was Herbert Spencer, incidentally—is that the recipient of education is a human person with a given nature, emphatically including a given pattern of growth. Dewey's revolution has by no means been fully consummated in America. Most parents still, even most highly educated parents (for instance, professors and physicians), continue to be nonempirical, unobserving, insensitive to the ever-changing natural patterns of development of their children. They are so because they want their children to excel, but it is a poor excuse. If we wish to see those whom we love excel, our first task is not hurrying and pressuring them, but understanding them.[6] Dewey knew this and thus solved the riddle, "why Pericles had mediocre sons." Pericles did not have time and patience for understanding them.

It has been said that America won the last war with a generation of youngsters brought up according to the principles of Dewey. We may need to go beyond those principles in one way or the other; but shall we win the next war with frenzied, competitive intellects, and without co-operation, emotional health, a habit of deliberation, and individual and group responsibility?

The highest responsibility of all of us as educators—and as the financial supporters of education—is not the manufacture of electronic brains on two legs, but the manufacture of excellent minds and responsible persons.

## EDUCATION OUTSIDE THE SCHOOL AND FAMILY

We are responsible as a nation not only for classroom education but also for the level, intensity, and general excellence of the information held by our adults. We do not do as good a job as we might.

The average family TV set is on six to seven hours a day. Then

[6] The same parents who will accept the presence of an allergy in their child, if the doctor says so, may stubbornly refuse to recognize the presence of a six-month "delay" in reading readiness and lose patience with the child. I have fraternal twin sons—very "even" ones; but they obviously see-saw in their development. First one is braver, brighter, stronger, more musical, taller, more outspoken, better dispositioned—and then three months later the other one is. Of course, these superiorities do not move in unison. Of the corresponding "inferiorities," I affirm that there is nothing to do about them but to wait them out.

there are car radios and other radios. But how much good material is transmitted? Unfortunately, psychologists and other social scientists have made the great and important discovery that profits can be made by giving the people what it wants. The yellow press already was operating on that hypothesis. But the consequent degrading of democracy is profoundly irresponsible.

### RESPONSIBILITY FOR A VIABLE ART

One of the most significant and touchy sorts of higher responsibility is that of the artist. The public has a certain disposition to look on artists as inherently irresponsible, but such is by no means the case. Bohemianism is nothing more than a lateral effect of the artist's responsibility; only in the mind of outsiders is it the crux.

What is, then, the responsibility of the artist? It is to see and to paint or sculpt what he sees. And what is the artist required to see? He is required to see what he sees, when his sensibility has been cultivated and brought to the highest pitch. We may hope that his intelligence has been brought into full play along with his sensibility. That which we cannot legitimately hope for is that we should be able to tell him in advance or in distinction from his artistic activity what he should see. For this reason, censorship and every totalitarian, or even authoritarian, movement aimed at controlling or limiting the artist is mistaken in its very intention. It is also the reason why a capitalist despite all the bourgeois ideology and philistinism has turned out to be, after all, an artist's best friend. For just *one* capitalist who seriously recognizes the value of his work can bake the artist's bread. And this lone patron is easier to discover under capitalism than under any other economic order.

The highest responsibility of the artist is clearly not to his patron. It is to his own envisagement of reality—or envisagement of whatever it may be that absolutely consumes him, completely intrigues and fascinates him. This *has* generally turned out to be some face of reality, as it did, notably, in the case of Impressionism, which was at first widely accused of taking no interest in the real. The protection and encouragement of the arts, however, cannot be left to depend on historical argument. *We* need the contemporary artist.[7]

### RESPONSIBILITY FOR EXCELLENCE

Dr. Gardner proposes that we consider this little schema:

1. Emphasis on individual performance.

[7] Marx seems to have enjoyed no art but literature.

2. Restraints on individual performance.
   (a) Hereditary stratification
   (b) Equalitarianism

Both equalitarianism and hereditary stratification "try to keep a lid on individual performance."

> There is evidence . . . that the critical lines of tension in our society are between *emphasis on individual performance* and *restraints on individual performance.* This tension will never be resolved and *never should be resolved.* Failure to accept this reality has led to a lot of nervous indigestion and unnecessary commotion.[8]

Mr. Gardner has the good sense to see that some realities *are* tense, and he set himself the problems of *excellence in society* and of *excellent society.* "The problem is to achieve some measure of excellence *in this society,* with all its beloved and exasperating clutter, with all its exciting and debilitating confusion of standards, with all the stubborn problems that won't be solved and the equally stubborn ones that might be." [9] But as Mr. Gardner says, with our opposing emphases on individual performance *and* equalitarianism, we do need to do what we have not done: Candidly and incisively explore the implications of each contesting emphasis.

We have been—in consequence—terribly faddish in respect to standards of excellence. Now we favor the true democrat whose only extreme is extreme mediocrity, and again we favor the rugged Horatio Alger who gets places but perhaps ends up frustrated at not being adopted by the Four Hundred. Horatio Alger should have known from the beginning that, at least to the Four Hundred, money is not everything. Again, we favor the intellectually gifted —that's where we are now. And how we suffer when some lad of more than 140 I.Q., duly registered, does not come through! But we ought to have known from the beginning that intelligence is not everything. Parents and schools that bring up their intelligences and intellects, instead of their children, are bound to produce a wan lot of pedants: As if one could make spice cake from spices alone.

The trouble is multiplied in the child and in the child's career, but the trouble itself lies in the one-sided standard. Why should a physician *insist* on his son becoming a physician? Why should not the son of a professor become a banker or an undertaker? Whether he should or not ought to depend on him and society, not on archaic notions irrelevant to him as an individual. According to the General

[8] *Excellence, loc. cit.,* pp. 27–28. Reprinted by permission.
[9] *Ibid.,* p. xiii.

Electric Company, C. P. Steinmetz did not at first distinguish himself in school. He had some difficulty with multiplication tables.—The first question we ought to ask ourselves, however, is not how come a Steinmetz should have trouble with multiplication tables, but rather how come one associates multiplication tables with mathematics and mathematicizing anyway.[10]

## AN EXAMPLE

A first-class college aims to bring together the best available students and the best available teachers under optimum conditions for learning and teaching. A major problem for any such institution is its admissions policy, and it is a problem infused with added emotion, because of the tempo of the national "talent hunt." Hard thinking is invested in weighing the considerations that should bear on "calculated risk-taking in admissions" and the use of scholarship funds. The carefully wrought Ford [11] Committee Report on Admission to Harvard College states:

> Our concern . . . is not simply whether a given applicant would benefit from being at Harvard, but whether he is one of those individuals for whom Harvard can do something not available elsewhere. To deprive a man of the opportunity to attend Harvard is a serious matter . . . only with respect to those individuals who could profit uniquely from having been at Harvard.[12]

The Committee, of course, opts for intellectual promise and disfavors the admission of any candidate unless he appears to possess "the requisite intellectual ability to take advantage of the opportunities and to meet the demands inherent in undergraduate education for a highly selected student body forming part of a university community."

That which Harvard does not want to miss, above all, are candidates possessing "certain qualities of mind which transcend precision, retentiveness and logical consistency, qualities such as the ability to perceive the most complex relationships, incisiveness and

[10] There are other unforgettable lessons in the career of Steinmetz that draw attention to standards: (1) Steinmetz escaped the German police, who were chasing him because he was a Lassallean socialist. (2) He almost failed of admission to the United States, because the immigration officer was unfavorably impressed by his appearance and lack of funds. False standards—or even good standards perhaps—can easily slam the door in the face of vitally needed talent.

[11] For Committee Chairman Franklin Lewis Ford.

[12] *Admission to Harvard College,* A Report by the Special Committee on College Admission Policy, Faculty of Arts and Sciences, Harvard University, February, 1960, p. 8.

originality in the formulation of questions, unorthodox daring in the search for answers." [13] Of course, only one or two per cent of accepted candidates will meet that standard. Warmth, good motivation, tenacity, moral courage and practical judgment are further stated criteria. Harvard College is "greedy" for quality of many different kinds, and it accepts not only responsibility for producing good citizens, but a major special responsibility for producing some great ones. Selection and admission are not themselves college education, but the education wants to be offered to the right individuals: The great critic and art historian Bernard Berenson said, "[My years at Harvard] set the trajectory that I followed all the rest of my life."

Not only at Harvard, but in all colleges having selective admissions, the problem is not only one of concern with safe minimums and prerequisites, but also: "How far should we reach for unevenly developed talent?" Or it can be put in declarative form as, "Intelligent chance-taking is the golden talent of college admissions." [14] There is also the problem of pressure for admission, although no one seems to exert undue pressure on Harvard College Admissions (except perhaps members of the Faculty of the Harvard Medical School).[15]

## THE IMPACT OF SCIENCE

The rather pessimistic impression of Professor Feibleman is that:

> *The primary effect of science is to intensify social behavior outside of science.* It does this by applying to social situations the tools and techniques of pure and applied science. Such intensification is without regard for the moral consequences; more efficient methods of lifesaving, but also more efficient methods of killing: anaesthetics and antibiotics, but also poison gases and ballistic missiles. More often than not the first effects of any new instrument are bad. The earliest practical airplane was used for bombing before it was used for commercial transportation, and the atomic bomb was used at Hiroshima before the construction of the first American plant for production of atomic energy at Shippingport, Pennsylvania.[16]

[13] *Ibid.*, p. 9.

[14] *Ibid.*, p. 10.

[15] One of the most interesting phenomena among Harvard undergraduates is their tendency to shift concentration from natural science to social science. Of the class of 1959, 50 per cent initially declared for natural science and engineering, but 28 per cent completed their degree in them; 19 per cent initially declared for social sciences but 43 per cent completed degrees in them.

[16] James K. Feibleman, "The Scientific Philosophy." *Philosophy of Science*, Vol. 28, No. 3 (July 1961), p. 258. Reprinted by permission.

The natural tendency may be even worse than what we might call "Feibleman's destructive first effect of science." For the absence of control over the beneficial effects may negate the benefits. Thus, an increase in food production tends to lead at once to an inordinate increase in population.

The relations of science with society and government are fascinating, as dealt with by Don K. Price [17] and by C. P. Snow.[18] We have moved far and fast. Dr. Millett has said,

> . . . it is no exaggeration to say that since 1940 federal contract-research income alone has enabled higher education to advance notably its research activities in the physical sciences. There is scarcely a first-rate physics or chemistry department providing graduate instruction in our universities which could maintain its present standing or personnel without federal income.[19]

Dean Price, after insisting on the importance of sustaining free science in and by a great many strong and independent institutions, concerns himself with the problem of the application of science to practical problems. "For it is of no use to imagine that you can defend pure science alone."

> Science, in short, cannot exist on the basis of a treaty of strict nonaggression with the rest of society; from either side, there is no defensible frontier. We can, and must, maintain strong and independent universities and research institutions and insist on their right of freedom of research. But we cannot insist on their freedom on the argument that they are engaged only in basic science, which does not interfere with public affairs or bear on controversial issues. This has not been a useful argument since the scientists came out of the monasteries, and since we gave up the ideal of separating society into distinct "estates," with all those who could read and write claiming the privileges of the clergy. Our argument for the freedom of science must rest instead on the conviction that such freedom is justified both by the importance of freedom for its own sake, as the fundamental value in political society, and by the historical evidence that only free science can play a dynamic role in furthering human welfare. The scientists of Germany, who thought that science was so separate from politics that it could prosper no matter what political philosophy dominated the government, discovered their mistake under Hitler.[20]

[17] *Government and Science: Their Dynamic Relation in American Democracy.* New York: New York University Press, 1954.

[18] *Science and Government.* Cambridge: Harvard University Press, 1961.

[19] John D. Millett, *Financing Higher Education in the United States.* New York: Columbia University Press, 1952, pp. 354–355. Quoted in Price, p. 79. Reprinted by permission.

[20] Price, pp. 106–107. Reprinted by permission.

Many Americans mistakenly think of "science" as representing a consensus that does not exist. C. P. Snow, in an early novel, wrote:

> [The lecturer] mentioned the nucleus and said, "Rutherford has suggested a constitution for it, but I'm not sure that he's right." Before that, I had never imagined that these new concepts were anything but unanimous; I had heard of controversies in the past, but the science I was studying had seemed without people or contradictions.[21]

Yet just where science is most interesting and effective, it is people and contradictions. If undergraduates are fed science in solution with truth serum, they are given a body of dogmatic cognitive results, not real science. Even where science begins and where it ends —or that, especially—is not well established. Price remarks

> I shall always remember with particular pleasure the medical research doctor in one of the military departments who assured a Catholic chaplain that the problem of birth control was one that was purely scientific and thus by definition one with which the chaplain had no concern. I thought at first that he was making this argument with his tongue in his cheek, but I am afraid that in this quarrel the theologian had the greater sense of humor of the two. . . . most scientists are working with tools and methods that give only a partial glimpse of the real nature of any complex human and social problem.[22]

Although both Snow and Price agree that we need more science and scientists in government, they seek not to underestimate the difficulties of preparation. Price quotes the elevated conception of administration of Brooks Adams—with the following comment:

> Administration is the capacity of co-ordinating many, and often conflicting, social energies in a single organism, so adroitly that they shall operate as a unity. . . . Probably no very highly specialized class can be strong in this intellectual quality because of the intellectual isolation incident to specialization; and yet administration or generalization is not only the faculty upon which social stability rests, but is, possibly, the highest faculty of the human mind.[23]

Many scientists, especially those from universities, never feel the need for such a function! [24]

Snow is specially concerned with such problems as how so great a

[21] C. P. Snow, *The Search*. New York: Charles Scribner's Sons, pp. 26–27. Copyright 1934, 1958, Charles Percy Snow. Reprinted by permission.

[22] Price, p. 131.

[23] Brooks Adams, *The Theory of Social Revolutions*. New York: The Macmillan Company, 1913, pp. 207–208. Reprinted by permission.

[24] Price, p. 184–185.

scientist-administrator as Sir Henry Tizard could have been swept aside by the conservative government of Winston Churchill. But I shall quote Price to show, in simplest terms, how science, especially in application, leads to ever-larger policy issues.

> Just as you permit a clerk to handle money because you can audit his accounts, you permit a junior bacteriologist to inspect the water supply on which the health of a city depends because you can tell him (on the basis of definite professional standards) exactly how many and what varieties of bacteria can be tolerated.
>
> But then we come to questions that, step by step, become less objective in their nature. How many bacteria can the water system tolerate? How much should the city spend on reducing infant mortality by public health measures? How much salary should it pay the public health officer? These questions become progressively more difficult to answer in precise numerical or objective terms; more difficult to answer in ways that others can readily check by methods on which there is a professional consensus; more dependent on factors on which research does not give a conclusive and verifiable answer and on which the scientist's opinion may be as prejudiced as any layman's.[25]

### HIGHER ADMINISTRATIVE AND BUSINESS RESPONSIBILITY

One of the most important changes in modern times is shortened hours of labor—important in terms of increased opportunity for happiness and health, and in many other ways. The history of the work week is one of sudden leaps. Before the Civil War, men, women, and children worked almost around the clock. Teamsters, like the father of James T. Farrell, worked eighteen hours a day until after the First World War. Most factory workers in cities, however, worked six ten-hour days, from the Civil War on, from seven A.M. until noon, and from one to six. This system prevailed until Woodrow Wilson promoted legislation enforcing an eight-hour day on the railroads.

Executives sometimes make decisions that startle the trade. President Kinsey decided to reduce the hours of work at Marshall Field & Company, cutting the women's hours from forty-eight to forty. When such decisions are carefully thought out and accord with changing attitudes, they may quickly change custom. The incumbent President of Field's says, "I don't recall that it had any very violent effect on anyone, including our competitors. The work schedules of retail employes have been fairly well standardized for years." [26]

[25] Price, pp. 166–167. Reprinted by permission

[26] Mr. J. L. Palmer, by letter.

A great advantage of our pluralistic society is that various individuals and corporations can try out policies. If Mr. Kinsey's company had been unsuccessful in its change to shorter hours, the shortened hours would not have become customary. When Myron Taylor introduced Big Steel to collective bargaining, not all steel companies made contracts with the United Steel Workers. Keystone Steel is not C.I.O., and Armco has plants that are and plants that are not: A result is further economical and advantageous diversification and more kinds of operations and management in the American steel industry.

One of our greatest problems concerns devices for maintaining at once administrative responsibility and administrative discretion, and that paradox of responsibility, responsibility *for* administrative initiative and discretion. The excellent formulation and development of these responsibilities and powers are manifestly of the greatest value—and necessity—to big government and national defense, big business, big labor, *etc.*

PLURALISM

Our system, requiring that organized men not only perform their regular function but also assume responsibility for the defense of the *conditions* under which they can effectively do their jobs, protects the public indirectly by eliciting such group defense. The American Medical Association in striving to protect medical practice against "socialization" is in exactly the same boat with Hoffa's teamster organization trying to protect teamsters' hours, pay, and other conditions of work. Who is better equipped to protect airline pilots against undue stress than a union of airline pilots? Yet what could be more important to the safety of airline passengers? The government should be involved as overseer, or potential overseer, of "the public interest," but the government cannot initiate the multitude of actions, nor provide the human energy that protects detailed conditions of performance all through the economy. Pluralism is not a luxury: It is a characteristic essential to any economy of our tempo, intense specialization, and complex cooperation. Conflict among private interests is not in principle harmful to the public and may be beneficial.

The requisite diversity of leadership, also, could only be provided by an open society that allows leadership to emerge field by field, interest by interest, industry by industry. Our leaders do not so much form a class, an aristocracy of merit, as they do represent phase after phase of performance. In almost every case, leadership means leadership of a faction, a specialized interest, a corporate concern. In the legislature, representatives represent geographical interests and often also functions associated with committees, like defense, foreign affairs, agriculture, or labor. The Presidency is in some ways an exception, since, besides representing the *government* interest as head of the government, including the armed forces, the President represents the *national* interest as a unity more than does any other branch of government. Nor should a President's successes and failures be too quickly judged. Was Wilson a failure? Or did he represent the national interest despite the ignorance and unimaginativeness of his opposition? To be ahead of (or behind) the times does not entail failure or success in performance—from a long-term perspective.

Excellence is difficult to judge, and experts themselves by no means agree. They fall into classes, traditions, like the French intellectuals of the early nineteenth century with their cabals and battles. The difficulty of judging excellence is in itself an immense consideration weighing in favor of the open society and libertarianism, especially if combined with the capacity to reach practical agreement and working unity.

## POLITICAL RESPONSIBILITY

Political responsibility in the modern, democratic sense has not been widely understood. In this connection, Professor Leys points to a hole, not only in the philosophy of Plato, but also in the philosophy of John Dewey.

Plato has been widely accused of indifference to accountability and of "a penchant for master-minding." Dewey's contention was that Plato's idealism and every other idealism tends to establish an ideal so far beyond practice that they take men's minds away from real problems and run them up into a delusive heaven. If nothing is good unless it is perfect and if perfection is unattainable, men will look on accepted practice as adequate and incorrigible. The defenders of Plato have stressed his insistence on objective standards and his contribution to the natural law tradition.

But Mr. Leys takes a third course, more interesting than the others. He finds Plato neither an advocate of irresponsible nor of responsible government, but an advocate of no government at all. "*The Republic* is, for the most part, the description of a society without conflict; hence, it describes a society that does not need government, law, or political activity." [27] Plato's rulers are simply administrators, who make decisions on their merits. Plato consistently denounced sophists, politicians, barristers, propagandists, and negotiators. *Advocates* are represented as having no capacity except to make the worse reason appear the better.[28]

The pragmatists in their turn have been accused of promoting a kind of Nietzschean irresponsibility, because they objected to fixed standards. The pragmatist orientation puts stress on open-minded problem solving. Dewey wanted to locate responsibility and real morality in intelligence, in honest confrontation of the concrete situation and deliberate response to it.

However, Mr. Leys finds little philosophic support in Dewey or James for any system of politics and law, responsible or irresponsible.[29] Pragmatic philosophers have shown zest for solving problems and corresponding "impatience with institutions that were not geared to problem-solving." But as Mr. Leys then points out, a "scientific" or "intelligent" or "problem-solving" approach to social conflicts is rarely possible in government and politics; typically, pragmatic reference to politicians is slurring. Mr. Leys discovered the following "give-away" of Dewey's impatience with anything on the order of political method:

> Experimental method is not just messing around nor doing a little of this and a little of that in the hope that things will improve. Just as in the physical sciences, it implies a coherent body of ideas, a theory, that gives direction to effort.[30]

For Dewey and James, responsibility was awareness of consequences and decision based on science. The pragmatists tried to dissolve formalities and rigidities in the interest of a changing good, attainable by the application of open-minded, creative intelligence. The question is: Is this sort of responsibility *political* responsibility? For Hobbes and Machiavelli, and today for most political scientists, *political* responsibility is "dependability in controlling conflict situations." Such writers are not interested so much in value realization as they are in power. For them, "The responsible man is the man who preserves the decision-making machinery and secures the survival of people and agencies."

From the perspective adopted by these political scientists and by

[27] Wayne A. R. Leys, "Platonic, Pragmatic, and Political Responsibility," *Nomos III: Responsibility*. New York: The Liberal Arts Press, 1960, p. 72.

[28] *Ibid.*

[29] *Ibid.*, p. 74.

[30] John Dewey, "The Future of Liberalism." *The Journal of Philosophy* 32:228 (April 25, 1935). Leys, *loc. cit.*, p. 74, n. 11.

most behavioral scientists, irresponsibility lies in acts which weaken the hold of the government, or of the party, or of a political or administrative agency. Irresponsibility is acting, or not acting, so that the established order is shaken or undermined.

Hence, we have two rough classifications of citizens and thinkers, the "Machiavellians," whose attention and interest is focused on survival value and power, and those whose attention and interest are focused on good works and the realization of value. Mr. Leys calls them the game-lovers and the game-haters, respectively; and he wants us to believe that many men come to enjoy litigation and politicking for their own sake.[31] But such prejudices apart, Leys says, *nonpolitical* responsibility is relevant whenever there is substantial agreement on goals. When there is disagreement on ends but agreement on procedure, on due process, then legal responsibility is appropriate. But when the decision-making machinery of society is "in low gear," when disagreement or uncertainty extends to ends *and* procedure, then, short of civil war, political responsibility takes over.

The consequence is that political responsibility, if not the highest responsibility, is in any case the most basic one, from a social perspective. It stands between men who are in stark disagreement among themselves, divided into factions which cannot take one another's conceptions seriously, and which can perhaps hardly respect one another—it stands between them and civil war. In international diplomacy, by the same token, political responsibility works to stave off hot war. Realistically, it seeks to keep internal or external disputes from undermining national strength on a globe that develops much torque and tension in spinning on its axis.

Professor Leys summarizes his analysis:

> Plato's responsible man was responsible for the common good but not accountable to any part of society that might oppose him. Dewey's responsible man was responsible for maximizing shared goods, but his accountability to the opposition was limited by a profound prejudice against contentious debate and propaganda. Machiavelli's responsible man was responsible for dealing with all actual and potential oppositions, but tended to be indifferent to the merits of the particular policies through which he could deal with his opposition and survive. Each of these philosophies treats a criterion as an imperative.[32]

[31] This "politics for politics' sake," for instance, is present in regulatory agencies that make concessions, initially to increase their survival value and soften political opposition, but eventually forget their regulatory function and the factions that instituted them in the first place. Leys, *loc. cit.*, p. 79, n. 18.

[32] *Ibid.*, p. 82. Reprinted by permission.

The peculiar relevance of the definition of political responsibility, the justification for discussing it in a book on social ethics, is that the broader scientific community tends to share Dewey's reluctance, in this area, to take the properly political questions with sufficient seriousness, while at the same time many *political scientists* and theorists these days tend to give them even more than their due weight, thus depreciating values other than survival value.

The broader public tends to divide into two camps, following the scientific community. We lump together in one camp those frenzied anti-Communists who are extremely impatient of the federal government's patience in dealing with Communism—and the impatient "radicals" who want the executive branch of federal and state governments to provide solutions for all problems right now—very likely without due appreciation of the amount of force that would have to be exerted to do so. In the other camp are the optimists and the milder progressives, those who, like Dewey, will not face the fact, for example, that a vast majority of citizens and voters cannot understand complex considerations that must be taken into account in decision-making.[33] In Mr. Leys' terms, these are the people who stress the destination of the navigator, but who are not fully mindful of the rocks and shoals *en route* to it. That this position is one of weakness is obvious. These are the people who tend to underrate the importance of politics and politicking and who systematically depreciate that fundamental merit in business administrators, that they keep their corporation in good financial health. The intellectualist disposition to avoid looking political and economic problems full in the face can lead to a profound immorality; it can, namely, cause the intellectuals to cast their lot with whatever powers that be, with whoever will give them what they want.[34] For sometimes the only plausible alternative to political achievement is coercion.

### "WHO, ME?"

John Gardner says:

> The very fact that leadership is so widely dispersed, that it is broken down into so many fields, that it is not signalized by badges of rank—all of these things reduce the self-conscious sense of re-

[33] Faced with this problem, Dewey "diverted the discussion to the question whether, if society were reorganized, the low I.Q. citizens might not turn out to be quite intelligent." *Ibid.*, p. 81; Dewey, *The Public and Its Problems*, p. 209.

[34] Compare again de Juvenel, "Indeed, the intellectual has been known to call upon tyranny for the propping-up of his schemes." "The Treatment of Capitalism by Continental Intellectuals," *loc. cit.*, p. 118.

sponsibility of individuals and groups who are actually exercising a powerful guiding hand in our national life. They lack a sense of their role as leaders, a sense of the obligations which they have incurred as a result of the eminence which they have achieved. They exercise the power but have no keen sense of exercising it. Or they may well recognize their leadership role with respect to their own special segment of the community but be unaware of their responsibility to the larger community. If you suggest to the influential American that he occupies a position of leadership, his most predictable response is "Who, me?" [35]

I agree with Mr. Gardner that leaders should lead, should be aware of *all* their obligations, both of their more immediate obligations and of their obligations to the wider community. It is one of the great functions of leaders to help a society to achieve the best that is in it. The recalcitrant, tight-lipped and tight-pursed, unimaginative leader does on occasion block action critically required in the interest of the larger community. Men have to fight their way uphill to positions of leadership in our society, and sometimes they develop a grit inside and a shell outside that make them too balky and too narrow. These are the conservatives who will not pay the piper and the radicals who will strike at the drop of a hat.

On the other hand, can we not all too easily prove false to our pluralism? Many people who consider themselves responsible and who would deny having anything resembling Calvinist views are, nevertheless, forever urging sacrifice to what they consider "the national interest." Odds are, their conception of the national interest is a hazy one. We see clearest that which is in the foreground and not too far away.

When I was twenty-two, I was Executive Secretary of the Code Authority of the Artificial Flower and Feather Industry of America. We had an industry-wide strike, which led to my having a long conversation with Rose Schneidermann. I have not forgotten her remark, "Best that labor represent labor,"—even if it did hurt my feelings at the time. Walter Reuther recently said, "After all, I am the legally constituted and duly elected representative of a million automotive workers." Mr. Reuther is generally admitted to be a man of national scope. Can there be any serious question, however, that his primary responsibility to the nation is *to represent his men,* and *not* to represent the nation, just as the Ford Motor Company is responsible, from day to day, for the welfare of the Ford Motor Company? The public interest is extremely difficult to get clearly in view. It is an aggregate of individual and corporate interests, a harmoniza-

[35] *Excellence, loc. cit.,* p. 125. Reprinted by permission.

tion of the most disparate concerns. It is *not a priori,* not something that the simple-minded can easily grasp, not something that can always be conjured up to relate and organize subordinate interests.

We therefore have need of our distinction between political responsibility as the most basic responsibility and responsibility for excellence as the highest responsibility. The responsibility for excellence is the responsibility of the expert, the specialist, the artist. Political responsibility may itself fall under that category only in the case of statesmen and other expert political negotiators. Political responsibility as a *basic* responsibility is the responsibility of all of us. "Who, me?" is a fitting response, properly modest. But the answer to "Who, me?" is still, in the end, and for all of us, affirmative. We must insist on working unity by negotiation and compromise, even when universal agreement in our beliefs is unattainable.

# 15

# JUSTICE AND MERCY

The three-millennia-long discussion of justice has conceived a widespread doubt of its having any cognitive meaning at all. Yet it is easy to show that justice has *too many* meanings, including contradictory meanings. It is easy to show that conceptions of justice play a major role in social action and change. Men have in all kinds of experience and social circumstance a sense of "fairness" that affects what they do, and what they will or will not tolerate. Modern psychology and psychoanalysis, far from eliminating justice as a component of human personality, confirm its decisiveness for healthy feeling and acting. However, the definition of justice is a matter of *clear expression of human intent,* of response to the world and mankind; it is not something that is discovered, in the sense in which gold is discovered or in the sense in which a physical principle is discovered. It may be discovered in the sense in which a man becomes aware that he has a habit, or an addiction, or in the sense in which a people discovers that it has a tradition that tugs it in a certain direction.

Let us look at a very simple case of human relations that may titillate our sense of justice. Rudolph, Utah, is a county seat, with a population of 4,500. It has little civic-mindedness, but it is very sports-conscious, thanks to the tradition of winning high school teams built and maintained by Coach Held. Coach Held has not only produced winning teams, but he has built up and improved Rudolph's athletic fields and equipment and put Rudolph on the map in state athletic programs. The high-school enrollment runs around 500. The school is locally noted for its science department; for the rest, its staff and facilities are "average." The school, like the rest of the community, is athletics-minded, so that an "A" student has no more prestige than a failing athlete.

Mrs. Tanner flunked a number of students in Latin at the end of the first semester, and among those who failed was Herman Held. Herm is a reasonably good student, and he is under constant pressure from his father, the coach, to do well both in his studies and athletics. He reported to his father, with some chagrin and indignation, that he was being failed in Latin. He repeated what his father already knew, that Mrs. Tanner is a Latin scholar but runs an untidy, disorganized course and does not return papers and exams. Herm made clear that he was by no means the only complaining student.

Herm is conscientious in every way. Some of the positions he plays may go beyond his desert, according to some of the other athletes. However, the other students and athletes do not blame Herm personally.

Coach Held goes to the principal, Dr. Snow, to register a strong complaint. He is quietly aware that he outranks both Dr. Snow and Mrs. Tanner on the real, if informal, rating scale of the Rudolph community. Dr. Snow calls in Mrs. Tanner and listens impassively as Coach Held protests her treatment of his son, Herm. She says that Herm did not complete the required work, and that much of what he did turn in was unsatisfactory. At five and again at nine weeks, she had marked him "Incomplete."

The upshot is that Herm gets a "B" in the course. The other students, especially those who themselves flunked, find it out, and they are annoyed. They will be annoyed again in June, when Herm again gets a "B," while many of them fail a second time. However, Dr. Snow is able to account for the discrepancy, and he considers the doing so a routine, if mildly unpleasant, part of his job as principal. Like the students, he is fond of Herm; and he longs for the day when Herm will graduate and move on to Logan. At the same time, Dr. Snow strongly supports Mrs. Tanner, pointing out that she has a master's degree in Latin, has taught for many years, and knows how to grade and to deal with students.

We may wonder, however, just how deleterious are the consequences to the other students of Latin at Rudolph High. Do they hereby learn the facts of life, so that we can write it all off as experience, as a wholesome lesson in realism? Or do they learn that "justice" is meaningless? Will some find their idealism actually strengthened and, later on, do their best to introduce more equity into the local educational plant? Will some find their sense of values subtly re-oriented in the direction of a healthy and athletic nation? Will some, particularly those who flunk Latin—and stay flunked—under Mrs. Tanner, be aware of tasting a bitter taste? Will a few perhaps revise their ambitions and their standards of choice and of personal conduct? Will a few perhaps find that, let justice be what it may, they are anyway not seriously addicted to it?

## AN ACTUAL CASE

Houston, Texas, is in an area long considered pro-segregation.

A few years ago it was the home of W. E. Worthing, a white man who owned numerous apartments and houses for rent to Negroes, who in connection therewith maintained profitable loan offices. When he died, Worthing left a million-dollar estate. His will established a scholarship fund exclusively for the use of students of the three Negro high schools in Houston.

On one of these scholarships, Joe Billy McDade came up to Bradley University. The basketball coach had not even heard of him; he first spotted him standing there, six foot five inches tall, in the registration line.

Thanks to the McRoberts law scholarships, administered by the Commercial National Bank of Peoria, Joe Billy has been able to go on to the Law School of the University of Michigan.

## PLATONIC JUSTICE

Let us look very briefly at a few historically important conceptions of justice. One of the most famous of these is that of Plato, as expressed in *The Republic*. It is generally admitted that Plato was analytical (or pre-analytical) to the extent that his conception of justice emerged out of an old and strong Greek tradition. He stated what many Greeks already felt or thought about "justice."

Plato's most frequent expression for "just" is the Greek, "DIKÉ." This word meant "straight," "right," in the sense of a right line; by symbolic extension, it came to mean "correct" and, finally, "just." There is doubtless a broad divergence between Plato's DIKÉ and *our* intuitive sense of justice. Both his sense of justice and our own, however, relate themselves to "equality" and "equity." But his equality relates to quality. There is in the back of his mind a potent feeling for retribution and desert, a feeling that one should get a just reward for performance, for function and status and work. Our own sense of justice presumably gives more weight to persons as persons, to universal human personality. "All men are created equal," and discourse on justice begins logically for us, with that proposition. In brief, Plato's justice and equality are characteristic of aristocratic thought; *ours,* of democratic thought.

A set of virtues sometimes stressed by the Greeks included temperance, courage, wisdom, and justice. Plato had no difficulty, in his own mind, at least, in ascribing meaning to the first three. Temperance he understood to be control over the appetites in the interest of good sense, honor, and the welfare of one's life as a whole. It is not far removed from our prudence, or providence. Courage he called a kind of knowledge: knowledge of which things really ought to be feared, namely, cowardice and the reputation of a coward, treason, and failure to preserve one's freedom of action. Wisdom is the exercise and use of mind, the reflective application of knowledge to achieve well-considered ends. What, then, is justice? Justice is the actualization of the other virtues, the dynamo, the "go," the energy that inspires the individual man to be temperate, courageous, and wise, and so to act; and it is the energetic, positive performance of *his* function by each citizen, artisan, and slave in the state. Negatively, it is not trying to do the work of someone else, not being a busy-body and kibitzer. In their negative character, temperance and justice are alike, and both are aristocratic versions of the liberal thesis that men should mind their own business. A class should do its own work. Thus, workmen, foreign traders, navigators, all do their jobs and do them well, if there is justice in the state (navigators avoid shoals *and* sail toward their destinations); but they do *not* govern and do *not* make war and peace. Regular and auxiliary troops fight, but they do not compete with tradesmen and workers and certainly do not try to govern. The rulers govern. Of course, one may be somewhat sceptical about the justice—in our sense—of Plato's system. Government, with associated intellection and contemplation, is an activity that gratifies nobility and intelligence. Men of gold, in Plato's view, should be offered golden opportunity, and men of brass, brazen opportunity. Plato favored the meritocracy, and he was willing to recognize merit even in unlikely places, *e.g.*, in women. Such was Plato's aristocratic conception.

If one approaches the Platonic conception only from the angle of instrumentality and the implementation of policy, it will not vex him. Can we seriously intend to let plumbers or television repairmen who have never passed outside the city's gates apply their wrenches to the nation's constitutional law or its foreign policy? If such difficult concerns are to be well managed, the right men must be found and educated to manage them. Plato would foster, as a matter of life and death, the search for high abilities. And he would excellently cultivate these abilities for full and free exercise in the service of the state.

If we Westerners seem too quiet about the necessities of selection and seem to deny the implications of education for the gifted, we are really—at most—mincing words. We would not dare neglect recognizable capabilities nor refuse them full development.

> Thomas Jefferson would have talked of an "aristocracy of talents" and Vilfredo Pareto, of the need for social mobility to nurture and reinforce an "intellectual elite." Yielding to the popular distaste for terms such as "aristocracy" and "elite," we can just as well state our ideal as one of seeking to break through all barriers which separate gifted boys from the chance to capitalize on their gifts.[1]

Justice requires that there be *excellent performance* all up and down the land and in all walks of life. That which we shrink from is interlucation and pruning. But the responsibility of society here is to offer fair shakes. No one should be pulled down, but not everyone should be pushed up the ladder. Even granting native intelligence, indeed, we can easily ask a talented boy or girl to climb higher or faster than his background will permit. How many of our young men suffer, for instance, in trying to get a medical education for which they are ill-adapted? And why? Because the medical profession has been glamorized to the degree of absurdity. This is not to say that recognizable talent does not also suffer from lack of funds. Funds should be provided as far as is humanly possible; (and with no encumbrances on the spirit, such as test oaths). There is no better investment of federal or any other money.

> This mournful truth is everywhere confessed,
> Slow rises worth by poverty depressed.
>
> —Johnson.

That idealist Plato was then, in this respect, much more realistic than we have sometimes been. He would offer fifty years of training, education, and apprenticeship in order to assure the state of top talent and attainment. Nor would he wince, because he had to adopt a principle of selectivity.

Plato, of course, knew nothing of intelligence quotients, person-

[1] *Admission to Harvard College,* p. 35.

ality tests, profiles, nondirective interviews, and all the other apparatus of modern placement. But if such tests are honest and helpful, they should be used to the hilt. In fact, they do not replace the record of a man's career; there is higher correlation between high school grades and college grades than between intelligence quotients and college grades. But they can help a man find himself and sometimes keep a square peg from a round hole. They are devices, and not much more than that. Even interview technique rarely discovers the awkward and inarticulate genius or reveals neuroses in the smooth and articulate one.

Plato was seeking results; and to get the best results from human material requires investment, time, and steady, appropriate nurture. Plato did not seek intelligence only. He wanted health, proved temperance and courage, intellectual development, and a wisdom that can be born only of experience. To these rare qualities, add justice; and "justice" in the rulers means complete devotion to the real interests of all subjects of the state.

One of Plato's major limitations has already been discussed: the lack of any sense of distinctly *political* responsibility. He thinks of conflict as something that can be settled by his rulers on the merits of the case. But we have seen that political conflict exists characteristically among parties who take absolute stands on grounds of interest or moral principle that they will not allow to be sacrificed. From this point of view, Plato's work is not complete. He offers us an administrative unit, not a true polity.

The only other limitation that inescapably concerns us is intimately associated with the first one. Our universal interest in justice is not instrumental only. To say that only gifted and educated specialists can adequately implement policy is not to say that they alone have a substantive interest in the determination of policy, in the overarching ends of society and the state. Plato wanted his rulers to feel responsible and to act responsibly toward all subjects of the state, but he did not make them *accountable*. Perhaps in the circumstances of the Greek city-states, Plato was not back-sliding; but given our own position in history, such an absence of accountability to all would be back-sliding. That this is so is confirmed by the Khrushchev program for the Soviets. Khrushchev wants to see the dictatorship of the proletariat ended.

> The party considers it essential to perfect the forms of popular representation and promote the democratic principles of the Soviet electoral system.[2]

[2] Program proposed to the 1961 Congress, translation by Tass News Agency. From *The New York Times.*

For all our faults, and for all the talk about our bourgeois ideology, we are politically much more advanced; and that means, we enjoy long-established accountability to the people. The big political decisions are made by men who have been chosen by the people to represent them. Governments derive "their just powers from the consent of the governed," according to the Declaration of Independence. When we fail to maintain accountability and free, popular election by the entire adult population, we are back-sliding. The Russians can't back-slide, because they aren't yet up there. Something similar may be said of Plato and the Greeks, whose political experience he expressed. Whatever their virtues otherwise, they did not have the political acumen of the Romans nor have acquaintance with the political form of constitutional democracy in the modern sense.

### MARXIAN JUSTICE

Hegelian that he was, Marx took a dim view of unhistorical abstractions. He often ridiculed moral principles and justice as mere objectifications of class feeling. It is hardly to be denied that this ridicule is sometimes well warranted. Principles are often the abstract form in which private interests clothe themselves for presentation to the public. However, *general* objections against bourgeois principles of justice, *e.g.*, that they really represent a surreptitious class interest in an historical situation, can be turned *mutatis mutandis* against the Marxian and Leninist ethics as well. For the proletarian interest is also a class interest (at best it is the interest of wage laborers as wage laborers), and the conception that this interest is a univeral one rests on an historical presumption. Historical change has indeed, in recent years, worked against this presumption of Marx: Labor has become more and more skilled, and its interests less and less "proletarian." For instance, our chief labor problem is no longer the conditions of employment, but rather what to do about our unemployables; but the appeal for a solution to this problem is directed rather more to our compassion and to our aversion against waste than to our sense of justice.

However much Marx aimed to conceal his animus behind historical and economic science, he nonetheless had one; and his animus was directed against capitalism, because he thought it a system unjust to workers. Not only did he believe that the workers were underpaid, but he thought all the power was unjustly concentrated in the hands of fewer and fewer and greedier and greedier capitalists, so that they could lay off workers, move plants to new locations, *etc.*, all with manifest arbitrariness. The alleged injustice was also attitudinal. He thought the owners looked on the workers as de-humanized commodities and avoided accountability to them by hiding behind a screen of stock shares or disappearing altogether by the magic of corporate anonymity.

Marx overlooked the superiority of the camouflage devices available to governmental bureaucracy. One can say, he hadn't seen anything yet. He underestimated the humanity that is universal and that extends even to hardened capitalists. But above all, he brought to his concept of justice a miserable sense of equality. As an intellectual, he must at some level of mind really have known better. The sense of equality here called "miserable" is that which would equate any given hour of work with any other hour of work. This is to let one's desire for a mechanical measure cancel out his sense of proportion and justice altogether. Anyone who has worked knows that one hour, even of his own work, is not in reality equal to any other hour, except in terms of clock time. The Soviets themselves have by no means managed to operate on such a basis. The new program of the Soviet Communist Party mentions the motto, "From each according to his ability, to each according to his needs." But when it gets down to business, it changes this to read, "From each according to his abilities, to each according to his work"—and this implies variability in the value of work.

This is not to say that the new program is not full of double-talk, particularly in reference to liberty and justice:

> Socialist democracy includes both political freedoms—freedom of speech, of the press and of assembly, the right to elect and to be elected, and also social rights—the right to work, to rest and leisure, to education, to material security in old age and in case of illness or disability; equality of citizens of all races and nationalities; equal rights for women and men in all spheres of political, economic and cultural activity. Socialist democracy, unlike bourgeois democracy, does not merely proclaim the rights of the people, but makes it really possible for the people to exercise them. Soviet society insures the real liberty of the individual. The highest manifestation of this liberty is man's emancipation from exploitation, which is what primarily constitutes *genuine social justice*.[3]

The absence of exploitation, broadly conceived, may indeed be the core meaning of justice. But a genuine communist order would exploit those whose productivity was above the median; and the actual Bolshevik order exploits workers and farmers generally. The presumption that workers are exploited under capitalism is belied by

[3] From Part One, "Socialist Principle." Italics added.

their earnings, their hours, and their contracts that result from collective bargaining. The liberty and justice claimed for Soviet Russia are little more than words in a propaganda assault. To give credit where credit is possibly due, however, the political experience of Premier Khrushchev may have led him to appreciate the merit of liberty.

There is, moreover, no reason to doubt that Marxist policies and propaganda have stimulated the capitalist West to great accomplishments and to at least speedier justice. The greatest competition and contest today is that between these two orders. War and the threat of war are not inevitable and exclusive outcomes. An alternative possibility is that this competition should lead to a fairer opportunity for all men. Not through either capitalist nor Communist imperialism, but through the competition between them.

There is no justice, Bentham said, without publicity. Today there is more publicity than ever before. The stage is set and lighted. The Communists can withhold or publish news at will, striving to create the image that they wish to show the world. Our government can broadcast its own perspective, but it cannot withhold either news or opinion. Although this may hurt us in detail, its more profound and lasting effect is demonstration abroad that "Liberty is what the West upholds."

## NIETZSCHE ON JUSTICE

"Population explosion!" "Seventeen million Americans are mentally disturbed." "Seventy-six million Europeans are starved for truth." "We will blast you off the earth."

How terrible is the state of the world, and how dreadfully inadequate are our morals to the trials we face. This inadequacy particularly, the remarkable difference between need and potentiality on the one hand and sad actuality on the other, has led many people to take an interest in the work of Friedrich Nietzsche.[4] Nietzsche called for a transvaluation of all values; he attacked at its foundations the morality of modern man. He attacked middle-class morality, and he detested exaggerated historicism and nationalism.

Nietzsche's thought was unseasonable. That means, he criticized

[4] Some Americans have associated Nietzsche with Hitler. Nietzsche lost his mind in 1890 or 1891, but Hitler was born only a year earlier—1889. The claims Hitler made on Nietzsche were supported, it is true, by Nietzsche's aged, foolish sister. There is vast evidence that Nietzsche detested the sort of middle-class German nationalism to which Hitler made his appeal.

from the perspective of a classical scholar, the accepted imbalances in moral and intellectual judgments. Thus, Nietzsche presented the historical culture of his time, something of which one could be "rightly proud," as a fault and a defect.[5] For we develop our faults at the same time as our virtues; "and an excess of virtue can obviously bring a nation to ruin as well as an excess of vice." In particular, "forgetfulness is a property of all action," and we must fix limits to "the memory of the past, if it is not to become the gravedigger of the present . . ." Education, with its stress on knowledge for knowledge's sake, loyalty to our ancestors and their values and ways, and the essential, unavoidable economies of thinking in slogans, formulas, and principles, all combine to distract our attention from the living, concrete present. Nietzsche compares unhappy man with his gnawing sense of a role to play in history with the contented cows in the pasture who are equally ignorant of past and future; but his work, especially his early work and his criticism of historicism, is not a paean to the bucolic and the pastoral, but to youth and the spirit and energy and immediacy of youth. He speaks disparagingly of Germany as *"the land of little-by-little."* It is a normal and healthy characteristic of youth that it does not dawdle on the diving board but swings itself gracefully through the air and into the pool. Youth is not so circumspect that its circumspection obstructs action or tapers pleasure. It does not settle for a little moderation when an excess of change is in order; it does not *a priori* or from temperament prefer evolution to revolution. Youth takes its life and lives it. All that fitting, matching, shaving, and "beautifying" that go with middle- and old-age are spared it.

That is, of course, no description of youth; nor is it an idealization of youth. Nietzsche's objective was to express sharply the difference between a natural and timely movement toward value and excellence and a movement handicapped by historicism, by traditional concepts and concepts of tradition, by barnacles that quickly attach themselves even to those very virtues that have—in the past—plated the prow of moral progress.

Justice itself is a product of strength and living sensitivity. The weak, the tradition- and hide-bound, the inward- and backward-looking may smugly conserve "principles of justice." But their principles of justice do not look to present and future human consequences. What they really conserve are their prejudices and privi-

[5] All references are to *The Use and Abuse of History,* trans. Adrian Collins. New York: The Liberal Arts Press (rev.) 1957. (First published in German in 1873.)

leges. Nietzsche put his thesis this way: "Only strong personalities can endure history; the weak are extinguished by it." [6] The weak personalities do not do and think what is right and adequate, but what used to be right and adequate, or, worse still, what they "think" was in the past right and adequate. To wreak justice implies commitment to values and commitment against disvalues. Only a man who hates injustice can wield the saber of justice. But a man who hates injustice is necessarily a man of vigorous, "youthful," intense conscience. ". . . a cold detachment may mask a lack of moral feeling."

"The search for truth is often thoughtlessly praised; but it has something great in it only if the seeker has the sincere unconditional will for justice." Objectivity can be a lacquer covering weakness. This negative objectivity can do nothing, least of all accomplish justice. Although we frequently think of Nietzsche as a blind voluntarist and irrationalist, he said:

> Few in truth serve truth, as only few have the pure will for justice; and very few even of these have the strength to be just. The will alone is not enough. The impulse to justice without the power of judgment has been the cause of the greatest suffering to men.[7]

The application of Nietzsche's position to ourselves (and his position is here but hinted at) calls for an entire volume. But we can see that he raises doubt concerning the breadth of our humanity, when we are *haunted* by the injunction to be our brother's keeper, when we choose as our way out to dehumanize enemies or scorn allies as "gooks," "wogs," or "slopeys." When we seek to maintain our superiority by an array of racial theories, or to support them with the evidence of carefully hedged-in Southern—or for that matter Northern—experience, whom do we deceive? Ourselves least of all. Who is fooled when all, or the majority of, or the leadership among, desegregationists are labeled "Communists"? Justice requires that the capitalized word "Communist" be applied only to Communists. Otherwise its use is figurative and not incisive. The principal injustice is to the indiscriminate user, to us; and it wears the form of confusion and diminished morale and teamwork. But also it gives body to "the spectre of Communism": The more phe-

[6] "History unsettles the feelings when they are not powerful enough to measure the past by themselves. The man who no longer dares trust himself, but asks history against his will for advice 'how he ought to feel now,' is insensibly turned by his timidity into a play-actor, and plays a part or, generally, many parts—very badly, therefore, and superficially."

[7] *The Use and Abuse of History.*

nomena are feared under the label of Communism, the greater and more *material* is its thrust. In a similar way, labeling neutralists "Communist" pushes them away from us; and labeling *their* feudal enemies "democrats, and our friends," pushes the neutralists farther still.

After one of Mr. Khrushchev's appearances before the United Nations General Assembly, the Chief of the Public Studies Division of the U.S. Department of State [8] asked.

> Does it take the visit of a world-famous figure, having a vivid personality, to arouse the American people from their "usual apathy"? Or do our fellow countrymen have serious thoughts about our foreign relations year in and year out? Are their opinions sound and stable, or do the people shift about like weathervanes, from one quarter to the other, in response to the latest blast of hot air? Are the people sharply divided among themselves, creating a serious lack of national unity on matters which are of critical importance in this era of rocket and nuclear weapons?

As the quotation perhaps suggests, but contrary to popular opinion, the highest level foreign problems await the solution of domestic "problems." What an animal can ingest and digest of its environment depends on what kind of animal it is. What an animal can *do* also depends on what kind of animal it is. A kangaroo can jump and box, a chameleon change its color. By the same token, if we practice justice at home, along with firm self-discipline and shrewd judgment, we are well on the way toward taking the foreign hurdles. *Our* foreign situation is made at least as much here at home and by us as it is over there. The diversion of attention from domestic problems can be a kind of escapism, "Afghanistanism." Objectivity comes cheap, if it's vice and virtue in Afghanistan we're haggling over.

The objectivity with which both the Russians and we ourselves speak of thermonuclear war—as we might speak of the league pennant in 3003 A.D.—may be a too inexpensive objectivity. Subjectively speaking, the prospect is remote; and "Distance makes the heart grow fonder." From close up, however, there is nothing humanly desirable in nuclear war. Since the ultimate strength of the United States and that of Russia are reciprocally related, it could only weaken us both. Yet it is hardly conceivable that our colliding should benefit some third party. What the world requires is strength and peace and justice.

[8] H. Schuyler Foster, on October 15, 1959.

## JUSTICE AND LIBERTY

*"Every usage of 'freedom' apart from expressing a political social relation is (of course) metaphorical."—T. H. Green.*

Both liberals and conservatives can agree with Professor Hayek that "the ultimate decision about what is good or bad will be made not by individual human wisdom but by the decline of the groups that have adhered to the "wrong beliefs." [9] But the *practical* problem is how to learn sufficiently in advance which are the "wrong" beliefs and how to put them down far away from our group.

The libertarian is convinced that it is absurd to look to reason and experience for enlightenment, but to prescribe beforehand which side they must favor. He therefore permits and encourages criticism of every general presumption and is willing to look on the lives of men as so many "experiments in living." He is jealous of truth and therefore not jealous of his opinions. A society the orientation of which is fixed beforehand is dangerously committed to its opinions, which it will call "truth." But the truth is what it is, and not opinion.

The libertarian makes a habit of judging political and social relations and institutional devices and procedures by the criterion, Do they foster liberty? If they do not, he questions their claims to being just. Unless there is freedom of criticism and correction, how can he know if the claims are meaningful and true? Subjective justice—the mere feeling that one is acting justly, or equally the feeling that one is being justly dealt with—may come easy. But the libertarian is not satisfied with that: He wants the kind of comparison and check that can be made only on an open market.

## JUSTICE IN ENGLAND

England holds the highest reputation for the administration of justice in its courts. The work of administering divine justice rests, however, in human hands.

Sir David Maxwell Fyfe once stated that there is "no practical possibility" of an innocent man's being hanged in England. A book by Ludovic Kennedy, *Ten Rillington Place,* nevertheless tells of what may have been such a case of capital miscarriage of justice.

In 1950, Timothy Evans, a little Welshman, twenty-five years old and illiterate, was executed for having strangled his wife and infant daughter. The chief witness for the prosecution was a Mr.

[9] *The Constitution of Liberty,* p. 36.

John Christie, who lived on the ground floor, below the Evans' flat.

In 1953, Christie was himself arrested, and it was established that "this necrophilic ghoul had strangled six women for pleasure and managed to stow them away in the back yard. . . ." He confessed to the murder of Mrs. Evans.[10]

JUSTICE AND MERCY

> Tannhäuser was a Frankish knight and famous minnesinger, who, travelling at twilight past the Hörselberg, "saw a white glimmering figure of matchless beauty standing before him and beckoning him to her." Leaving his horse, he went up to meet her, whom he knew to be none other than Venus. He descended to her palace in the heart of the mountain, and there passed seven years in careless revelry. Then, stricken with remorse and yearning for another glimpse of the pure light of day, he called in agony upon the Virgin Mother, who took compassion on him and released him. He sought a village church, and to priest after priest confessed his sins, without obtaining absolution, until finally he had recourse to the Pope. But the holy father, horrified at the enormity of his misdoing, declared that guilt such as his could never be remitted: sooner should the staff in his hand grow green and blossom. "Then Tannhäuser, full of despair and with his soul darkened, went away, and returned to the only asylum open to him, the Venusberg. But lo! three days after he had gone, Pope Urban discovered that his pastoral staff had put forth buds and had burst into flower. Then he sent messengers after Tannhäuser, and they reached the Hörsel vale to hear that a way-worn man, with haggard brow and bowed head, had just entered the Hörselloch. Since then Tannhäuser has not been seen."
>
> . . . This sad legend, in its Christianized form, is doubtless descriptive of the struggle between the new and the old faiths. The knightly Tannhäuser, satiated with pagan sensuality, turns to Christianity for relief, but, repelled by the hypocrisy, pride, and lack of sympathy of its ministers, gives up in despair, and returns to drown his anxieties in his old debauchery.[11]

Given our severe puritanical background, we can well afford to strain a little in the direction of sympathy and mercy in our judgment on new men, new institutions, and new nations. The rod of justice can put forth buds and burst into flower. We do not have to go so far as Father Flanagan when he said, "There is no such thing as a bad boy." We need not charge upon the field, like the

[10] *The New Yorker,* February 11, 1961, pp. 85–89.

[11] From John Fiske, *Myths and Myth-Makers.* Boston: Houghton Mifflin and Company, 1886 (ninth edition), pp. 29–30.

Six Hundred at Balaclava, of whom French observers remarked, "C'est magnifique, mais ce n'est pas la guerre." Let mercy, like bravery, be tempered by judgment and purpose. We need not, and ought not, confuse mercy with justice. But mercy, if superadded to strict justice, is a virtue.

# EPILOGUE: CHOICE AND CONFLICT

## CAN MAN CONTROL HIS FUTURE POWER AND LIBERTY?

The first question in this connection is hardly whether or not we can maintain the individual liberties that have been traditional in the West. The question is rather: How could we possibly afford *not* to maintain and even to enlarge and extend these individual liberties?

The power available to society collectively is much greater than in the past, but power to crush the individual and to commit liberticide is not newly achieved. Our forefathers, however, gradually augmented the sphere of the individual, from motives of social utility and welfare, because they associated liberty with dignity and because indeed they frowned on the invasion of individual right as the basest immorality.

The more power we have and the easier it is to engage it by the mere flick of a switch, the more poignant and immediate becomes our need of the soberest and most enlightened judgment and foresight. Such judgment and foresight grow only on the soil of free men and, even there, require the finest cultivation.

Do the demands of present-day institutions and their administrators radically change the picture?

> Remember, administrators are by temperament active men. Their tendency, which is strengthened by the nature of their job, is to live in the short term, to become masters of the short-term solution. Often, as I have seen them conducting their business with an absence of fuss, a concealed force, a refreshing dash of intellectual sophistication, a phrase from one of the old Icelandic sagas kept nagging at my mind. It was: 'Snorri was the wisest man in Iceland who had not the gift of foresight." [1]

Pontius Pilate was a good administrator, and, by accepted institutionalized criteria, his hands were washed clean. The desire for control and discretion so natural and appropriate to the administrator must be gratified, but it must be gratified by a public that maintains ultimate responsibility for the decisions and operations of its administrative agents. Administrators will agree that this responsibility cannot be faithfully carried out unless the conditions of optimum judgment are maintained and that first among those conditions is liberty to learn and know the facts and relevant considerations, to criticize, to publish criticism, and to propagate alternative insights, theories, and solutions.

Do the existence of Communist states, the threat of thermonuclear and biological warfare, and the needs of the military establishment, diminish the social utility—among civilized peoples—of individual liberty? Some of our best intellects have gone astray in trying to answer that question. Thus, Bertrand Russell has said that "only the prevention of war gives outside states a justification for interference," and that no world federal authority "ought to impose freedom of the Press or any other freedom upon any subordinate State." [2] But is it not morally regressive to say, even in our new through-the-looking-glass sort of world, "I am *not* my brother's keeper"? It is in any case unrealistic. Is the world's safety assured by turning over to any and every military junta the privilege of silencing its subject people?

There is an empirical law of social psychology to the effect that external pressures create internal pressures, that they make for the garrison state. But if we are talking about the health of society, we cannot agree with an application S. C. Pepper makes of his

[1] C. P. Snow, *Science and Government.* Cambridge: Harvard University Press, 1961, p. 83. Reprinted by permission.

[2] Bertrand Russell, *Common Sense and Nuclear Warfare.* New York: Simon and Schuster, 1959, pp. 68–69.

"practicable ideal" of an *adjustable society* that adapts itself readily to changes of social conditions and the impact of varying social pressures.

> There is the ideal of the functional society for which Plato's *Republic* is the classic example. And there is the ideal of the open individualistic society for which the political writings of Locke and Mill are classic examples. These are clearly, on our analysis, utopian extremes. Each would be appropriate only under conditions of extreme security or extreme danger. But they serve an important function in exhibiting the extremes and suggesting that the appropriate social structure at any time depends on the degree of social pressure—the greater the pressure the more the functional organization needed, the less the pressure the more room for individual freedom and the open society.[3]

But Mill meant that the civilized state which stands on the principle of liberty *is stronger*. It is precisely under circumstances of terror that impoverishment of mind, inhibited communication, and hysteria are most risky. To look once at the matter with a cold, military eye, those are garrison state characteristics [4] that lead to military fiascoes, logistic failures,[5] failures of defense and of offense.[6]

Conflict and the new dilemmas are here to stay. Granting the problems of war or coexistence with Communism, weapons dealing megadeaths or diplomacy dealing deuces, threes, and fours, assisting underdeveloped nations or surrendering them outright, integrating within at quick tempo or wearing the ugly, segregated look within and without; granting all these problems, the paramount issue is: What kind of persons, operating with what quality of information, judgment, nerve, and moral standards shall we send out to face and solve them?

So we live in a time of great choices. Our central problems are less problems of knowledge and capability—in their traditional reference to nature—than they are problems of conflict, choice, and control. Our great and "cursed" questions are questions of the distribution and use of knowledge and power, questions of interest shared or in conflict, of the clarification of intent, of emotional health and balance, of judgment, and of decision and decisive action.

[3] Stephen C. Pepper, *Ethics*. New York: Appleton-Century-Crofts, Inc., 1960, p. 331. Reprinted by permission.

[4] It was not the Athens of Pericles that lost the Peloponnesian War.

[5] "Blankets in the tropics, bikinis in the arctic."

[6] The Japanese military hierarchy infamously attacked Pearl Harbor and infamously did not realize any serious military objective.

Now, choice can be determined in many ways. If we may group these ways into major classes, they are (1) by imagination and fantasy, (2) by accordance with fact, and (3) by principle.

(1) Imagination naturally enters into deliberation and choice: It *is* conceived or imagined human consequences that deliberation must weigh, along with alternative routes to or away from them. But imagination can be controlled and fact-related, or it can be illusory, fantastic. "The world of imagination is infinite." Nothing is more vital to men and nations than morale, but morale that rests on illusion rests on sand. Foresight without imagination is uninspired; but projections and programs when *led* by imagination are inefficacious, unrealistic, and hence perilous. Constructive imagination is necessary to social and political compromise, but fantasy is the road to death.

(2) Although choice can be determined by ignorance and illusion, it can equally be determined by knowledge and insight. Acquaintance with fact and informed self-reflection can prevent us from pursuing ends that can't be reached and from adopting futile or awkward means and methods. Knowledge can favorably influence our perception of opportunities and obligations.

We accordingly take our stand for objective science in all areas and aim to accept the implications. The behavioral sciences have been severely unwilling to concern themselves with values. To the extent that knowledge is their aim, they are correct in affecting this reluctance and unconcern. Attitude and the validity of like and dislike are not their primary business. A true conception and an accurate description of fact and devices imply the energetic extrusion of subjectivity. Only the expert who has tried and enjoyed a modicum of success knows how difficult to attain is a consistent habit of objectivity. Not even the physical scientist can easily distinguish his knowledge from his feeling and his moral position, but surely the knowledge of a social scientist and his position as a man can be kept distinct only by policy and sustained, self-conscious effort.

(3) Our paramount thesis is that choice ought also to be guided by principle and commitment to value. Our presuppositions should be rendered as transparent as we can make them. Consistent commitment to carefully wrought principle is a component of choice no less crucial to soundness and viability than is knowledge.

The basic lines of social policy should be well secured. Otherwise, long-range programs are not feasible. The social use—and the point—of ethical principle in particular is that men shall know they will be treated as ends and squarely dealt with; then they are liberated to reflect, plan, and work constructively.

However, so long as the clock runs, situations and values will be changing. Given our ignorance of the future, and of the needs and likings of new generations of men, efforts to hamstring the future are not justifiable. Persistent search for new values is a component of the good life. In consequence, new principles will have sometimes to be admitted, and old ones altered. Principles should express our highest insight and deepest reflection.

Although the community of the good knows no national nor sectional boundaries, still the libertarian tradition evokes more good will. The disposition normal to authoritarianism and to totalitarianism is ignoble. It tends toward impatience and arbritrariness and thus also toward inhumanity. Other traditions may manage to exercise very forcefully some part of the intelligence available to them, but the libertarian tradition has the greatest likelihood of achieving sound judgment. It has the greatest likelihood of bringing into social use all available human powers; for we do not look on intelligence and knowledge, narrowly defined, as the only significant characteristics of excellent human beings.

Expressions like "policy science," "administrative science," "domestic science," and "secretarial science," may be injurious. Better to let science retain its narrower signification, better to let science satisfy our cognitive interest. "When Eric Fromm . . . defines emotional health in terms of the capacity for love, he is not reporting empirical fact; he is propounding an ideal for living." [7] Human living and the actions of legislators, courts, and administrators are not all science. Valuing, judging values, and philosophical reflection are not science; but it is difficult to say today whether philosophical reflection is a lost mode of thought or whether it has not rather permeated—and perhaps confused—a large domain that had better be reserved for pure science.

Knowledge is a component, but not the whole, of practical wisdom. The division between the sciences and the humanities may be no more than a mark of our fallibility, of our inherent human provincialism and inadequacy. But limitations must be taken into account and given their due. Politics, the arts, and ethics themselves have an established interest in that kind of objectivity aimed at by the behavioral scientists. But mankind also has a great stake in that kind of objective consensus, which is quite properly tentative, aimed

[7] Raphael Demos.

at by the humanities. The perception of values and ordered consideration of value problems are the specialty of the humanities and of philosophy.

Certainly it matters in whose interest choice is made. Conflict concerns choices no more than it concerns who shall make and interpret them and for whose sake. A great moral strength of liberal democratic and republican political and economic forms is that decision tends to be just, tends to be in the interest of all interested parties. Expert and detailed knowledge is the province of scientific specialism, studied reflection is the specialty of the philosopher; but, in the end, the orientation of social policy is the business of everyone.

The rise of man to his present position of power and potentiality is owing to many factors. It is owing to the quiet industry of the ordinary man in his "quiet desperation," to his thrift, his generous hopes for a better world to come, his wonted decency. It is owing to long series of good choices made by individuals and nations, series that reach back into the history before history. It is owing to ridicule by the incisive wit. It is owing to the conquest of terror and the slow advance in physical and then in moral courage. It is owing to the sensitiveness and expressiveness of the poet, to the stamina in thought and experiment of the scientist, to the analysis of the philosopher, the logician, the mathematician.

Let all patriots conspire to insure that no epilogue—or *epitaph* —wants writing to the rise, decline, and fall of that one, sometimes noble, species that has known power, choice, and freedom.

# Index